# Tigers in the Trenches

The Leicestershire Regiment
on the
Western Front

1914-1918.

Robin P. Jenkins

In Memory of

**No. 22609266 L/Cpl Eric Anthony Jenkins**

'D' Company, 1st South Staffords

First published in the United Kingdom in 2024 by **The Lookout Press (Leicester),** 31A, Victoria Street, Fleckney, Leicester LE8 8AZ.

www.heritageco.co.uk

©Robin Jenkins and Jess Jenkins 2024

All rights reserved. No part of this publication may be reproduced, stored in a retrieval system, or transmitted, in any form or by any means, electronic, mechanical, photo-copying, recording or otherwise, without the prior permission of the publisher and copyright holders.

The views expressed ion this publication are those of the author and are not necessarily endorsed by the publishers.

British Library Cataloguing in Publication Data.

A catalogue record for this book is available from the British Library.

ISBN 978-17395815-1-0

Typeset in 12/16 point Calibri

# Introduction

This book has been well over a decade in the making. I first began to gather and study stories of the Leicestershire Regiment as senior archivist at the county record office; responsible (amongst other duties) for collecting and taking care of the many military documents and photographs, including the Royal Leicestershire Regiment's archive there. By good fortune, my time there included the centenary of the Great War, which saw a massive surge in public interest and active involvement in commemoration and remembrance.

It always seemed to me that the official records, those generated by the Regiment itself, could be supplemented and enhanced by seeking out the material created and kept by individual soldiers; their papers, letters home, memoirs and photographs. As a result, much significant material was both rediscovered and made widely and readily accessible and under my direction, in happy collaboration with Jenny Moran, senior archivist responsible for public services, the Record Office devoted much of its collecting, cataloguing and 'outreach' efforts to the accumulation, dissemination and interpretation of these new archival resources. In answering enquiries, researching exhibitions and preparing talks and even dramatic reconstructions, I found myself amassing, somewhat incidentally, a wealth of knowledge with too little time to deploy it all to its full potential.

The essays that follow attempt to bring together those different archival strands. To tell the story of the Leicestershire Regiment on the Western Front through the official histories and battalion war diaries but enlivened, as it were, by adding the experiences of those ordinary fellows who did the fighting and dying over the four terrible years of the Great War.

In 2015 I was honoured to be invited, by the Royal Tigers Association, to speak at the cathedral in Leicester at a service of Remembrance on the centenary of the attack by the Leicestershire Regiment's territorial battalions on the Hohenzollern Redoubt. I was also asked, the following year, to speak at Uppingham School as part of Rutland's commemoration of the war, on the Leicestershire Regiment on the Somme. Those talks are partially preserved here.

Now, in retirement, I find that I have much ground to make up in making full use of all my research carried out over the centenary period. This volume follows upon a study of Leicester's Base Hospital and the R.A.M.C. unit which ran it and its many satellites. In due course I hope to return to the experience of the Great War on the Home Front but here my concentration is upon the Leicestershire Regiment on the Western Front, from mobilisation until the final shots of 1918.

It would be impossible, if not impertinent, to try to chronicle the movements and actions of every battalion throughout the war. It would take many volumes to tell the full story of each battalion. There are, in any case, many excellent histories – both written by participants in the events they record and by more modern historians. Instead, my intention is to focus upon key events from the Western Front, from France and Flanders, which will nevertheless enable me to visit the Regular, Territorial and Service battalions.

Here I have attempted to give a flavour of the Tigers' war through a few brief glimpses of different battalions from mobilisation to the Armistice. This, again, reflects a mass of research done over the Great War centenary; putting together a series of exhibitions, events and lectures held at the Record Office in Wigston Magna and elsewhere. That research has never really ceased, as additional material still comes to light, constantly adding to knowledge and understanding.

Some chapters here will be concerned with fairly minor affairs or even routine life in the front line while others describe a part played in great events. Two chapters in particular, respectively concerning discipline and trench life in general, will depart slightly from my generally chronological approach. My intention here, however, is to give an impression of life at the front as it was experienced, in quiet sectors as well as those truly at the 'sharp end' of the war. A third chapter looks at trench raiding, as experienced and as it developed, with examples drawn from early and late in the war.

My main intention has been to give an account of the Leicesters in their own words. To allow the officers and men to speak for themselves, no matter how unfashionable some views may seem or how damning or shocking an odd comment might seem. All will be seen from the soldier's point of view; recounting what he saw and felt, as often as possible in his own words. This is an account of the Great War seen through the eyes of those soldiers whose cap bore the Tiger badge of the Leicestershire Regiment. We are fortunate that enough of those Tigers wrote home, or wrote memoirs and, in a few cases, that others, including their enemies, wrote about them to make this possible. We can only marvel at the courage and resignation of ordinary men faced with extraordinary challenges and horrors.

In all this research and preparation, I have accumulated a long baggage train of debts, for records loaned or pointed out, and for help given. The Regiment itself, in the form of the Royal Tigers Association, has always given me great encouragement and, I hope, will see this unassuming volume in part as an effort to repay many kindnesses. I am grateful to archival colleagues over many years and to Laura Taylor, the current Chief Archivist in Leicestershire, for permission to reproduce material from the Regimental archive.

To Jess Jenkins I owe the greatest debt; for encouragement and guidance, for technical expertise in producing the book, and for her companionship in visiting so many of the places which feature so prominently in the following pages. I look forward to further trips and more books.

I am a firm believer that he who never made a mistake, never made anything. In this case the blunders are mine.

Robin P Jenkins<br>
Fleckney<br>
June, 2024

*Machine-gunners of the 11th Leicesters, the 'Midland Pioneers', halt at Ribecourt on 20 November 1917. [IWM: Q6279]*

# Contents

Introduction

| | |
|---|---|
| 1. Mobilize! | 9 |
| 2. "Playing at Soldiers" | 31 |
| 3. Over by Christmas | 43 |
| 4. "Hot as Mustard" | 59 |
| 5. "Trying to hold on" | 78 |
| 6. "It was a bomb business…" | 110 |
| 7. "The Tigers' Bloodiest Day" | 133 |
| 8. "Come on the Tigers!" | 163 |
| 9. "Bored to tears and covered in mud" | 180 |
| 10. "Kudos if it succeeds…" | 199 |
| 11. "The Flood Breakers" | 220 |
| 12. "Come along Tigers…" | 238 |
| 13. "Worthy of Everlasting Remembrance" | 260 |
| Sources & Bibliography | 267 |
| Index | 271 |

*A draft for the 4th Leicesters marches up Leicester's Newarke Street on their way from the Magazine barracks to the Midland Railway station, Winter 1914-15. [ROLLR; DE3736]*

Mobilize!

## Chapter One

# Mobilize!

Britain's response to the threat of war had been defined for her army since 1912, with the publication of the War Office's *War Book*, detailing the procedures for national defence and mobilisation. The first response was to deploy sufficient troops to secure naval bases and vital elements of supply and communication. Then, following a Royal Proclamation, full mobilisation could take place, including requisitions of animals and vehicles and government control of the railways.[1]

Leicestershire's first indication that the European crisis was coming to a head, was the click-clacking of the county's post office telegraph sounders on 29 July 1914, relaying orders recalling reservist officers and all troops on leave and warning headquarters that mobilisation was imminent.

The Leicestershire Regiment's regular battalions were overseas; the 1st Battalion at Fermoy in Ireland and the 2nd at Ranikhet in India. The Depot at Glen Parva was alerted however, and messages sent to the training and territorial battalions, the 3rd and 4th at The Magazine on Oxford Street in Leicester and the 5th Battalion in Loughborough.

The word passed along this telegraphic chain, spreading out from the battalion orderly room to company headquarters and detachments' isolated drill-halls, and with it the news of war. Policemen tacked up mobilisation posters and reservists dug out their instructions, with attached warrants for advanced pay and railway travel.

The telegrams sent, on 4 August 1914, by the adjutant of the 5th Battalion at Loughborough, to 'B' Company at the drill hall in Oakham, survive at the county record office. Just after 7p.m. it was *"mobilization imminent warn your company"* and at 9pm, a stark *"mobilize"*.[2] Throughout Leicestershire and Rutland mobilization messages were being carried

---
1 Charles Messenger *Call to Arms: the British Army 1914-18* (London) 2006, pp. 29-30
2 Record Office for Leicestershire, Leicester and Rutland (ROLLR): ref. 22D63/147/1-3

ever deeper into the countryside. From Oakham the adjutant's warning was taken to detachments at Uppingham, Cottesmore and Whissendine; while 'A' Company, at Ashby de la Zouch notified Coalville, 'C' Company at Melton Mowbray told Bottesford, Harby and Wymondham, and so on.[3]

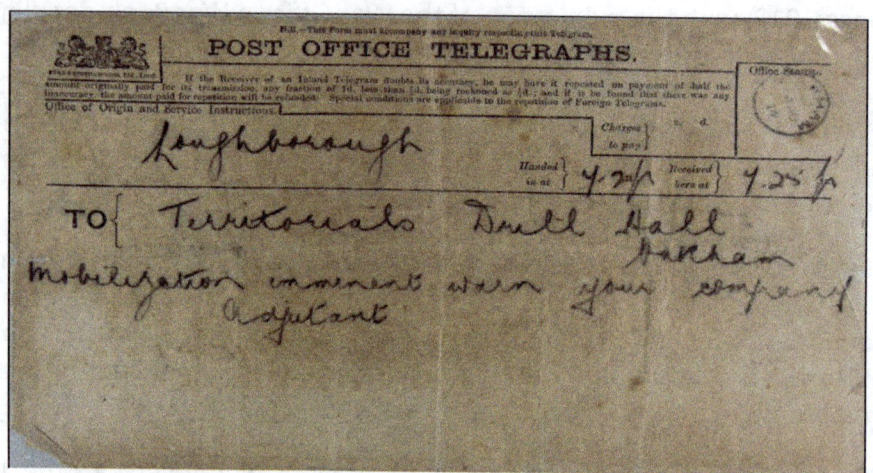

More urgent than the mobilisation of the Territorial Force however, was the vital need to gather Britain's reservists; the pool of trained and experienced manpower which would bring the Expeditionary Force up to fighting strength. These were the old soldiers, some 145,000 in number, who were recently discharged from active service but liable to recall – for which they received either a shilling or sixpence a day (depending upon their skills and liability for recall).[4]

Reservists, whose active service with the Leicestershire Regiment may have ceased anything up to nine years before (since Reserve service – and the pay it attracted - could be extended up to four additional years) were required to report without delay to the regimental depot at

---

3 Ray Westlake *The British Army of August 1914* (Staplehurst) 2005, p.82. The 5th Battalion's eight companies (as the territorials had not yet adopted the regulars' four company organisation) were based at Ashby, Oakham and Melton, as above, with 'D' at Hinckley, 'E' at Market Harborough (Kibworth and Fleckney), 'F' at Mountsorrel and Woodhouse Eaves, 'G' at Shepshed (Barrowden, Bisbrooke and Ketton) and 'H' at Loughborough.
4 Charles Messenger *Ibid.*, pp. 21-22

# Mobilize!

Glen Parva. Trains arriving at South Wigston were met by mobilization staff and the reservists marched up the hill to the Depot. There, they were formed into sections and taken for medical inspection. The unfit were sent home; the fit were provided with uniforms, equipment and weapons (and the cleaning materials to make them usable!). After a night in barracks, the reservists were put on a train once more, bound for the 1st Battalion of the Leicestershire Regiment in Ireland.

The depot at Glen Parva and nearby South Wigston had been, as one local reporter observed *"in one continual buzz of excitement since war was declared. The first batch of Reservists left the barracks on Thursday evening and on Saturday a large number of the friends of the soldiers from Leicester and the surrounding villages visited the barracks to bid farewell...Eleven hundred Reservists have been equipped and sent off, and recruiting is in progress."*[5]

*Mobilization staff at the Glen Parva depot, 1914*

Mobilization of Reserves was always the clearest sign, to allies and enemies alike, that war was anticipated and imminent. The disappearance of reservists from their traditional employments was also a signal for confusion and domestic disruption. Leicester was no different, the

5 *Leicester Daily Post*, 10 August 1914

# Tigers in the Trenches

*Leicester Daily Post* noting as early as 4 August 1914 that: *"The calling up of the reservists brings home more pointedly than anything else the gravity of the situation. There are many hundreds of reservists in Leicester engaged in various ways, and their withdrawal means dislocation in the working arrangements of many undertakings. For instance, there are 75 Reservists in the postal service of the town, 14 in the police force, a large number on the local railway systems, and an even larger number are engaged in various industrial concerns...Should the Proclamation be issued by noon it is anticipated that between one and two thousand men will have left Leicester to rejoin the colours."*[6]

*A reservist collects his uniform, kit and rifle from the Magazine, early August 1914 (ROLLR: DE3736)*

Although many Leicestershire men had served with their county regiment, it was by no means the rule. Consequently, while some men travelled a couple of miles to Glen Parva, others faced longer journeys

---
6 *Leicester Daily Post*, 4 August 1914

## Mobilize!

to wherever their old unit was based. Thomas Alderman Nourish, for example, had served with the 3rd Coldstream Guards in Egypt until his discharge in 1908. He had returned home to Fleckney, where he worked as a carter for a coal merchant until mobilised in 1914. He had reported to his old battalion at Chelsea Barracks and by 13 August was disembarking at Le Havre.

The Leicesters' 1st Battalion at Fermoy, in County Cork, was notified of the impending war by telegram at 5.50pm and instantly began to prepare for active service.[7] Detachments were recalled from Bantry and Berehaven, where they had presumably been guarding the Admiralty's deep water anchorages. The Bantry detachment reached Fermoy at 2p.m. on 7 August, followed two hours later by 296 Reservists from Glen Parva. The next day, at 3.15 a.m., the arrival of the Berehaven detachment, followed by another 230 Reservists at 5.15 a.m., brought the battalion to almost full strength.

On 9 August 1914 the battalion was inspected by Brigadier-General Edward Charles Ingouville-Williams, commanding the 16th Infantry Brigade of the 6th Division. On 10 August a further draft arrived from England, adding two non-commissioned officers and thirty-three other ranks to the battalion. The appearance of Captain Julian Bacchus from Aldershot, where he had been Superintendent of Gymnasia, on 11 August, completed the battalion's mobilisation.

That the battalion could be at full strength, fully equipped and taking part in Brigade training within a week of the declaration of war is a tribute not only to the Leicestershire Regiment but also to the Civil Servants of the War Office, who had masterminded the mobilisation plans, as well as the postal service and railways of the United kingdom which had made such an achievement possible. The 1st Battalion's historian, Colonel H. C. Wylly noted: *"Considering that the 1st Battalion...required no fewer than 579 non-commissioned officers and men to bring it up to war strength, the rapidity with which mobilization was completed is a fine tribute*

---

7 The Regimental History records that there is some dispute over the timing of the receipt of the mobilisation telegram at Fermoy, the Divisional History giving 10p.m. and the battalion War Diary 5.50 p.m. I have opted for the earlier time.

to the smartness with which the reservists rejoined on the declaration of war, and also to the business-like way in which the reservists were equipped at the Depot and passed on to the Battalion at Fermoy..."8

The Leicesters moved first to Queenstown (now Cobh) on Friday, 14 August, where the battalion's four companies were divided between the town's skating rink ('A' Company), the church ('B') a rest camp ('C') and Mistleigh House, on the Lake Road. At some point 'B' Company moved further out of town to take up quarters in Rushbrooke Docks.

On Saturday morning the battalion's transport, nine vehicles with one officer and forty-five men, with thirty-eight horses, embarked on the Belfast Steamship Company's express steamer, *S.S. Heroic* for Holyhead. The next day, 16 August 1914, the bulk of the battalion embarked upon the steamer *Londonderry*, brought down from the Midland Railway's service from Heysham to Belfast. A small party of four non-commissioned officers and forty men, under Lieutenant J. W. E. Mosse, boarded the *S.S. Kilkenny* which operated the City of Dublin Steam Packet Company's service to Liverpool.9

A photograph taken on 16 August shows the upper deck of the *Londonderry*, with men of the 1st Battalion gathered sitting or lying beneath their blankets around the cowl ventilators; their rifles and equipment carefully stowed about them on the deck.

---

8 Colonel H. C. Wylly *History of the 1st & 2nd Battalions the Leicestershire Regiment* (Aldershot), 1928, p.7.
9 1st Battalion War Diary (National Archives: WO95/1611/2)

## Mobilize!

Unlike Guardsman Nourish, however, the 1st Leicesters were not to join the British Expeditionary Force; not immediately at least. Instead, the 6th Division was deployed on the east coast, to counter any attempted invasion across the North Sea, and then concentrated in camps on Coldham Common, between Cambridge and Newmarket. The War Diary thereafter records a pattern of battalion and brigade training, punctuated with route marches and a church parade. A final draft of reservists arrived on 25 August to make good those no longer fit for active service.

On 27 August the Battalion moved to Grantchester, where 'night operations' were practised by the whole division on 29-30 August. It was only on 7 September, more than a month since the declaration of war, that the 1st Battalion marched to Royston, to entrain for Southampton. There, at 7 a.m. on 8 September they boarded the troopship, *Braemar Castle* for the crossing to St Nazaire (the German advance through Belgium having made the shorter crossing to Le Havre or Boulogne too hazardous).

The 2nd Leicesters, the Regiment's other regular battalion, was stationed in India in 1914; one of fifty-two British Army battalions on the sub-continent.[10] The Leicesters were one of four battalions (one British, one Gurkha and two Garhwali) in the Garhwal Brigade of the 7th (Meerut) Division. Their mobilisation telegram reached the battalion headquarters at Ranikhet, a cantonment in the Himalayan foothills, at 11 a.m. on 9 August 1914.

Warned for service in Europe, the battalion spent the following days in a near frenzy of activity. One company, 'C', on detached service in Delhi, was recalled while bayonets were sharpened, boots newly hobnailed and every man medically inspected. Wisely, the battalion was also ordered by the Quartermaster General in India to *"take winter scale clothing with one blanket"*.

On 12 August the battalion left Ranikhet, marching the fifty-two miles to the railhead at Kathgodam, where it entrained for Bareilly.

---
10 This figure includes India and Burma. Wylly, *Ibid.*, p. 105.

# Tigers in the Trenches

There mobilisation continued, marked by a succession of increasingly desperate telegrams requesting, as the war diary for 17 August recorded: *"Component parts Machine Gun & 2 mules, frogs and pouches, web equipment, Balaklava Caps, mittens, warm coats, waterproof sheets, spare boots"*.

*The 2nd Battalion leaves its depot at Ranikhet. ROLLR: DE6007/158*

Repeated telegrams bombarded those responsible for clothing, ordnance and remounts. To equip an entire Army Corps of troops, normally supplied with lighter khaki drill and equipment for an Indian climate, was clearly beyond the powers of the Indian Army however and on 18 August the war diary despairingly notes: *"Should be ready but following not yet received. 250 pouches for web equipment. All Balaklava Caps & mitts. 160 p[ai]rs boots. 116 British warms. 87 waterproof sheets. Component parts M[achine] Gun"*. To cap it all, the battalion's Medical Officer also had not yet arrived.[11]

By 24 August the battalion was ready to move, having been equipped with complete sets of up-to-date webbing and needing only the 160

---

11 War Diary 2nd battalion The Leicestershire Regiment; National Archives WO95/3945/2

## Mobilize!

pairs of spare boots, which the Arsenal unhelpfully deemed *"should be provided regimentally".*[12] Ten days later the battalion was warned for departure and on 5 September entrained at Bareilly for Karachi. There, after another week of delays, the battalion embarked aboard the transports *Devanha* and *Elephanta*: the former carrying the 10 officers and 437 men of the Headquarters and 'C' and 'D' Companies and the latter 'A' and 'B' Companies' 9 officers and 417 men.

Although the mobilisation of the Indian Army Corps does not bear comparison with that of the B.E.F., which was at sea within eleven days of mobilisation and in action at Mons on 23 August 1914, it is only fair to recall the greater distances involved and remoteness of supplies in India. The 2nd Leicester's commanding officer, the redoubtable Lieutenant-Colonel C. G. Blackader, was clearly neither satisfied with the Indian Army's performance, nor disposed to let the matter drop. His summary of the battalion's experience of mobilisation is both an indictment and a record of triumph over the odds:

*"although it left its Peace Station at 69 hours' notice, and although all requisitions were despatched immediately to complete equipment and also reckoning the Battn. was 4 days marching to Bareilly, it took exactly five weeks to get on board ship. The men in the mean time in the middle of the hot weather and the rains were in camp and suffered consequently in their health. At Bareilly 2 companies were put under shelter and although the C.O. urged that buildings should be requisitioned, such buildings being available, in order to get the men under cover from the heat and wet, this was refused by the O.C. Bareilly. It was only by dint of repeated telegrams and memorandums that the requisitions were complied with, both by the Arsenal and Clothing factory. On the 22nd August the last requisition was complied with, so had it been necessary to embark the Battalion at once, it would have gone only partially equipped."*[13]

At home, the Royal Proclamation which mobilised those reservists whose military service was still comparatively fresh also called up the Special and National Reserves. The former had been created from the

---
12 Ibid., 24 August 1914.
13 War Diary: 17 September 1914.

old militia, in the case of the Leicestershire Regiment forming the 3rd Battalion, which was designated a training battalion. On mobilisation the battalion was despatched to Portsmouth, for a time occupying Fort Widley, on Portsdown Hill, before joining the Hull garrison in 1915.[14]

G. R.

**To all Ex-N.C.O's.**

EX-NON-COMMISSIONED OFFICERS of any branch of His Majesty's forces are required for the duration of the War, their assistance in training the New Army being urgently needed.

**TERMS OF SERVICE.**

Promotion to non-commissioned rank immediately after enlistment. Age no obstacle so long as competent. No liability for service abroad if over 45, or in special cases 40.

**PENSIONERS.**

Pensioners may draw their pensions in addition to pay of rank at Army rates.

Apply for information or enlistment at any recruiting office, or ask O.C. depot to re-enlist you in your old Corps.

**GOD SAVE THE KING.**

The National Reserve was another creation of the 1907 Territorial and Reserve Forces Act. An unhappy compromise, the National Reserve allowed the War Office to keep a list of nearly a quarter of a million men whose assistance, as old soldiers, might be needed in a crisis but whose increasing age rendered them less valuable in reality. Those under the age of 42 might be accepted for active service, while a second class, of officers, warrant officers and sergeants under 55 and rank and file under 50, if fit, could sign up for *"home defence, for duty in fixed positions or for administrative work".*[15]

In fact, August and September 1914 abounded with mixed and conflicting messages from the military authorities. Territorial force recruitment continued alongside that for the regular army and Kitchener's New Armies. While newspaper readers were bombarded with advertisements for "EX-NONCOMMISSIONED

---

[14] The legislation of 1907, which had created the Territorial Force, in effect swept aside the old militia, yeomanry and volunteers. The territorial cavalry however inherited the titles and traditions of the old Yeomanry and the legislation to raise volunteers, though unused, remained in law. *Manual of Military Law (1914)* p.179.
[15] Manual of Military Law p.211

## Mobilize!

OFFICERS...To drill and instruct Recruits"[16] or for "Ex N.C.O'S...chiefly required as drill instructors...Age no obstacle so long as competent..."[17] the Territorial headquarters in Leicester's Oxford Street found itself issuing and then recalling arms and equipment.

On the afternoon of 8 August about a thousand National Reservists gathered at the Magazine drill hall in Leicester to hear Colonel J. E. Sarson and Lieut-Colonel R Dalgleish, representing the Emergency Committee of the Territorial Association. *"Colonel Sarson stated"*, reported the *Leicester Daily Post, "that at present 200 men had registered in the first class for foreign service and about 500 for the second (for home service) but they hoped many more would yet come in..."*

Nine days later, the same 'paper printed a letter from 'J.M.', one of those class one reservists, who complained that he was one of those who had reported to the Magazine, *"enrolled, were passed by the medical officer for active service and actually received their kit, only to be informed by postcard that their kits must be returned."* The affront, at least in J.M.'s case, was compounded by the loss of the £10 bounty to which he would have been entitled on 'mobilisation'.

It is hard not to sympathise with the staff of the Territorial Force at the Magazine and its adjacent buildings in Leicester. The minutes of the Territorial Forces Association Emergency Committee reveal something of their desperation in the first months of the war: *"...constituted to deal with purely Territorial matters concerning those units already administered by the Association [the Committee] has as time went on, been obliged to take into consideration a much wider outlook...the War Office has asked that the Territorial Associations should...take over and feed, clothe, and train as many recruits as the local military Authorities are able to cater for...dealing with 3,000 men, and as the depot buildings themselves are only capable of accommodating with tents and hutting – say 1,000 men – the Association may be called upon to provide accommodation for some 2,000..."*[18]

16 *Leicester Daily Post,* 4 September 1914
17 *Leicester Daily Post,* 8 September 1914
18 Record Office for Leicestershire, Leicester and Rutland (ROLLR) DE819: Territorial Forces Association Emergency Committee Minutes, 1914.

# Tigers in the Trenches

Bearing the brunt of the National Reservists, the Territorials' staff were understandably blunter in their response. Having issued rifles and kit only to recall them for more deserving and useful causes, the manuscript War Diary of the 4th Leicesters records that the *"National Reservists created a great deal of trouble. Original Organisation of same evidently incomplete – many physically unfit."*[19] The Reservists eventually found themselves protecting railway viaducts against saboteurs, guarding prisoners of war at Donington Park and elsewhere, and acting as orderlies at Leicester's Base Hospital, though (at least in the latter two cases) they all too often proved sadly lacking due to physical inability and infirmity.[20]

National Reservists with their newly issued kit outside the Magazine Barracks in Leicester, August 1914 (ROLLR:DE3736)

---

19  ROLLR: 22D63/136
20  See Robin P Jenkins *The Base Hospital* (Leicester) 2022, p. 21 for an account of National Reservists as orderlies and the same author's 'Luxury galore: The Officers' P-o-W Camp at Doningto Park, 1914-1919' in *Leicestershire Archaeological and Historical Society Transactions 95*, 2021 for an account of the Reservists at Donington.

## Mobilize!

It was hard enough to provide for the 4th Battalion of the Leicestershire Regiment, the North Midland Mounted Brigade (comprising the Leicestershire Yeomanry, the Leicestershire Royal Horse Artillery and its Ammunition Column as well as the Army Service Corps' Transport and Supply Column) and the two Royal Army Medical Corps units (2nd North Midland Field Ambulance and 5th Northern General Hospital) without an influx of elderly reservists and the sudden, unexpected and almost overwhelming responsibility for Lord Kitchener's New Army.

As luck would have it, however, most territorial units were already embodied, as the August Bank Holiday weekend, 1-3 August, was also the start of their summer camps. The War Office's initial warning telegrams had therefore pursued the Leicestershire Regiment's 4th and 5th Battalions to Bridlington, catching up with them soon after 5a.m. on Monday 3 August. By early afternoon they were on their way home.

It had been a wearisome weekend. The 5th Leicesters had arrived at Bridlington station at about 12.30 on Sunday and had marched the one and a half miles to camp, their band almost drowned-out by torrential rain and thunder. Their sister battalion had reached the East Yorkshire resort at 4p.m., missing the rain but with even less time to recover from their journey before packing-up once again to return.

Compared to other units of the territorial North Midland Division, the two battalions may have considered themselves fortunate. The Divisional Signals Company had been due to spend the week at St Asaph, some 130 miles away. The unit had reached St Asaph at about 10p.m. and finally took to their beds at midnight, only to be roused an hour and a half later and to be back aboard the train to Leicester by 6 a.m. The Leicestershire Royal Horse Artillery reached their training ground at Oswestry to find it deserted; the regular units having already departed for active service – the artillery towing their guns away behind motor lorries.[21]

The 4th Battalion returned from Bridlington to Leicester divided between two special trains, reaching the Great Central Station in quick succession, soon after 8.30 p.m. on 3 August. The *Leicester Daily Post's*

---
21 *Leicester Daily Post*, 4 August 1914.

reporter seemed quite carried away by the occasion:

*"Not since the outbreak of the Boer War have such animated scenes been witnessed in Leicester as those which took place last night on the return of the 4th Battalion to their headquarters in the Newarke. Many persons lined the streets leading to the Great Central Railway Station, and around the Magazine a comparatively large crowd assembled. As the battalion marched along, to the martial music of their band, cheers were raised and the utmost excitement prevailed."*[22]

Leicester in wartime was a strange mixture of careful planning and chaos. Crowds gathered around the territorial headquarters on Oxford Street and at the town's railway stations, eager to remain close to relatives in khaki and to know what was happening. Sentries were posted for the first time at the Magazine, with orders to admit only Territorials.

*Territorials of the 4th Leicesters brave heavy rain beside the Magazine Barracks*

The keys to Leicester's schools, empty for the summer holidays, were

---
[22] *Leicester Daily Post*, 4 August 1914.

## Mobilize!

taken by the borough police in case the buildings were needed as temporary barracks. The 4th Leicesters, in fact, had been dismissed to their homes on their return from Bridlington and told to report at 9 o'clock the next morning, in drill order, for training on Western Park. After a morning of what the local 'paper called 'musketry' their commanding officer, Colonel W. A. Harrison, sent them home for lunch, with orders to report again at 3p.m. for 'special drills' at the Magazine Drill Hall.

While the 4th Battalion skirmished across Western Park, and the local Royal Horse Artillery battery practised on the Filbert Street Recreation Ground, more trains arrived at Leicester's stations, bringing territorial units home. The *Daily Post* reported "animated scenes" as the 2nd North Midland Field Ambulance arrived from Bridlington, presumably at the Great Central Station, and the 5th Northern General Hospital, another Royal Army Medical Corps territorial unit, returned from an interrupted training week at Netley Hospital on Southampton Water.

The 5th Leicesters, being the county rather than city and suburbs battalion, had the added aggravation, or inconvenience, of having to travel a little further beyond Leicester to reach home. 'C' Company, for example, returned to Melton Mowbray at 10 o'clock on the morning of Tuesday, 4 August, being dismissed from the Asfordby Road drill hall with a warning to be ready for mobilisation at any time.[23]

The call came that evening, in response to which all but one of the company reported for medical and kit inspections at 8.30 a.m. on 5 August. Seven men were eventually rejected on medical grounds and the following morning the 127 Melton 'terriers' (or sometimes 'terrors') marched to rejoin their battalion at Loughborough.

At Loughborough the 5th Leicesters found themselves billeted in the town's elementary schools, drilling and parading, while strenuous efforts were made to equip the battalion for active service. The headquarters company made do with the drill hall. It was a process described in J. D. Hills admirable account of the battalion as *"the purchase of horses, the collection of stores, the requisitions for food and the sharpening of*

---

23 *The Pork Pie Crunchers* (typescript account of the battalion), 1.

# Tigers in the Trenches

bayonets..."[24]

The following days were spent on route marches, to toughen-up the soldiers and accustom them to marching in ammunition boots, carrying rifle and kit. That week the machine-gun section arrived from Ashby de la Zouch, with their maxim machine guns, and over a hundred of Loughborough's horses, vanners and hunters, were absorbed into the Army.

The 5th Leicesters parade in Loughborough Market Square on the eve of their departure from the town (ROLLR: DE3736).

The holiday atmosphere prevailed, aided perhaps by the payment of a £5 mobilisation bonus. In Loughborough, the Memorial Baths and Church Insititute rooms were both thrown open for troops, while, on Saturday evening, a free concert was held for mobilised forces in the Town Hall, followed on the Sunday by Divine Service conducted by Rev. H. Cyril Luxmore and the battalion chaplain, Rev. Canon Blakeney, in the open air. Loughborough's Queen's Park resounded with such appropriate hymns as "Onward Christian Soldiers", "Fight the Good fight" and "O

---

24 Captain J. D. Hills *The Fifth Leicestershire* (Loughborough) 1919, p.2.

## Mobilize!

God our help in Ages Past".[25]

The Territorial Force, like the old militia it replaced, had been created primarily for home defence; the *Manual of Military Law* spelling out that *"Any part of the Territorial Force shall be liable to serve in any part of the United Kingdom, but no part of the Territorial Force shall be carried or ordered to go out of the united Kingdom."*[26] As a consequence, on 10 August 1914, it had been necessary for Lord Kitchener, the Secretary of State for War, to begin a laborious process to ascertain which territorial units would consider overseas service.

Seen as substitutes for remote imperial garrisons, enabling regular troops to be brought back to the Western Front, territorials were to be asked to commit to an 'Imperial Service Obligation'; only units which proved over eighty percent willing to serve overseas being considered. As a consequence, both 'Tigers' battalions had to be paraded and addressed by the commanding officers, appealing to their men to waive their right not to serve overseas.

While both of the Leicestershire Regiment's territorial battalions continued to recruit, the 4th Battalion taking on an extra seventy men within a few days of the outbreak of war, plus sixty 'gentlemen cadets' from public schools, military service was not always a matter to be taken lightly, many 'terriers', sincerely believing there to be a difference between home defence and foreign adventures. Others, no matter how convinced of Britain's cause, were not able to leave domestic commitments – and had joined the Territorial Force *because* it allowed service without having to abandon family and business. While many men flocked to join the 4th or 5th Battalions, calculating that it was the quickest route to uniform and training, others fretted whether to take the Imperial Service Obligation or not.

On the morning of 11 August the 4th Battalion paraded in Magazine Square, Leicester, forming a hollow square around its commanding officer, Lieutenant-Colonel Harrison. William Augustus Harrison had over

---
25 *Leicester Daily Post*, 10 August 1914
26 War Office *Manual of Military Law* (OHMS) 1914, *p.763*

# Tigers in the Trenches

twenty years' service with the Volunteers and Territorial Force, including active service in South Africa against the Boers. Now, he addressed his battalion, as the reporter of the *Leicester Daily Post* recorded:

*"...the men of the 4th Battalion of the Leicestershire Regiment were asked if they were willing to undertake active service abroad, and responded splendidly to the appeal...The men who were willing to go were asked to step one pace forward, and practically the whole of them did so. The numbers were taken, and Colonel Harrison announced that although figures could not be given...he would be able to take the battalion. The announcement was received with cheers."*

The 4th Leicesters march through watchful crowds on their way to the railway station, 12 August 1914 (ROLLR: DE3736).

The 5th Battalion was not asked for its views on overseas service until 13 August, by which time it had moved from Loughborough to Duffield. Captain J. D. Hills considered the rough estimate that seventy percent

# Mobilize!

would consent to serve impressive, arguing reasonably that *"at that stage it was not perfectly certain that everyone would be wanted, and when the question of war service abroad was raised, and other men were not serving at all, it is only natural that the thought passed through some men's minds that the appeal was not for them."*[27] In any case, asked again at Luton, on 17 August, the county battalion was ninety percent resolved to serve.

Under the benign stare of John Biggs, on his plinth in Welford Place, Leicester's Territorials wind their way to the Midland Station (ROLLR: DE3736).

The 5th Battalion had departed Loughborough on 11 August with a ringing endorsement from Alderman Mayo, the mayor, in their ears. The 4th Battalion enjoyed what the *Daily Post* termed a "splendid send-off" the following day. Having marched to Magazine Square from their school billets, the companies assembled in double ranks, where they were joined by a party with the battalion's Colours, from St Martin's

27 Captain J. D. Hills *Ibid.*, p. 4

church, and a Boy Scout band. Colonel Harrison stood at the centre of the Square, with *"a small and select company of civilians"* including the Mayor, the Duchess of Rutland (whose son was an officer with the battalion) and the Bishop of Peterborough, who had chosen to come to Leicester rather than see off his son-in-law, who was departing for active service with the Coldstream Guards.

After an address from the bishop and a short speech by the Mayor, the battalion marched along Newarke Street, Granby Street, and the London Road to the railway station. The town's journalists knew that this was a momentous occasion:

*"The streets were lined with people of all ages from the Magazine to the Midland station, and it was no ordinary crowd that watched the progress of our citizen army. None assembled merely as sightseers, or out of curiosity. Scores of women made themselves useful by religiously asserting their right to assist in the carrying of kit bags to the station. All the way up London Road some of the "weaker" sex trudged along merrily, remaining with the battalion as long as possible."*

The station gates had been closed to the public, although trains continued to run and passengers arrived to board and alight. The station was therefore thronged with observers.

*"After marching to No. 1 Platform where a special train was in readiness, the 'Terrors' stood at ease for about ten minutes, during which time numerous music-hall songs were 'rendered' in lusty style. 'Dolly Grey' was revived but up-to-date ragtime songs were not forgotten."*[28]

Despite being far longer than the platform, the train was swiftly loaded and shortly after 3.25p.m., the Leicestershire Regiment's 4$^{th}$ battalion was on its way, the ribald shouts of the troops lost amidst the steam and pistons' noise of the straining locomotive.

Plans had already been laid however for an entirely new military force in addition to those which were mobilised by proclamation on 4 August. On 6 August, within hours of taking up his new post as Secretary of State

[28] *Leicester Daily Post*, 12 August 1914

## Mobilize!

for War, Lord Kitchener, had declared his intention to form a completely new force of at least half a million volunteers. Anticipating a war on an unprecedented scale and a duration of at least three years, Kitchener proposed to supplement the Regular Army and Territorial Force with new, 'Service' battalions, batteries and squadrons; creating a succession of 'New Armies' alongside but distinct from the existing military organisation.[29]

No sooner than it had processed its own reservists, the Leicestershire Regiment's depot found itself, like all other depots around Britain, engulfed in a tidal wave of new recruits; answering the call of Kitchener's grim visage and pointing finger, and eager to 'do their bit' before it was too late. The resulting 'service battalions' we shall encounter later, though the queues of keen or determined civilians impatiently awaiting uniforms and up to date rifles often rubbed shoulders with newly mobilised reservists or territorials.

Meetings were held throughout the Leicestershire, promoting the cause of military service. There were soldiers everywhere; on troop trains, billeted in schools, buying horses at fairs and sales, and drilling or marching wherever there was space. No-one was exempt, as calls went out for 'ANOTHER 100,000 MEN' and for retired NCOs to help drill new recruits, 'Public School Cadets and other gentlemen' to serve as officers, and ambulance men to join the Royal Army Medical Corps. Motorists offered up their cars and older men and young women their time, to serve in Volunteer Aid Detachments for military hospitals.

Recruitment never ceased and local newspapers were filled with reports of mobilisation. On 28 August over 700 recruits were fed at Glen Parva, where 3,000 men had been 'processed' in twenty days. A meeting at the Rothley Liberal Club, on 30 August brought 35 men for Kitchener's New Army. The following day a further 80 recruits attested at the Magazine for the Territorials and, at Wigston, 25 employees of the 'Two Steeples' marched to the Depot behind the son of a director of the company.

---

29 Clive Hughes 'The New Armies', in Ian F Beckett & Keith Simpson *A Nation in Arms* (Barnsley) 2014, p. 100

# Tigers in the Trenches

Had there been enough of the cloth to go around, Leicestershire would have been a sea of khaki!

*"The entraining was carried out most satisfactorily...as each moved out hearty cheers were given, the band playing 'Auld lang syne'. The responding cheers could be heard from the trains some distance after they had steamed away..."*

## Chapter Two

# "Playing at Soldiers"

Although Leicestershire's Territorials were waved off from the railway stations in Loughborough and Leicester, as the local newspapers put it, "for the front"[1], there was in reality a long period of acclimatisation and of training for modern warfare ahead of them. The two Territorial battalions were conveyed first to Derbyshire where they joined the 4$^{th}$ and 5$^{th}$ Battalions, The Lincolnshire Regiment in what was to become 138 (Lincoln and Leicester) Brigade of the 49$^{th}$ North Midland Division.

The enthusiasm of those weekend soldiers seems to have carried them through the initial confusion and shocks of military life. They were often hungry, tired and bewildered. The 'Terrors' survived the long training marches and uncomfortable quarters however; accepting the discomfort of sleeping on the floors of school halls and, for the 4$^{th}$ Leicesters in Belper, even part of the Union Workhouse.

There were compensations, however. At Belper, where they found themselves billeted in chapels and private houses, the public baths, provided by local industrialist, Herbert Strutt, were thrown open to the soldiers. As one tired 'terrier' recalled: *"and after parading in the hot sun with your pack on your back, and 150 rounds of ammunition in your pouches, you can understand what a boon it is to stand under a spray or to have a plunge in clear cool water. The attendants treated the 'Boys' as if we were conferring the favour and not them..."*[2]

The local population proved generous with food too, the same correspondent to the Leicester 'papers reporting that *"you will see the 'guard' enjoying a cup of tea and some cakes or bread and butter supplied by the 'missus' next door."* Cooking facilities were, in any case, often deficient anyway as few buildings were equipped for mass-catering: *"our cook makes a fire in the gutter and cooks our meals."* Opportunities were also there to be seized, Aubrey Moore (serving with 'D' Company of the

---
1 *Leicester Daily Post*, 8 August 1914 (amongst others)
2 *Ibid*, 18 August 1914

# Tigers in the Trenches

5th Leicesters) recalling that he celebrated his twenty-first birthday at Luton with two fellow officers by buying a seven shilling and sixpenny bottle of champagne at the Royal Hotel on Mill Street.[3]

Leicester Territorials on a route march accompanied by locals *(ROLLR: DE3736)*

From Belper and Duffield, the Leicester battalions were transported by train to Luton in Bedfordshire, where the Third Army (Home Forces) was gathering. It was their first real encounter with the unexplained and interminable delays which were to become typical of army life. At first, even the approach to the station was clogged with transport and the

---

3 Aubrey Moore *A Son of the Rectory* (Gloucester) 1982, p.120

# "Playing at Soldiers"

troops found themselves forced to stand and wait, as the grass of the verges was too long and wet to permit them to fall out and lie down. As Captain J. D. Hills observed: *"our train was timed to start at 11p.m., and seeing that we arrived at Luton at 2 p.m. the next day, the rate of motion was about 6 miles an hour, not too fast for a train...that was our first experience of such delay...and it counts one to the number of bars we said our medal should have."*[4]

The Territorials were slowly being introduced to the lessons learned by their comrades of the British Expeditionary Force at the front. War had become a matter of hard marching and digging-in. Our correspondent with the city battalion reported: *"We had an interesting morning's work today. We marched out about four miles to a piece of land to practice trench digging and to examine the transport and Maxim team, stretcher bearers etc."*

*Men of a Tigers' service battalion practise trench digging at Wokingham*

Slowly, August gave way to September and then October. A soldier of the 4th Leicesters' 'C' Company wrote home describing how warm days of drill, physical training, and route marches gave way to cold nights, spent twelve men to a tent, each one with his own groundsheet, wrapped in

---
[4] Captain J. D. Hills *The Fifth Leicestershire* (Loughborough) 1919, p.4 The battalion left Derbyshire on 15 August.

three blankets and an overcoat. The routine was enlivened by pay day and the antics of the fledgling Royal Flying Corps: *"overhead we have five aeroplanes. There have been as many as ten machines up all together. It's just like being at a flying meeting..."*[5]

By December 1914, the lessons learned from the Aisne and then around Ypres were beginning to reach the training camps and the refinements of siege warfare were becoming as prominent as the hitherto dominant marching and musketry. On 14 December, the *Leicester Daily Post's* correspondent 'with the 4th Leicesters' reported that *"we were engaged digging a new type of trench, a very elaborate system which has been designed from experience gained by our troops at the front and are quite different from anything we have seen before. They comprise sleeping apartments, latrines, and the firing trenches..."* The novelty was swiftly followed by the usual complaints of wet weather and praise for the morale-raising qualities of cigarettes.

*Service battalion orderlies under canvas, Autumn 1914 (ROLLR: 22D63)*

Food, too, was a popular topic of conversation. The correspondent from 'C' Company approved of breakfasts of *"ham and bread and butter or kippers or sausages",* supplemented by 'dinner' of boiled beef or

5 *Leicester Daily Post,* 5 October 1914

# "Playing at Soldiers"

mutton and 'tea' of bread and butter, cake or jam. He was also pleased to see 'dinner' occasionally enlivened with *"stewed plums by way of a dainty"*. The 5th Leicesters found themselves billeted in Luton, either in council schools or lodged, three or four men to a room, in the ground floor fronts of long domestic terraces. Cooking, like washing, became communal once more, in cook-houses and wash-tubs erected on the orders of Major R. E. Martin.[6] The adoption of a cat, with suitably tiger-like markings, completed the domestic arrangements.[7]

Parades soon grew from battalion to brigade and then divisional exercises, giving senior officers and their staffs experience of deploying and manoeuvring ever larger numbers and formations of troops and their attendant artillery and supply trains. No doubt many valuable lessons were learned, although the benefits do not always seem to have filtered down to the rank and file. Private W Holt, a signaller from Hinckley, serving in the 5th Leicesters' 'D' Company, clearly appreciated every aspect of one two-day exercise, which began at first light on Thursday, 8 October. He is worth quoting at length:

*"We were off at 5.30 with blanket and water proof sheet in addition to all our other clobber. We had a six-mile march to the manoeuvring district, where the trenches were…Then the chaps started making cover and finishing all the trenches while we were signalling, sending and receiving orders and message running, all in full kit…the trenches were dug all along this ridge and commanded a vast extent of country in the plain below. The trenches were finished off by boughs cut from trees and were made to look like bushes and hedges…"*

*"The artillery had their gun entrenched and covered behind the infantry higher up. You would see a little bush…but these were really cannon. Each piece had four blank shells to fire. The RFA [Royal Field Artillery] chaps told us that operations did not begin until two in the night, and finished at six…About eight o'clock things slackened down a bit so we got out our blankets and tried to get a bit of sleep…we had to lie where*

---

6 Hills, *Ibid.*, p. 5
7 The kitten was adopted by the 4th Battalion's 'E' Company, subsequently over-fed and much photographed! See the *Leicester Daily Post*, 24 August 1914

we were. I got a nice place in the hedgerow but did not get to sleep, and then about ten they fetched us up for some tea. I had had nothing since dinner...At eleven the whole battalion moved off just as Sergeant Diggle had got a loaf and pot of jam..."

The Division then marched, "dickens only knows how far", in a vast circling movement, passing through a number of slumbering villages and hamlets.

"We marched for hours and hours...marched and marched to our utter endurance, some of them walking in their sleep almost. At one of the ten-minute halts we got every hour, one of the officers' horses fell down asleep... We then came to a railway bank...No sooner were they over than firing commenced in all directions. The big guns boomed away and the rifle fire cracked away, the noise being deafening."

"By then it was nearly light and we moved over the [railway] line and found that sticking up about a mile in front of us was the rise where our trenches were made...the point we started from. The enemy were occupying our trenches and it appeared to us that we had been all that terrible way round and back again just for fun."

"I have no idea who won, or how it came out...Talk about playing at soldiers..."[8]

---

8 *Leicester Daily Post*, 12 October 1914. The night exercise is also described by J. D. Hills (p.8) who also records the fatigue of over-worked and ill-fed men.

# "Playing at Soldiers"

The North Midland Division, already contemplated as possibly the first territorial unit to be deployed at the front, was also subjected to frequent inspections from senior officers and even the King, who showed great interest in their progress.⁹ The progress was easy to see; the companies, battalions and brigades were accustomed to working together and the troops took everything in their stride. Even by the end of August if the pace of a column was too slow, a cry would reach the drummers, *"give us something quicker, chips"* and dust was kicked up in clouds.

The Territorials were learning. The *Daily Post's* correspondent, 'embedded' with the 4th Leicesters described a scene of efficient routine: *"After marching five miles each battalion marched into the large fields allotted to them for exercise. Arriving there we piled arms, took off packs, and each section commander took charge of his section and put them through their facings. The Maxim gun team of the 4th and 5th Leicesters were engaged in range finding and taking their guns to pieces."*

The correspondent was struck, on that hot August day, by the appearance of the division; the effect of the troops' shirt-sleeve order: *"the kaleidoscopic effect produced by the varied coloured shirts. There were reds, blues, whites, but the predominant colour was green, most of those served out to us being of that colour. It was a fine sight whilst on the march. As far as the eye could see was a long line of various colours of khaki soldiers, in all colours of the rainbow, and the few bands could only be faintly heard owing to the length of the column...the scene...*

---

9 On 11 October 1914, speaking at Ilkeston, the Duke of Devonshire had made public the decision that the North Midland Division had been given the signal honour of selection as the first Territorial division to serve at the front.

*gives one a fair idea of the value of khaki; it is the least discernible cloth for active service."*[10]

One lengthy route march took the division past the home of Sir Evelyn Wood, formerly Quartermaster General and Adjutant General of the Army (left). As the creator of a marching and shooting competition, the elderly Field Marshal might have been expected to appreciate the gesture, although one aspect of the experience grated upon the, presumably, footsore Lieutenant Aubrey Moore:

*"Sir Evelyn…was very keen that all troops on the march should sing, so we were told to sing loudly when we got to him. He was also stone deaf. So, an officer stood close to him and at intervals bawled into a sort of ear trumpet "the men are singing". For this privilege we marched over twenty miles. It was good exercise for the staff in moving a division."*[11]

Second-Lieutenant J. D. Hills, of the 5th Battalion's 'D' Company, soon wearied of the inspections and their concomitant drills, exercises and expenditure of spit and polish. *"Twice"*, he recalled, *"his Majesty the King honoured us with a visit, and in addition General Ian Hamilton, Lord Kitchener, and others."*[12] Ian Hamilton had assumed command of the 'Home Army' of Territorial forces on the outbreak of war and would have led the defence of Britain had an hostile army landed.

The King was as much an object of curiosity for the men of the 4th and 5th Leicesters as the newly mobilised units were to their royal visitor. At Luton Hoo, on 18 September, *"his Majesty walked the whole length of the brigade, front and rear accompanied by his staff. He was keenly interested in all he saw. The staff then lined up, and we marched off, the 4th Leicesters going by the King first. We went by quite close to his Majesty, so we all had a good look at our Sovereign, most of us for the*

---

10 *Leicester Daily Post*, 24 August 1914
11 Aubrey Moore, *Ibid.*, p. 122. Stephen Manning *Evelyn Wood VC* (Barnsley) 2007, p. 235.
12 Hills *Ibid.*, p.7 The 'others' included General Sir Alfred Codrington, who succeeded Sir William Franklyn as commander of the Third Army.

# "Playing at Soldiers"

first time. He wore serviceable khaki."[13]

The Leicesters returned to their camp for rifle and foot inspection, followed by a night exercise: *"rather a cold job – but we are all in good health."* They could not have known how serious was the debate over the future use of the Territorials, nor how perilous the plight was of the B.E.F. on the Aisne and in West Flanders.

*A draft for the 4th Leicesters marches up Leicester's Newarke Street from the Magazine Barracks, en route to the Midland Station, probably late in 1914.*

It was not only questions of the readiness of the soldiers which delayed the departure of territorial divisions to the front-line however. Much of their equipment was antiquated and reports from the front expressed severe doubts over weapons, such as the 15 pounder field guns, which were largely phased-out amongst regular units but still standard issue with Territorials. The decision, too, to 'cherry-pick' key battalions for

[13] *Leicester Daily Post*, 19 September 1914

service in Gibraltar, or India, had also put back the preparation of entire divisions for front-line deployment.[14]

In reality, however, there was no-one else to send. The Service Battalions of the Leicestershire Regiment, by the Autumn of 1914 moved for further training to Aldershot, were nearly a year away from readiness. Unlike the Territorials, the Leicesters' 6th, 7th, 8th and 9th Battalions had had to start from scratch; with virtually no weapons, uniforms or equipment and officers either enticed back from retirement, diverted whilst on leave from colonial forces, or newly commissioned.[15] For at least one battalion rifles appeared in October but khaki uniforms and leather equipment was not issued until March 1915.[16] What Kitchener's Army lacked in equipment, however, it made up for in spirit and enthusiasm.

'B' Company of the 8th Leicesters drill in mufti, September 1914. (ROLLR: DE8402)

A Whitwick man with the 9th Leicesters clearly appreciated the need for urgency, telling his late employer: *"We are all trying to keep the old regiment's name up. Our officers are very good to us. They want us to try <u>and be ready as</u> soon as we can. They don't want us to be left behind."*[17]

14 Charles Messenger *Call-to-Arms(London)* 2005, pp. 82-3
15 The newly raised 8th Battalion, for example, was commanded at first by a volunteer captain of the Singapore Artillery (I. L. 'Dick' Read *Of those we Loved (Barnsley)* 2013, p.504
16 C.A.B. Elliott records taking 50 men to collect rifles from the railway sidings in Aldershot. They were "in a shocking state" and two men had to be "detailed off to walk behind and pick up small parts, bolts, magazines, etc which became unattached."
17 *Leicester Daily Post*, 9 November 1914

# "Playing at Soldiers"

Sometimes the considerate behaviour of officers took a curious turn. Lieutenant Charles A. B. Elliott, serving with the 8th Leicesters, noted in his dairy how *"Our first C.O. was only about a fortnight with us, and was away from Thursdays to Tuesdays (week ends). He came on parade once for certain and having had the Batt[alio]n. drawn up in mass told us through a megaphone that there was too much noise after lights out, which interfered with his thoughts, as most of the night he plotted & planned for the good of the B[attalio]n."*[18]

Lieutenant (later Major) C. A. B. Elliott, 8th Leicesters, with a feline friend. (ROLLR: DE8402)

This was a Major H. McEwan, who was swiftly replaced by Lieutenant-Colonel Hugh de Berdt Hovell, lately retired from command of a battalion of the Worcestershire Regiment. Hovell enjoyed a reputation for innovation and eccentricity as well as a D.S.O. awarded for gallantry during the South African War.[19] Charles Elliott, though, was clearly

18 Diary of Lieut. C.A.B. Elliott, ROLLR: DE8402/1
19 https://www.angloboerwar.com/forum/5-medals-and-awards/8425-hovell-h-de-b-hugh-de-berdt . There are many references, on-line, to Hovell's peculiarities of conduct as well as to their unfortunate consequences.

unimpressed by some of his commanding officer's methods:

*"Col Hovell altered the P.T., and made us do it for 1/4 hr 4 times a day whenever a big gong which he had erected was struck. This led to much grumbling, confusion and incidentally amusement as the men had orders to leave off whatever they were doing, with no word of command and start doing P.T. as soon as they heard the gong...He [Hovell] would ride up to a man suddenly, and ask him if his tent flap was kept open at night, or if he had any dubbin etc. For this last question, which he was asking frequently, he was nicknamed 'Old Dubbin'.*

Lieutenant Elliott, presumably breathed a sigh of relief when 'Old Dubbin' was himself replaced by Colonel C. H. Shepherd. The battalion was to have two more commanding officers before, in July 1915, it too was finally considered ready for active service.[20]

*Lieut. Elliott's snapshot of his platoon at bayonet drill (ROLLR: DE8402)*

---

20 Readers anxious for more detail of the preparation of the service battalions will not do better than to read Matthew Richardson's admirable *The Tigers (Barnsley) 2000.*

Over by Christmas

## Chapter Three

# Over by Christmas

There are many telling photographs from the Great War. This one was taken, late in September 1914, presumably by an officer, of the 1st Leicesters' 'B' Company. The scene is a familiar one as far as that war is concerned; half-a-dozen 'tommies' resting in a hastily scraped fire trench cut into the side of a hill. It is somewhere near Vailly, overlooking the Aisne River. One of the soldiers, an amused, younger fellow, stands upright as a lookout, while the others sit or crouch with loosened equipment, though their SMLE rifles are clean and bright. All are gazing at the camera, only the sentry smiling, the others seem older and more wary or expectant. They have been less than a week on the front-line but are already learning the ways of trench warfare: its hazards and 'rules' but more than anything its capriciousness.

ROLLR: DE6201/36

Private Herbert Bailiss, a Nailstone reservist serving with the Leicesters, sensed both the turning tide of the German offensive and the new ways

# Tigers in the Trenches

of warfare: *"We are winning all along the line. If things go on like this, I think that the war won't last long, as we seem to have them bottled up. I have just witnessed a war in the air. It was a sight never to be forgotten. We are smoking tea-leaves and brown -paper, as the Germans have looted all the villages round here, and 'pinched' all the tobacco and eatables. We are having it very stiff, but I don't mind, as I think it will end all the quicker, as we have got them on the move 'a treat'. I cannot tell you where I am, although I should like to. We have some nice music here. I am on outpost duty, and the guns are banging away a treat."*[1]

The 1st Battalion of the Leicesters had reached the front-line on the evening of 21 September, relieving the 3rd Worcesters and 2nd Royal Irish Rifles just before midnight. They were to occupy the hastily scraped trenches above the Aisne until the early hours of 13 October, when men of the blue-coated and red-trousered 106th French Infantry arrived to take over the line. There had been no serious assaults on either side but that brief spell in the line, through shelling and sniper-fire, had cost the lives of Captain Robert F. Hawes, a lance-corporal, drummer and four privates.[2]

*Lieutenant Hugh Barrington Brown and Captain Julian Bacchus, both of the 1st Leicesters, retain an older style of warfare, Brown still wearing his sword, while Bacchus wears the spurs of a mounted officer. ROLLR: DE6201/61.*

---

1 *Leicester Daily Post*, 30 September 1914.
2 The *War Diary* (National Archives: WO95/1611) does not record the name of the officers killed and wounded but H C Wylly *Ibid.*, p. 10, does, the wounded being Major B. C. Dent and the Adjutant, Captain E. S. W. Tidswell. The Other Rank casualties were: 9238 Drummer Bernard Pegg (of 'B' Company), 9640 Private J Goadby, 7087 Private Arthur Horace Skinner, 9468 Lance-corporal T W Bray, 8443 Private James Stephen Graham, and 7600 Private William Robert Bradford.

# Over by Christmas

Company Sergeant Major Frederick Diggins, of the 1st Battalion, adapted swiftly to the routine and privations of the new trench warfare:

*"We are in 'em', and have been for weeks – the trenches, I mean, nothing else. Still busy sparring with our chums. We have a pound now and again to show we are still alert...The barber would do a roaring trade if he came here, no-one having shaved for weeks. Consequently, beards vary according to the age of the individual, and the length of time he has not shaved. Mine for instance, is something to gasp at and remember. They are not by any means what a writer in a lady's novelette would describe as a perfect dream. They are scattered over my chivvy-chase in anything but order, nineteen on one side, fifteen on the other, and thirty-five on the chin, intermingled with a small smattering of down and dirt. Dirt did I say? That doesn't describe it. For three solid weeks I haven't broken my caste. Water is at a discount, except for drinking; soap something to read about and wonder when you last used it, and when you will see it again. I can safely say 'three weeks ago I used your soap, since then I have used no other'."* [3]

The trenches dug by both sides along the valley of the River Aisne were a physical sign that the war of movement was coming to an end. Further attempts were made that Autumn to break through into open country, but all were eventually thwarted by an impregnable combination of spadework and firepower. As the trenches extended along the entire front-line, the British Expeditionary Force was moved northwards; closer to its supply bases and the Channel ports.

Eventually, the Leicesters were placed in the line at Rue du Bois, a hamlet some six or seven miles south-west of Armentières at the centre of French Flanders. They were to remain in the trenches, or 'resting' in Armentières, from mid-October until May 1915.[4] As the year drew to its close, the B.E.F. with its French and Belgian allies faced the final attempts of the Germans to break through in 1914; first racing the Belgians to the sea and then in a series of assaults around Ypres. Though the old Belgian

---

3 *Leicester Daily Post*, 20 October 1914. CSM Diggins' reference to breaking his caste refers to the Hindu belief that to cross water (to go overseas) will lead to a loss of 'varna', or class within the caste system.
4 War Diary

city was retaken by the Allies, it was to remain almost cut off at the tip of a salient.

*A hastily scraped trench of the 1st Leicesters on the Aisne. ROLLR: DE6201/48*

With every part of the B.E.F. under pressure, the 1st Leicesters found themselves hurried from one weak point to the next, digging in and expecting an attack at any minute. On 21 October the battalion was ordered to relieve the hard-pressed 1st West Yorkshires and for the following five days clung grimly onto a hastily scraped defensive line stretching from the crossroads and a chemical works at Rue du Bois to a nearby railway line.

The battalion war diary relates a story of almost constant shelling from the German artillery, punctuated by fierce, mass attacks and hand-to-hand fighting:

*"22 Oct Thurs. Held trenches. Heavily shelled by Shrapnel and Heavy Howitzers all day. Casualties Lt. Prain & Lt Dods killed. Lt Smeathman wounded and died. 11 other ranks killed & 25 wounded..."*

*"25 Oct Sun. Germans attempted to rush trenches at dawn but beaten*

## Over by Christmas

*back with great loss, shelled intermittently all day. 2 platoons of D Coy were driven out by enfilade fire about 9 a.m. but retrieved position by dusk..."*[5]

Like the other regiments of the British Expeditionary Force, the Leicesters were being slowly bled dry. The bitter fighting around Rue du Bois had, in less than a week, cost the battalion eight officers (four killed and four wounded) and forty-seven Other Ranks killed, 134 wounded and ninety-eight missing; a figure than must have included both dead and wounded left behind in abandoned trenches as well as those taken prisoner by the enemy.

A tired tommy of the 1st Leicesters shelters in his fox-hole like 'scrape' above the Aisne. ROLLR:DE6201/55

Private Wakefield, a reservist, recalled to the army from the Loughborough police, considered the Germans *"well equipped...excellent soldiers...with the exception of their dislike of cold steel"*. Evacuated after a wound to his knees, Wakefield particularly remembered *"October 25th when they had to relieve the Yorkshires. The Leicesters found the trenches full of water, and they had to begin digging fresh ones. Before a foot of earth had*

---
5 War Diary

# Tigers in the Trenches

been removed the Germans got the range to a nicety and began shelling with howitzers of the 11-in type and blew the Leicesters to pieces. This was the day the when the regiment's casualty list approached 550 men. It was impossible to hold the position and a retirement was ordered."[6]

The sudden shock of industrial-scale warfare was to remain with the 'Tigers' for many years. Private C. Ireland, of the 1st battalion's 'C' Company, wrote home that he should *"never forget the 23rd and 24th October as long as I live. From October 22 to October 26 we had it hot, and I think the regiment made a good name for itself..."*[7]

Another of the 1st Battalion's wounded was interviewed, recuperating at home in Leicester:

*"He was slightly wounded near Armentieres. He says the men are in good heart and although they have suffered losses they have given a good deal more than they got. Their shooting has been extraordinarily good especially considering the rapidity with which firing took place. Once or twice the Germans have attacked en masse, and the first volley from the Leicesters has wiped away the first line as if they were leaves blown down by the wind. The result was that the men behind 'bunched up', and the succeeding firing must have accounted for great loss, the target being such that it was almost impossible to miss. In connection with this he relates how he heard one of the officers, a very quiet reserved man, who was always very particular in his language, swear the first*

---

6 *Leicester Chronicle and Leicestershire Mercury,* 16 January 1915
7 *Leicester Daily Mercury,* 10 November 1914

## Over by Christmas

time any of the regiment had heard him. They were waiting for an attack and the waiting got a little upon their nerves. Suddenly the enemy were seen at a distance and there was an immediate cry of 'There they are', 'All right boys , all right', said the officer, 'Don't trouble to talk about it ---- well shoot 'em.'[8]

The shock and exhaustion no doubt felt in the crumbling, water-logged trenches [see opposite page] now spread to higher commands and general staffs and, as the 6th Division's history noted: *"active fighting now died away..."*[9] It was replaced with a horrific monotony (the word comes from the Regimental History) of periodic shelling, sniping and shoring-up the slimy, collapsing mud walls of trenches and rest periods out of the front-line. The appalling weather hampered any military preparations but also struck hard at health and morale.

Private Harry Burton, from Shepshed, serving with the 1st battalion, wrote home that *"the weather is so bad, owing to the continuous rain, that it makes it cruel for men to stand what they are doing"*.[10]

Even monotony came at a cost however as the battalion War Diary attests. In November alone, one officer (Captain C. C. Rolph) and fourteen Other Ranks were killed and twenty-one wounded; not including two soldiers evacuated with frostbite. Some eight days had been spent in billets behind the lines and twenty-two in the front-line. German shelling, though rarely heavy, had occasionally proved devastating. On the afternoon of 7 November 1914, a sudden bombardment had killed or wounded ten men of 'C' Company and on 11 November even the billets came under effective fire.

It is noteworthy that, in November, only once was it felt advisable to abandon the billets. This was on 3 November when the battalion relocated to a position five hundred yards away *"owing to 60 pr battery placing itself near"*. Presumably the Tigers had learned the hard way that a few shots from a Royal Garrison Artillery battery invariably brought upon its neighbours the wrath of the recipients and an uncomfortable

8 *Leicester Daily Post,* 9 November 1914
9 Quoted in Wylly, p. 13
10 *Leicester Daily Post,* 24 December 1914.

# Tigers in the Trenches

counter-battery fire.

December brought even colder, wetter weather. The War Diary often simply noted *"Quiet all day"*,[11] although whether that reflected exhaustion (of men or munitions) or a preoccupation with that common enemy, the Flemish climate, is unclear. Even a visit from King George V receives a bare half-dozen words, despite the hours which must have been spent in near fruitless cleaning and then marching to Bac Saint-Maur for the inspection.

No-where is the incongruity of this strange mixture of 'live and let live', shelling and sniping, better illustrated however than in the curious cessation of hostilities, the truce – or non-truce – of Christmas 1914.

Clearly, spirits were raised amongst the 1st Leicesters when, a few days before Christmas, the rain ceased and temperature fell; freezing the mud and water and allowing much needed repair work and cleansing. Christmas cards and presents arrived from home too, including a card and gifts from both the *Leicester Mercury*'s and Princess Mary's fund's. As the battalion's Lance-corporal J. Howard observed in a letter home, having received both: *"How nice it is to be thought of while out here doing our duty."*[12]

Major Stoney Smith also wrote from the trenches, on Christmas day, to thank the editor of the *Mercury* for its gift of *"11 boxes of gloves..."* adding *"that the men are very proud of the Xmas card and presents sent them by the people of Leicestershire and Rutland through the medium of your paper"*.[13] The major also listed many gifts of tobacco and cigarettes (mostly 'woodbines'), two parcels of footballs, and six bundles of socks from a variety of addresses in Leicester with the gratitude of the recipients and the hope that *they will understand that there is considerable difficulty in writing letters in the trenches and getting them sent back to the field post office."*

The spirit of Christmas had also reached the opposing front-line. Indeed,

---

11 On eleven occasions in December 1914
12 *Leicester Chronicle & Leicestershire Mercury*, 30 January 1915.
13 *Leicester Daily Post,* 28 December 1914

## Over by Christmas

it seems that expectations were high on both sides of all fronts, that Christmas – with its message of 'Peace' and 'Goodwill to All' – might take on an even greater meaning in 1914.

It was clearly not unknown for messages, some friendly and others more taunting, to be shouted across no-man's land where the opposing trenches were close enough to permit it. Private Albert Newby of the 1st Leicestershires, writing home on 20 December, recorded that *"on some occasions we have only been some 70 yards away from them. They shout 'Good-night, you English, have you had your rum?' Sometimes we ask them to sling us a German sausage over for supper, but they reply, 'Ver Der'* [Presumably 'wer da?' or 'who's there?']. *The night before...the Germans were as happy as kings, singing and shouting, blowing bugles and one thing or the other..."*[14]

---

[14] *Leicester Daily Post*, 1 January 1915. Private Newby also writes about a 'splendid battle last night' (19 December) with much destruction of the German trenches by artillery fire. The War Diary records 'Quiet all day'. Newby also describes the destruction of French villages and urges 'young men in England' to enlist.

# Tigers in the Trenches

For many of the 1st Battalion it is clear that Christmas Day passed peacefully and without hostility from the enemy opposite. Lance-corporal S. Morris, writing home to 29, Walnut Street in Leicester, reported *"things are very quiet here today (Christmas Day). The Germans have asked us not to shoot, and they offer to do the same. The men got quite friendly, singing songs alternately, and exchanging tobacco – in fact, they are visiting each other's trenches. But what's in store for tomorrow?"*[15]

Private J Lowe, of the 1st Battalion's 'D' Company, also wrote home to friends, describing an unofficial truce on both Christmas Day and New Year's Day: *"The Germans were quite friends with us on those two days. They left their trenches and came over to our officers and shook hands with them as they came along the railway line, but we didn't allow them in our trenches...It seemed a shame to start fighting them again after their giving us cigars and cigarettes."*[16]

*A view of the truce from the* Illustrated London News

There are many such letters. A corporal, un-named, but writing to his old headmaster at Leicester's Bridge Road School, also noted the change

[15] *Leicester Daily Post,* 30 December 1914.
[16] *Leicester Chronicle & Leicestershire Mercury,* 23 January 1915.

# Over by Christmas

to 'seasonable' weather: *"clear and frosty. Our troops and the enemy in front – a Saxon regiment – met on friendly terms and spent part of the day burying the dead. Many of the Saxons said they were sick of the war and longed for its end. I am sending you a parcel of curios and mementos of the war..."*[17]

The implication here is that our corporal had not only been collecting souvenirs of the war but also, perhaps, trading for buttons, badges and the like with men of the Saxon regiment occupying the opposing trenches. It is often Saxon troops who feature most prominently in accounts of Yuletide fraternisation. Private Harold Startin of the 1st Leicesters even recalled a voice in clear English coming from the enemy lines: *Hello there, hello there, we are Saxons, you are Anglo-Saxons. If you don't fire, we won't fire."*[18]

There are many accounts of the Christmas truce and no doubt most are quite true, at least as far as the observer was aware. The *Regimental History* records the singing of carols, begun by the Germans who then urged their opponents to respond; crying "Good! Good!" in encouragement. Elsewhere, enemies chatted in broken English, dead were buried, unhampered by sniping, and souvenirs or 'smokes' swapped.

Sergeant Arthur Illston, writing home to the parson of his church at Oadby, recalled a British invitation for the Germans to join them in no-man's land:

*"Everything had gone on as usual till 8 o'clock on Christmas eve when all firing ceased. A few minutes after the Germans commenced to sing their National Anthem, and then carried on with carols and songs. So one of our Officers organised a Concert and Glee party to sing carols. So things went on with no alteration until Christmas morning, 5 o'clock. One of our Officers chanced* [i.e. 'took the chance' or risk of going] *to go as far as the enemies trenches with a board of Invitation to the Germans, which was readily accepted by some of them who could speak English. They*

---
17 *Leicester Daily Post*, 20 January 1915 and *Leicester Chronicle & Leicestershire Mercury*, 23 January 1915.
18 Quoted in Malcolm Brown & Shirley Seaton *Christmas Truce* (London) 1994, p. 82

# Tigers in the Trenches

*advanced half-way between the two lines and met a similar number of our men. They exchanged Christmas greetings and souvenirs of every description, ands so the armistice went on until 12 midnight, when a warning shot was fired to let them know everything was as usual."*[19]

The position held by the 'Tigers', however, was opposite a point in the German line where two regiments met. Major Archibald Buchanan-Dunlop, [right] who was to achieve an unwanted and probably unwarranted notoriety as an instigator of the truce simply through the misfortune of having a detailed account of his carol-singing and modest fraternisation (in a letter home) published in a local and then national newspaper, noted the situation: *"The enemy on our left – Saxons – are still out hobnobbing with our fellows, but the folk opposite us – Prussians – are very vicious indeed..."*[20]

The same regional differences were identified by another 'Leicester soldier', in a letter which appeared in the *Leicester Daily Post* on 22 January 1915:

*"On our right was a regiment of Prussian Guards; on our left a Saxon Regiment. On Christmas morning some of our fellows shouted across to them saying that if they would not fire our chaps would meet them half-way between the trenches, and spend Christmas Day as friends. They consented to do so. Our chaps at once went out, and when in the open the Prussians fired on them, killing two and wounding many more. The Saxons, who behaved like gentlemen, threatened the Prussians if they*

---
19 No. 7760 Sergeant Arthur George Illston (1st Battalion Leicestershire Regiment, 1905-1915) letter 'from the front' to Rev Raine *Oadby Parish Magazine* Easter 1915. Illston was killed in action on 20 September 1915 and buried in La Brique cemetery, Ieper (Ypres).
20 Quoted in an excellent account and analysis of his involvement in the truce by Buchanan-Dunlop's great-grandson, Rupert Shepherd: *https://rupertshepherd.info/uncategorized/the-notorious-major-b-d*

# Over by Christmas

*did the same trick again. Well, during Christmas day our fellows and the Saxons fixed up a table between the two trenches, and they spent a happy time together, and exchanged souvenirs and presented one another with little keepsakes..."*

*Buchanon-Dunlop (right) with Captain Frederick Ingram Ford, during the winter of 1914-15. This image bears comparison with that on page 44.*

In fact, while the Germans to the left were almost certainly from either the 107th or 179th Infantry Regiments of the XIX Saxon Corps, the 'vicious

# Tigers in the Trenches

Prussians' seem actually to have been Westphalians of the 15th or 55th Regiments.[21] Although Westphalia is part of the kingdom of Prussia, 'Prussian' seems often simply to have been a shorthand term for less easy-going, more committed troops.

The Leicester Tramways' war memorial, which includes George H Sutton's name.

[In the care of the Leicester City, County and Rutland At Risk War Memorials Project].

---

21 Brown & Seaton p. 232

## Over by Christmas

The unwillingness of the Westphalians to suspend hostilities was to lead to one of the Christmas truce's sad incongruities. While to the left *"both sides were out of their trenches, shaking hands and exchanging tobacco for cigarettes and chocolate"*[22] as well as swapping buttons as souvenirs; on the right any movement drew the attention of enemy snipers and led to the deaths of not two but three men of the 1st Leicesters.

The War Diary recorded *"Cold. Quiet all day"* on Christmas Eve and a typically matter of fact *"Frost. 2 men killed one wounded"* for Christmas Day itself. The two killed were Number 7620 Lance-corporal George Henry Sutton, a twenty- seven year old tram-driver from Belgrave in Leicester, and Number 11419 Private James Farrell, a Birmingham man.

Not surprisingly, views of the fraternisation differed greatly within and between units. Captain Thomas Ingram, a medical officer attached to the 1st King's Shropshire Light Infantry (serving alongside the 1st Leicesters in the 16th Brigade, 6th Division) was distinctly outspoken in a letter home and can only have meant the Leicesters and the much misunderstood Major Buchanan-Dunlop:

*"All this friendly peace business at Christmas is rotten; we aren't here to pal up to the enemy and sing carols with him. One regiment especially distinguished themselves by their friendliness to the enemy at Christmas, and their second in command went and sang in the enemy trenches. This particular regiment is in our brigade and has not been so distinguished when fighting has to be done; in fact quite the contrary. Our men are awfully sick with them over the whole thing, and last night there was a bit of a scrap in the town between some of ours and the carol singing lot. Two or three other regiments who were too pally at Christmas have also had to fight their friends since; good thing too."*[23]

There is nothing in the casualty figures to suggest that the Leicesters had suffered less than their neighbours; indeed in December (bearing

---
22 Private F. Cooper, letter printed in the *Leicester Daily Post*, 2 January 1915.
23 Marc Ferro, Malcolm Brown, Remy Cazals & Olaf Mueller *Meetings in No Man's Land* (2007) p. 55

in mind the dead on Christmas Day) it is quite the opposite. Experience of war is clearly all too often a matter of luck and south of Armentières, on Christmas Day 1914, that luck could be nothing more than a matter of a hundred yards of trench. Arthur Slater, a private in 1914, but later a DCM-winning acting-sergeant, who had sung in response to the Germans, clearly did not see his fellow 'Tigers' as leading a charmed or easy life:

"I didn't get a change of clothing or a wash for 24 days, and everything I possess now is wet through. Under the circumstances I didn't enjoy my Christmas but the Germans did in front of us, for they were shouting and singing in some parts of the trenches. Some of our chaps exchanged fags and money with them, but it doesn't do to be too chummy with them at these times".[24]

*A group of 'Tigers' showing the ravages of the winter of 1914-15 in the trenches of the Ypres salient*

---

24 *Sheffield Daily Telegraph*, 11 January 1915: quoted in Rupert Shepherd.

## Chapter Four

# "Hot as Mustard"

On 1 December 1914, the day before he had inspected their sister battalion at Bac Saint Maur, the 2nd Leicesters paraded for King George V at Locom, some ten miles to the south-west. Afterwards the King spoke to both officers and men, questioning them about conditions and life in the trenches. As the battalion's War Diary recorded: *"Having only returned from the trenches at midnight they were very dirty, a condition described by the King as "looking war-worn".*

'War worn' was a description that applied equally well to the entire Expeditionary Force, which was clinging on, by its figurative finger-ends, to the sometimes freezing, sometimes mud-clogged trench line around Ypres. The irreplaceable old British Army, with its South African War and India General Service medal ribbons, was gradually being worn away and drowned in the Flanders clay.

Despite a winter of heavy losses around Ypres, the year 1915 brought new hope to the British and their allies. The French and Belgians were eager to recover territory under German occupation and to relieve pressure on their Russian allies. So, as reinforcements arrived for the BEF from the Empire and from Territorial units at home, and dumps of supplies were built up, plans were laid for the first serious British offensive of the war, south-west of Armentieres - where the German trenches curved around the village of Neuve Chapelle.

The area had seen bitter fighting already. In October 1914, the German offensive had only just been halted there after the B.E.F. had been driven back from the higher ground that stretched north-east from Aubers towards Lille. The former front-line was still marked by water-logged old British trenches to the east of the village. Now though, the German line bulged westwards in a salient that held the battered but still standing houses and church of Neuve Chapelle.

As early as February 1915, however, the planned attack had grown

# Tigers in the Trenches

beyond a simple matter of straightening-out a salient, with its savings in men and resources by shortening the distance to be held, and become an opportunity to smash through the German line and deep into enemy territory. With an overwhelming local superiority of guns and troops, the thinly held German salient at Neuve Chapelle could be snuffed out and then massed reserves poured through to seize the Aubers Ridge. Once there, British guns would dominate the landscape and all troop movements and positions on it, as far as Lille. Such a triumph would change the strategic balance on the Western Front.

The forces chosen for the assault were from General Sir Douglas Haig's 1st Army: two British divisions and two from the Indian Army Corps. The spearhead on the south was the Garhwal Brigade of the Meerut Division, which included the 2nd Battalion of the Leicestershire Regiment. Amongst many details of the impending attack, the battalion's War Diary includes Haig's exhortation: *"We are about to engage the enemy under very favourable conditions. Until now...the British army has, by its pluck and determination, gained victories against an enemy greatly superior both in men and guns. Reinforcements have made us stronger than the enemy in our front. Our guns are now both more numerous than the enemy's are, and also larger than hitherto used by any army in the field. Our Flying Corps has driven the Germans from the air...We are about to attack with about 48 battalions a locality...which is held by some 3 German battalions...At no time in this war has there been a more favourable moment for us, and I feel confident of success. The extent of that success must depend upon the rapidity and determination with which we advance."*[1]

Preparations were meticulous. For the first time the balance of forces was decidedly with the British. On a frontage of some 2,000 yards Haig proposed to deploy the massed artillery of both the Indian and IV British Corps: nearly four hundred field guns and over 130 pieces of heavy artillery plus the firepower of a naval gun and armoured train.[2] The German front line was held by a mere six companies, with two more in

---

1 ROLLR: 8D62/Box7/1.
2 *History of the Great War Military Operations: France and Belgium* 1915 p 83-85

# "Hot as Mustard"

immediate support; less than two thousand men in number[3].

*Tigers in the Rue de Bois, 1915*

The Leicesters had moved quietly up in drizzling rain from Richebourg St Vaast to the front line opposite Neuve Chapelle in the early hours of 10th March. The communication trench, which had been dug alongside the raised surface of the Rue de Bois, was crammed with troops shuffling along, each laden with 150 rounds of small arms ammunition, two spare sandbags, his emergency rations and what remained of that day's food. In addition, two machine guns, reserve ammunition for both rifles and machine guns, bombs (or grenades) and assorted tools were carried up the line. Everything had been thought of – even the order of march ('B', 'A', 'C' and then 'D' companies, followed by scouts, pioneers, signallers, machine gunners and finally, stretcher bearers) reflecting the eventual

3 *Ibid.*, p. 105

disposition in the front-line trenches.

By 5a.m. the 2nd Leicesters were in position. Two companies ('B' and 'A') were in the front-line immediately to the north of a strongpoint known as Port Arthur (from the long-besieged fortress of the Russo-Japanese War a decade before). The other two were in the communication trenches behind, ready to move swiftly forward once the attack began; 'D' Company lining a breastwork and 'C' Company, having found its allotted trench full of water, deployed outside it, along the northern side of the rear-facing wall or *parados*.

Little had been left to chance in planning the assault and the slender resources of the 1st Army were deployed, as far as possible, to their best advantage. The objectives were spelled out to brigade commanders and passed down to battalion and then company commanders. Everyone, in theory at least, knew their rôle in the coming battle.

*Brigadier General C G Blackader wearing the muddied boots of a front-line general.*

The Operation Orders of Brigadier General C. G. Blackader, commanding the Garhwal Brigade, are preserved in the 2nd Leicesters' war diary:

# "Hot as Mustard"

*"The INDIAN and 4th Corps are to co-operate in an attack on NEUVE CHAPELLE on the 10th March. The 8th Division is to attack from the 4th Corps front and the Meerut division from that of the INDIAN CORPS. The artillery of the two Corps will bombard the area to be attacked for 35 minutes before the assault. The bombardment will commence at 7.30 a.m. and cease at 8.5 a.m., artillery fire continuing with increased fuse and range."*

Blackader's brigade was to storm the German trenches which ran along the far side of the main road from Estaires south to La Bassée. To the Leicesters' right, the 1/39th Garwhal Rifles were to advance East from Port Arthur. The Leicesters themselves were to capture a cluster of houses at a crossroads on the outskirts of Neuve Chapelle; two companies advancing alongside the Garwhalis and the other two following the line of a natural ditch which ran towards the enemy lines. Further north, the 2/3rd Gurkha Rifles and 2/39th Garwhalis were to sweep up on either side of another road into Neuve Chapelle, where the Garwhalis on the left flank would, as the orders put it, *"join hands with the 8th Division".*

To avoid a counter-attack along any captured trenches *"all trenches leading towards the Enemy will be double blocked beyond bombing distance, and then cleared beyond the barricades made."* Captured trenches or buildings were also to be marked with coloured flags, pink for flank battalions and light or dark blue for centre battalions, to indicate the progress of the attack to aerial observation, artillery or other supporting troops. In an age before radio and given the uncertainty of field telephony, using wire uncoiled as troops advanced, it was the best that could be done.

The last hour of the night passed in grim silence. Fortunately, there was no concerted bombardment of the packed communication trenches by the German artillery, though shortly after 7 a.m., a few shells fell amongst the right-hand platoons of the Leicesters, where they met the 1/39th Garwhalis. The latter battalion's telephones were destroyed and several signallers killed as well as *"a large number of casualties among the 2nd Leicesters"*[4] including Captain Noel Morgan, wounded by shell

---
4 *Historical Record of the 39th Royal Garhwal Rifles*, quoted in Wylley, p. 122. The Leicesters' war diary

# Tigers in the Trenches

fragments in the chest.

Few of the waiting Leicesters can have taken much comfort from their surroundings. It was bitterly cold, with occasional flurries of snow or sleet and the enemy lines were shrouded in mist. The trenches were often barely scraped deeper than eighteen inches (at which point spades met the water-table) with sodden sandbags and wooden revetments built up above as a breastwork to provide cover against sniper or artillery fire.

At 7.30 a.m. the artillery bombardment began. While in both weight of shell and duration, the bombardment barely stands comparison with those of 1916, it was (as Gordon Corrigan points out) "nevertheless impressive, and many soldiers stood up to watch...as shells burst on the German wire and in the village of Neuve Chapelle."[5] Firing just over the heads of the Garhwal Brigade, the Indian Corps' field guns swept broad lanes through the German wire, while more than sixty howitzers and yet more field guns battered the enemy trenches and the houses of Neuve Chapelle beyond.

At 7.40 a.m. the heavy guns switched their attention to counter-battery fire, attempting to destroy or pin-down the German artillery. At the same time, the field artillery (the 13 and 18 pounders) shifted their aim to create a belt of swept ground some four hundred yards deep to the east of the village. No German could pass through it; to withdraw, to evacuate wounded, or to reinforce. For the first time staff officers spoke of a 'barrage', a French word meaning a dam, weir or other barrier, thereby introducing a new word for the British artilleryman.

The artillery fire was truly devastating: *"the artillery did deadly work"* remarked one of the Leicesters in a letter home.[6] Shrapnel and high explosive shells pulverized the German barbed wire and the front-line, collapsing the makeshift trenches and sending breastworks and their occupants high into the air.

---

does not mention the incident. Morgan's wound is described by Lieut-Colonel Gordon, quoted in Wylly, p.129.
5 Gordon Corrigan *Sepoys in the Trenches* (Stroud) 2006, p. 150
6 'Bridge-Road Boy at Neuve Chapelle', in the *Leicester Daily Post*, 8 April 1915.

# "Hot as Mustard"

At 7.45 a.m., the Leicester 'C' and then 'D' Companies moved up to the trenches which formed the northern part of the Port Arthur strongpoint's eastern edge. The battalion was ready to storm the German lines ahead of them. At 8.5 a.m. 'B' and 'C' Companies left their cover, advancing in two lines each of two platoons. With bayonets fixed, the Tigers charged through the devastated German lines: *"at a steady double. The first line of enemys [sic] trenches was carried and the advance was continued over several other enemy's trenches and communication trenches reaching the final objective...at about 8.20 a.m."*[7]

ROLLR: LS6174

Despite heavy fire from a few isolated strongpoints and machine guns on their flanks, the British and Indians had soon been amongst the German defences – bombing and bayoneting their way along the trenches and from house to house. As Private Arthur Beaumont wrote home to his mother in Leicester, from hospital in Rouen: *"We made a bayonet charge*

7 War Diary

# Tigers in the Trenches

last Wednesday morning, and captured three lines of trenches, drove the Germans through a wood, and captured a village on the other side. It was while we were in the wood that I got hit in the left arm by a bullet. It struck the bone, and turning over came out lengthwise on the other side...I have a trade mark now on both arms from the Germans, so I shall not forget them in a hurry..."[8]

ROLLR: LS6149 and LS6140 opposite

By 11 a.m. the bulk of the Garhwal Brigade had reached the old British trenches from the 1914 fighting, capturing five machine-guns and a couple of hundred dazed and demoralized prisoners. Lieutenant C. Tennant, hastening forward with the 1/4th Seaforth Highlanders to exploit the apparent breakthrough, gazed towards the sounds of battle: "Presently across the field came trudging a cocky little Tommy of the Leicestershires with fixed bayonet following a dozen young German prisoners. He was munching a ration biscuit and he was yellow with lyddite fumes. Soon other parties began to pass with prisoners, most of

8 *Leicester Daily Post*, 20 March 1915

# "Hot as Mustard"

*them looking very shaken and delighted to be out of the inferno..."*[9]

Unhappily, while the Leicesters had succeeded in their objectives, sweeping past the southern tip of Neuve Chapelle village and establishing themselves in a cluster of ruined house and a German trench which ran along a road, the 1/39 Garhwalis to their right had run into heavy machine-gun and rifle fire and bogged-down with heavy casualties. Similarly, on the far-left flank, a well-entrenched Jäger battalion had survived the bombardment to cut to pieces the advancing companies of the 2nd Scottish Rifles and 2nd Middlesex Regiments.

The Garhwali Rifles had also lost their way. Many explanations have been suggested[10] but whichever it was, possibly simply a natural inclination to

---
9 Quoted in Lyn MacDonald *1915* (London) 1997, p.95
10 See MacDonald, p. 102 for the fullest summary; ranging from the thick mist, the angle of attack (which was not straight ahead of their trenches) to the artillery bombardment's destruction of a tree which had been pointed out as their landmark.

# Tigers in the Trenches

PICTURE MAP TO ILLUSTRATE T

Scene of fight in Orchard

Rue de Bacquerot

ATTACK BY 4th ARMY CORPS

Rue Tilleloy

Orchard Farm

NEUVE CHAPELLE

Crucifix

Chateau

Brewery

River des Layes

Bois du Biez

Richebourg St Vaast

PORT ARTHUR

Rue du Bois

ATTACK BY INDIANS

To La Bassée

The Glorious Story of Neuve Chapelle.

**KEY MAP**

Estaires, Armentieres, Laventie, Fleurbaix, Lille, Aubers, Fournes, Neuve Chapelle, Richebourg St Vaast, Givenchy, La Bassée, Cuinchy

Scale of Miles

The large map indicates the approximate lines of advance of the British and Neuve Chapelle in relation to Lille, the

## "Hot as Mustard"

### THE BATTLE OF NEUVE CHAPELLE.

Indian troops against Neuve Chapelle. The small map shows the position of great French manufacturing town held by the Germans.

Printed and Published by the Associated Newspapers, Ltd., at the "Daily Mail" Buildings, London and Manchester.

# Tigers in the Trenches

**Previous pages:** *A bird's eye view of the battlefield, from the Daily Mail of April 1915. Although not entirely accurate, it gives a clear view of the bulge in the German lines around Neuve Chapelle and of key features, such as Port Arthur (almost worn away by fingers tracing the action!) Bois du Biez and Aubers Ridge beyond. On 10 March, the Leicesters attacked from the left of Port Arthur towards the Brewery. [22D63/197]*

turn towards the heaviest enemy fire, the battalion veered out of line, leaving a gap of between two hundred and two hundred and fifty yards[11] of enemy held trench between them and the Leicesters.

The stubborn, aggressive resistance put up here by the German defenders, from the 10th Company, 16th Infantry Regiment, shows how costly the assault on Neuve Chapelle could have been without the opening artillery bombardment. On both flanks of the British attack, small but determined parties of German troops stood their ground, disrupting the attacker's time-table and buying valuable time.

As the morning gave way to afternoon, two attacks from the Leicesters' 'C' Company were driven off and it was only a third assault by a platoon under Captain Francis Romilly, of 'D' Company, supplemented by a strong bombing party, that stabilised the position; building and holding a barricade across the open trench. It was, according to the Leicesters' commanding officer, Lieutenant-Colonel Herbert Gordon, *"the most beautiful bit of trench fighting I have ever seen, and, indeed, it became a model for a bombing attack."*

Having directed a machine-gun team to keep the enemy heads down, Colonel Gordon *"sent Romilly with a platoon to turn them out...Romilly was the keenest man I have ever met in a battle and bombs were a hobby to him. And in these early days it was not all joy handling a bomb! Under cover of the machine gun he rushed the north end of the trench and established himself there...and, with bayonet men in front and behind him, he himself advanced up the trench, throwing his bombs into the succeeding traverses."*

Eventually, tiring of the slow progress, Romilly leaped onto the parapet of the trench and worked his way along the top, followed by his runner,

---

11 The *Official History* suggests 250 (p. 95) while the Leicesters' War Diary records 200.

## "Hot as Mustard"

with a supply of grenades, which Romilly tossed at the enemy below. It was only a matter of minutes before the strongpoint was in British hands and about eighty prisoners were being marched back towards Port Arthur. *"It was a magnificent feat,"* observed Colonel Gordon, *"and won Romilly a well-deserved D.S.O."*[12]

While half the Leicesters and the Garhwalis fought what Gordon Corrigan calls *"their own private battle in front of Port Arthur"*[13] the remainder of the brigade was busily clearing pockets of the enemy from the ruins of Neuve Chapelle and *"improving the German trench & reversed the parapet"* to form a new defensive line.[14] The old British line, from 1914, was found to be too full of water for use and a new line was eventually created fifty yards or so back from it.

Although many of the German defenders were dazed by the furious bombardment and surrendered, others had fought on stubbornly. It was here, amongst the ruins of Neuve Chapelle's outlying houses, that William Buckingham (left), of the Leicesters, earned his Victoria Cross, repeatedly risking his life to bring in wounded men. Sergeant H E Ruckledge, Corporal R Keitley and Privates C Oakes and J Steeples also received the Distinguished Conduct Medal for their gallantry in helping wounded comrades. Private G Hill won the DCM for his courage in continually carrying messages across the bullet-swept no-man's land.

---

12 Lieut-Col. Herbert Gordon, quoted in Wylly, p. 130.
13 Corrigan, p. 154
14 War Diary. Soil – or more likely in this case – sandbags were removed from the parapet to the parados at the rear of trench to 'reverse' it.

# Tigers in the Trenches

To the Leicesters and the other battalions of the Garhwal Brigade to their left, the attack had proved a brilliant success. Neuve Chapelle was taken and patrols sent forward to the Bois du Biez, which was the next objective across the Layes Brook, reported that the Germans were nowhere to be seen.

In the front line, the Leicesters' Colonel Gordon could not understand the delay: *"The whole country in front was open to us – no wire – no enemy in sight and certainly a big enough gap to push through a mass of men and cavalry...no one who was actually in the battle had the slightest doubt that we could have been in Lille in a few hours."*[15]

It was certainly an unprecedented achievement of artillery and infantry co-operation. However, the overall picture was not so rosy as it appeared to the Indian brigades. While the Germans held grimly on in front of Port Arthur, on the far left of the attack, stubborn German resistance and the failure of some heavy artillery batteries, had held back the advance of the IV Corps long into the afternoon. Communication failures led to confusion and confusion to delay, so that darkness found the British in possession of Neuve Chapelle but the higher ground beyond remained tantalisingly out of reach.

While the British and Indian troops improved their new positions and exchanged a desultory fire with the enemy, General Haig's staff prepared revised plans for the following day. While the Indian brigades seized the Bois du Biez, the reinforced IV Corps brigades were to continue their advance onto the Aubers Ridge, largely according to the original scheme.

Sadly, the widespread impression that *"the enemy before us is in no great strength"*[16] was increasingly wrong. From as early as 10 o'clock on 10 March, reinforcements were being directed to the new front line behind Neuve Chapelle; a succession of trains pouring troops and artillery for the *"recapture of the village and the original trenches beyond it."*[17]

Thursday, 11 March 1915 was to prove no more conclusive than the

---
15 Wylly, pp. 129-130
16 *Official History*, p. 120
17 *Official History*, p. 116

# "Hot as Mustard"

day before. As the early morning mist thinned, observers in the British front lines noted grimly the appearance of wire and newly thrown up breastworks including a strongpoint where a small bridge crossed the swollen Layes Brook. The British attack was to be renewed, pushing on to the same objectives.

ROLLR: LS6159

Overnight fresh Gurkhas of the Dehra Dun Brigade of the Indian Army Corps had advanced past and through the lines of the Garhwal Brigade, ready for the renewed attack on the Bois du Biez. A fierce response from the new German defences drove the Gurkhas back to a new trench line slightly ahead of and partially overlapping that of the Leicesters. There they waited for a fresh attack from the IV Corps to their left, which they were to support by storming the wood.

## Tigers in the Trenches

The fresh attack never came. Once again, a series of errors, cut telephone wires and ill luck deprived General Haig of his breakthrough and hundreds of British and Indian soldiers of their lives. On the far-left flank, well entrenched machine guns cut down the attacking waves of the IV Corps, while the artillery struggled to zero-in on targets obscured by mist and rain. By dusk, the attack was called off and the battered battalions in the advanced trenches, including the Gurkhas, withdrawn – leaving the Leicesters once again in the front line.

Nightfall brought the advance of six fresh German battalions, including two (of Saxons) which were deployed opposite the Leicesters and Garhwal Rifles in the Port Arthur salient. With further reinforcements in support and in reserve, some sixteen thousand Germans (Bavarians and Saxon troops) were assembled, largely unsuspected by the British, to retake the lost ground around Neuve Chapelle.[18]

The German counter-attack came as something of a surprise. At 4.30 a.m., half an hour before the first glimmerings of dawn, the entire British line was subjected to a pummelling bombardment. Luckily, most of the shells fell upon trenches and breastworks no longer occupied; missing the front-line but falling instead upon support units. Pity the ration and supply parties struggling across open country, suddenly subjected to high explosive and shrapnel. The trenches around Port Arthur were also hit.

Soon after 5 a.m., the two Saxon battalions (of the 104th and 139th Infantry Regiments) supported by elements of the 16th and 56th Infantry, began their advance through the thick mist which blanketed the ground between the Bois du Biez and Layes Brook. It was an attack which belonged on the battlefields of the previous Autumn; long lines of infantry advancing at a steady pace, their officers (some even mounted) waving them on. As it emerged from the fog, the attack was, in places, barely sixty or a hundred yards from the British and Indian lines.

---

18 *Ibid.*, pp. 131 & 393. Listening posts had detected troop movements but it was not expected that so large a force could be detached from other fronts and moved so swiftly into position. It was the intention of General Haig to recommence the offensive with a half-hour artillery bombardment at 10.30 a.m. and an assault by the Indian Corps on the Bois du Biez at 11. (Army Operational Order No. 12, 11 March 1915).

## "Hot as Mustard"

Heard before it was seen, the onslaught of at least two thousand Germans, broke against a well-manned and prepared line of entrenchments. As the Official History recorded: *"as soon as dim forms in helmets appeared through the mist about a hundred yards away, followed by a dense grey wave of men, a violent fusillade was opened on them at point-blank range. It checked not only the leading lines, but also those still unseen, moving forward in support from the Bois du Biez."*[19]

The Leicesters' 'A' and 'D' Companies broke the attack, with the rapid fire of the 'mad minute'[20] a hundred yards from Port Arthur. To the left of the battalion, opposite the 2/3rd Gurkhas, the Saxons had occupied trenches abandoned the night before. From there they rushed to within forty or fifty paces of the British line, only to be checked by rapid rifle fire from the front and enfilade fire from the Leicesters' 'B' Company and one of the battalion's machine-guns under the command of Captain R. J. McIntyre.

Captain Donald Weir, who was to be awarded the Military Cross for his rôle in turning back the German counter-attack, played down the danger in a letter home:

*"It is sufficient to say that things have been quite on the warm side round here just lately, and that the Germans have taken a good hiding. I had the pleasure of accounting for a few with my own rifle this time, in daylight, and it was grand to see them flop over..."*[21]

While an old boy of Leicester's Bridge Road School told his headmaster:

*"On Friday the Germans came at us in droves but we were ready for them, and mowed them down like grass. In the paper I see it says that 2,000 Germans were counted in front of one battalion. That battalion was ours – we simply wiped them out."*[22]

Hundreds of dead and wounded covered the ground between the British

---
19 *Official History*, p. 135
20 The exemplary musketry training of the British Army included a devastating, aimed rapid fire; fifteen rounds in a minute.
21 ROLLR: DE2913
22 *Leicester Daily Post*, 1 April 1915

lines and Layes Brook. A party of Germans took cover in the abandoned trenches. There was even a sighting of a white flag but renewed firing greeted a party of Gurkhas who approached and so the area was assaulted and cleared by a company of the 1/4th Gurkhas and a party of the Leicesters under second-lieutenant A. S. MacIntyre. Many of the Germans fled northwards up the trench and into the hands of the 1st Highland Light Infantry.[23]

The battle of Neuve Chapelle was, to all intents and purposes, over. Although artillery fire continued and snipers became active, a renewed British advance was prepared but then abandoned. At midnight on 13 March, the 2nd Leicesters, with the remainder of the Garhwal Brigade, was relieved by elements of the Sirhind Brigade.

The first offensive of the B.E.F. had failed – but it had been close to a triumph, as Colonel Gordon's remarks, quoted above, make clear. Sadly, many of the lessons were misunderstood or not taken to heart. It was to be many weary months before generals and their staffs would truly appreciate the priceless value of meticulous planning, good communications, of a devastating, lightning barrage and quick reaction to unexpected opportunities.

The losses on both sides were in the region of twelve or thirteen thousand killed, wounded, and missing. The 2nd Leicestershire Regiment was by no means one of the worst affected battalions but even so had suffered heavily. Two officers were killed (or died of wounds) and five others wounded; while two hundred and fifty Other Ranks were killed, wounded, or missing. More significantly, perhaps, was the calibre of the men to be replaced; such as Private A. J. Robbins, wounded in the shoulder, a veteran of Ladysmith with twelve years' service; and Corporal John Davenport Sheffield, killed on 10 March, a South African War Volunteer.[24]

On 17 March the Leicesters were inspected by Lieutenant-General Sir James Willcocks. He expressed his pride and gratitude for the 'Tigers"

---

23 *War Diary; Wylly*, p. 124
24 *Leicester Daily Post*, 30 and 31 March 1915.

# "Hot as Mustard"

service and, turning to leave the parade in company with Brigadier-General C. G. Blackader, who had brought them from India, remarked:

*"By Jove! That Regiment fights well. Young fellows just coming out to join them ought to feel pretty proud of themselves!"*[25]

The last word will go, however, to a wounded soldier, his khaki "bespattered" and his boots "yellow with mud"; interviewed at Leicester's Midland Station on 15 March 1915:

*"We were in the big fight at Neuve Chapelle. The battle began on Wednesday, but our lot went in on Thursday. It was hot as mustard while it lasted."*[26]

25 *Wylly*, p. 127.
26 *Leicester Daily Post*, 16 March 1915

# Tigers in the Trenches

## Chapter Five

# "Trying to hold on"

It is a truism that soldiers who fight hard are also likely to play hard. Few memoirs of service in the Great War do not include some reference to cases of disobedience or disorder, usually arising from drunkenness, or exhaustion, or the stresses of warfare on an industrial scale. At times the perpetrator is seen as a victim of a hard system, perhaps at the end of his mental or spiritual resources. On other occasions he is portrayed as a rogue, justifiably caught and punished.

Records simply do not survive of the day-to-day exercise of discipline in the various battalions of the Leicestershire Regiment; the daily ritual (out of the front line) of 'company orders'. As Charles Carrington, an infantry subaltern, recalled: *"To be unpunctual, unshaven, idle, neglectful, insolent – or, worse than that, to have a dirty rifle, brought you hatless – which was the sign of military disgrace – before the company commander's table, with your sergeant giving evidence against you."*[1]

Minor infringements would usually receive 'fatigues'; requiring a defaulter to turn out for additional, irksome or unsavoury labour whilst his fellows rested or sought refreshment. More serious offences, yet still below the threshold for imprisonment, might attract Field Punishment No. 1., which permitted the use of *"fetters or handcuffs, or both fetters and handcuffs"*, or ropes where they were absent, and the attachment of the prisoner *"for a period...not exceeding two hours in any one day to a fixed object."* Field punishment No. 2 excluded attachment to a fixed object.[2]

In addition to the physical discomfort, the miscreant undergoing punishment would also suffer a loss of pay and be deprived of comforts such as tobacco and rum. He would also still be liable to 'fatigues' and see his prospects of leave diminish almost to invisibility.

---

1 Charles Carrington *Soldier from the Wars returning* (Barnsley) 2015, pp. 169-170
2 War Office *Manual of Military Law*, 1914, p. 721

## "Trying to hold on"

As might be imagined, the severity of such a punishment would depend to some extent upon the attitude of those supervising it. I. L. Read, serving with the 8th Leicesters saw the punishment imposed upon two men of his company, who had defied orders (designed to avoid typhoid or enteric) and filled their water bottles on the line of march:

*"Each was spread-eagled and tied hand and foot to the spokes of a limber wheel for two hours in the summer sun, under the surveillance of one of the Regimental Police...we watched with mixed feelings, but whatever else we felt, I'm quite sure that we would think twice before letting ourselves in for a similar fate."*[3]

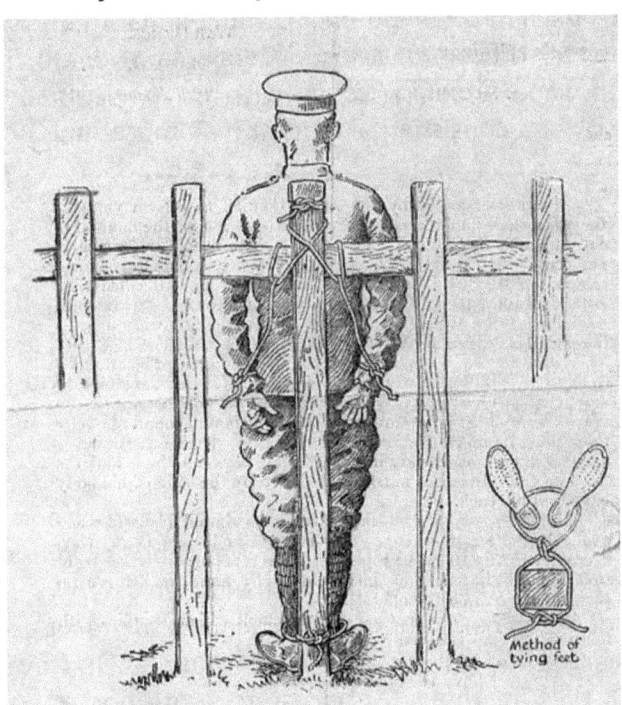

Many considered Field punishment justly deserved by the idle or defiant who received it and certainly a great deal less brutal than the flogging it replaced. Others, however, found it degrading and even shocking, as it must indeed have been to many Leicester lads fresh from school and church or chapel. The deterrent aspect of military justice is also clear.

3 I. L. 'Dick' Read *Of those we Loved* (Barnsley) 2013, p. 15

# Tigers in the Trenches

In cases where such summary justice was not appropriate, the Army Act (1881) provided an hierarchy of courts-martial, each with its own composition and jurisdiction.[4] At the lowest level was the Regimental Court-Martial, convened by any officer of the rank of major or above, and consisting of not less than three officers with at least one year's experience. The jurisdiction of the court was similarly limited, to Other Ranks, and its range of punishments to below forty-two days' imprisonment.

In peacetime, or at home, a District or a General Court-Martial would come next. The District Court-Martial also consisted of no fewer than three officers, each having held their commission for at least two years, and could not try officers or award a sentence of death. The General Court-Martial was the senior court, with full powers, summoned by Royal authority and consisting of at least nine more senior officers (five abroad).

However, the impracticability of summoning so extensive a court on active service, meant that almost all serious cases were dealt with by the far more flexible Field General Court Martial. This court could be summoned at relatively short notice and consisted of at least three officers, although two could hear cases not requiring more than field punishment, if the convening officer considered it impracticable to find more.

All officers were expected to be familiar with military law and its conduct. Every unit should have had a copy of the War Office's *Manual of Military Law* and *King's Regulations,* while the handy *Field Service Pocket Book* contained a digest of court-martial jurisdiction and procedure, as well as specimen charges and guidance as to punishments. In November 1915 Captain J. D. Hills, of the 1/5th Leicesters wrote home, describing his activities out of the firing line:

*"I am now trying to learn all the ins & outs & little intricacies of army acts & military law & how one manages Courts-Martial & all sorts of*

---

[4] The following account of courts-martial is drawn from the *Manual of Military Law (1914)* pp. 425-431 and from Cathryn Corns and John Hughes-Wilson *Blindfold and Alone* (London) 2001 pp. 90-91

## "Trying to hold on"

*interesting but difficult-to-understand questions of that calibre. Military law alone is enough to keep one employed for the best part of one's natural life, & when King's Regulations are added to that the task becomes quite impossible. Courts-Martial too are a constant source of worry, as none of these Territorial Officers have ever seen one before the war, & each has his own views on the best way of managing one. A good old muddle & a large number of mistakes is usually the result of this. Viccars the Staff Captain is rather an authority on the subject & I am learning the chief difficulties from him."*[5]

Military justice, viewed anecdotally over the past century or so, has not received the warmest reception. In large part this has been on account of the death sentences awarded by Field General Courts-Martial and concern that too many ill-educated, traumatised soldiers were put to death after only the most basic of hearings. The danger, of course, is that in deploring one perceived injustice, we commit another in condemning unheard so many tribunals which sought to do their judicial duty in the worst of times and circumstances.

From 1914 until the official end of the war in 1920, military justice was busy. Field punishment No. 1 was awarded in 60,210 cases, and over 300,000 courts-martial were convened, for all levels of crime, and 3,080 sentences of death issued. The British Army actually shot three hundred and forty-six of its soldiers; although it is worth noting that thirty-seven of those executed were convicted not of a military offence but of the civil crime of murder.[6]

The Leicestershire Regiment's active service battalions seem to have been no more licentious, nor more law abiding than other, similar British Army units.[7] From early December 1914 until mid-October 1918, thirty-four sentences of death were imposed upon men of the Leicesters, two men (Privates J Hackett and J Nisbet) being sentenced twice but only two

---

5 ROLLR: DEDE9672 Letter of J D Hills November 1915
6 Denis Winter *Death's Men* (Harmondsworth) 1979, p. 43; Cathryn Corns and John Hughes-Wilson *Ibid.*, pp 442-443; Richard Holmes Tommy (London) 2005, p. 558.
7 While the Leicestershire regiment lost two men to the firing squad, the South Staffordshire Regiment with slightly more battalions had three men executed, the Cheshire Regiment six and the much larger Sherwood Foresters also six.

were actually executed (Privates Ernest Beaumont and Joseph Nisbet).

The commonest crime, involving nineteen of the soldiers sentenced to death, was that of *"being a soldier acting as a sentinel"* sleeping at or quitting his post; one of the offences identified in the *Manual of Military Law* as *"punishable more severely on active service"*.[8] Although few would fail to sympathise with the level of fatigue felt by a soldier in the firing line, it is also obvious how important it was for the safety of the entire unit to have an alert sentry on duty.

The fact that not a single soldier of the Leicesters, found guilty of sleeping or quitting his post, was executed also suggests that those reviewing the sentences were aware of hardship and mitigating circumstances. It may also indicate how commutable, or expungable such sentences could be, that of the nineteen condemned to death, at least five (one of whom had also been promoted) are recorded as having died on active service well before the expiry of their purported sentences.[9] For example Private William Shortus, sentenced for 'sleeping' on 2 December 1914, seems likely to be the same Lance-corporal (number 7871) who died on 7 January 1916, serving with the 2nd battalion in Mesopotamia and 11861 Private John Thomas Mason, of 'D' Company, 7th Leicesters, whose death sentence on 4 December 1915 was commuted to five years penal servitude, died on 10 December 1917 and was buried at Villers-Faucon midway between Bapaume and Saint Quentin.

The service record of No. 11389 Private Wilfred Henry Hubbard, unusually, does survive.[10] Hubbard was a farm labourer from Wigston in Leicestershire, who enlisted, aged seventeen-and-a half, in the 3rd Battalion of the Leicesters (the old Militia) in May 1914; transferring to the 2nd Battalion on the Western Front on 10 November 1915. In

---

[8] *Manual of Military Law (1914)* p. 380

[9] It seems to have been widely accepted that soldiers would serve on in the hope that future conduct would expunge the (suspended) sentences given in place of the death sentence. Those not mentioned above are 15502 Pte Hargeave Brewin, 6th Battalion, died on 17 July 1916 having received 5 years on 25 October 1915; No. 4544 Pte Albert Smith, 4th Battalion, death sentence commuted to 15 years penal servitude on 30 September 1915 but died on 10 April 1916 and 2016 Pte. Frederick Rowland Ratcliffe who died storming the Hohenzollern Redoubt with the 4th Leicesters on 13 October 1915 despite having received a year's hard labour in lieu of his death sentence a month earlier.

[10] They are accessible through a number of on-line family history websites.

## "Trying to hold on"

December that year he moved, with his battalion, to Mesopotamia, where was tried by Field General Court Martial *"for – when a soldier acting as a sentinel, sleeping on his Post."*

Hubbard was found guilty and sentenced to death, on 16 July 1916. The court may have recommended clemency, the papers simply do not survive, but in any case, the sentence was commuted to two years' hard labour. However, just over three months later, Hubbard was dead – of wounds received in action – on 27 October 1916. The battalion's War Diary notes *"one man killed during the night by rifle bullet",* while working on trenches beside the River Tigris. With trained soldiers in short supply, it must have seemed a poor use of scarce resources to leave them in prison.

Desertion, a crime committed by nine of the thirty-four soldiers tried and sentenced to death, was another offence considered far more significant on active service. Indeed, the *Manual of Military Law* clearly stated that desertion on active service was *"one of the greatest of all military offences"*[11]. It differed from absence without leave only in the intention of the culprit to remain permanently away from duty.

Desertion was also undoubtedly one of the most serious of crimes in its effect and prevalence. As Corns and Hughes-Wilson observed in their study of those executed by the British Army: *"...during the war there were a total of 126,818 courts-martial for desertion and absence. In the field there were 7,361 courts martial for desertion and 37,034 for absence, and in the UK there were 31,269 courts martial for desertion and 51, 154 for absence."*[12]

By the end of the war, it was widely known that large bands of deserters inhabited the wasteland behind the lines. I. L. 'Dick' Read recalled how *"several gangs of men in various stages of khaki déshabillé appeared through the trees at the roadside as by magic"* to entice his men into games of cards or Crown and Anchor whenever they halted on a march.[13]

---
11 *Ibid.,* p. 522
12 Cathryn Corns and John Hughes-Wilson *Ibid.,* p. 216
13 I. L. 'Dick' Read *Ibid.,* p. 335

# Tigers in the Trenches

As we shall see, both of the Leicestershire Regiment's soldiers shot at dawn were convicted of desertion.

The other offences, each of which were committed by only two soldiers were disobedience, cowardice and mutiny. Disobedience, especially *"in such manner as to show a wilful defiance of authority"*[14], clearly could not be tolerated in an organisation as dependent upon unquestioning following of (legal) orders as the Army. Wilful defiance may suggest deeper causes than a simple break down of discipline of course but medical conditions and other mitigating factors could (and should) have been explored in the course of the trial.

Cowardice is as hard to prove as it is to define. Few normal soldiers will not have felt fearful in the face of mortal danger and many (the last being the admirable Harry Patch) admitted to feeling afraid. Cowardice, the giving way to fear, is therefore defined by the *Army Act* through its physical manifestations. For example, if a soldier: *"shamefully abandons or delivers up any garrison, place, post, or guard..."* or *"shamefully casts away his arms, ammunition, or tools in the presence of the enemy"* or *"misbehaves or induces others to misbehave before the enemy in such a manner as to show cowardice."*[15]

Sadly, the records of the Leicestershire Regiment trials do not survive, so it is not possible to know what conduct earned Private G Fagan, of the 2nd Leicesters, three years penal servitude in March 1917, or Private H. Waring, of the 7th Leicesters, five years in August 1917. In each case, on the dates of the awards, their respective battalions were at rest, or at least out of the front line, though the 2nd Leicesters had just stormed into Baghdad while the 7th Leicesters' War Diary, on the night of 24-25th July 1918, records the failure of an attempted trench raid, *"on account of one party finding the wire not properly cut..."*

For a glimpse of what close companions heroism and cowardice could be, there are few accounts to compete with that of No. 17411 Private John W. Horner, of the 8th and then 6th Battalions. Horner recalled, having

---

14 *Manual of Military Law (1914)* p. 387
15 *Manual of Military Law (1914)* pp. 378-9

## "Trying to hold on"

recently returned to active service from hospital: *"I had nerves of steel before...but now when the guns were firing and a shell burst anywhere near I shivered and trembled with unknown fear. My nerves had gone. At night I was out with a wiring party repairing the wire and I stood holding the spade petrified and shaking with fear. The Lieutenant asked me if I was all right. I explained to him that I'd been in the 8$^{th}$ Battalion for about ten months and had been wounded...and that I was the man who had been nearly hit by the gas shell that morning and that had shaken my nerves. He asked me if I would like to go back to the dugout but I said 'No – I can't let the lads down' and he understood I was trying to hold on..."*[16]

It is obvious how differently that incident in no-man's land might have ended had Private Horner been a little weaker or his officer a little less sympathetically astute. It is also clear to what extent an individual's natural courage can become eroded, or degraded, through experience and ill-luck and how important is morale or *esprit de corps*.

The remaining two Leicestershire Regiment capital sentences were for mutiny, Privates Bennett and Knight of the 7$^{th}$ Battalion exchanging death at the hands of their comrades for fifteen years penal servitude apiece on 14 October 1918. There is no indication of what had provoked this double-act of collective insubordination, nor of the form it took. The battalion's war diary is silent, recording only a period of training and recovery after the exertions of harrying and pursuing the retreating Germans.

Curiously, the first Great War courts martial for mutiny were of thirteen private soldiers of the 3rd Leicesters from the garrison at Portsmouth.[17] Although no detailed record survives of the case, it seems likely to have been sparked by the clumsy handling of troops who felt aggrieved at finding themselves suddenly in khaki again despite being within a few hours of the expiry of their (reserve) enlistments. One of those sentenced was No. 7355 Private George Morris, a Hallaton man,[18]

---

16 Private J W Horner *Private memoir* (Liddle Collection - University of Leeds) quoted in Cathryn Corns and John Hughes-Wilson *Ibid.*, pp. 461-2. Horner's notebook is in the Imperial War Museum: Documents 14156.
17 Charles Messenger *Call-to-Arms* (London) 2006, p.399
18 See Max Bridgewater (ed) *Hallaton in the Great War Vol 2* (Hallaton) 2018, pp. 608-611 for a full ac-

who had enlisted into the Leicestershire Regiment on 2 June 1904 for the customary period of three years with the Colours and nine on the Reserve. Although after the expiry of his period of service, Morris was mobilised on 5 August 1914. This may have been frustrating to Morris and other reservists so trapped, but it was also quite legal; the Army Act permitting the extension of the period of service by another twelve months if a state of war existed.[19]

With his dozen or so fellow mutineers, Private Morris and was convicted by Field General Court Martial on 27 August 1914 and sentenced to a year's hard labour. In desperate need of trained manpower however, the Army wisely remitted Morris's sentence after a month and he was posted to the 1st Leicesters. He was killed-in-action on 25 or 26 June 1915.[20]

Fortunately, the records do survive of the two men of the Leicestershire Regiment shot at dawn. Their cases bear scrutiny, not only as interesting records in themselves of courts-martial but also for what they tell us of contemporary conditions and attitudes.

Much has been written concerning the inadequacy of military justice, from A. P. Herbert's novel, *The Secret Battle,* in 1919 onwards. Writing a veiled account of the trial of Sub-lieutenant Edwin Dyett, Herbert described the court-martial process from the point of view of a barrister serving temporarily as an infantry officer of the Royal Naval Division. He (and many others later) saw military law in the hands of honourable, well-meaning officers, sometimes somewhat out of their depth and lacking legal advice.

The criticism isn't altogether unfair. As the war went on and the Army expanded, great efforts were made to provide military courts with officers suitably qualified in law and to ensure that all medical grounds for acquittal or clemency were explored. We have seen already how

---

count of Morris's life and military service, including a portrait of the unfortunate soldier.
19 *Manual of Military Law (1914)* p. 187
20 While most sources record his death as 'killed-in-action' on 25 June, the War Diary of the 1st Battalion shows a period out of the line preceding 25 June and only "Intermittent shelling" for that day. On 26 June it records "two men killed, Capt Waller and one man wounded".

# "Trying to hold on"

Captain J. D. Hills, of the 1/5th Leicesters, tried to get to grips with the *Manual of Military Law*. He also records the arrival of trained help, in December 1915:

*"On getting back I found the Court-Martial expert had arrived & a long discussion was going on about some case that had cropped up - it seems very doubtful whether we could get a conviction though it is absolutely certain that the man is guilty. That is just like the law. He might of course plead guilty – it would then be plain sailing, but there is always the chance of his pleading Not Guilty & the proceedings might be quashed, a very ignominious finish for us & quite useless."*[21]

Courts-martial were held when the battalion concerned was out of the firing line and fitted in alongside drills, training, and whatever entertainment had been arranged, from concert parties to sporting fixtures. It is not recorded where the two Leicestershire Regiment hearings were held but they were likely to have been in buildings not unlike those described by A. P. Herbert for his fictional trial:

*"The Court-martial was held in an old farm lying just outside the village. There was a large courtyard where the chickens clucked all day, and children and cattle roamed unchecked in the spacious midden. The court-room was unusually suitable to its purpose, being panelled all round in some dark wood with great black beams under a whitewashed ceiling, high and vaulted, and an open hearth crackled heartlessly all day. Usually these trials are conducted in the best bedroom of some estaminet, and the Court sits defensively with a vast white bed to their backs. But this room was strangely dignified and legal: only at first Madame persisted in marching through it with saucepans to the kitchen – all these curious English functions were the same to her, a Christmas dinner, or a mess–meeting, or the trial of a soldier for his life."*

The court-martial of No. 8710 Private Beaumont, of the 2nd Leicesters, took place at the headquarters of the Garwhal Brigade, which was still a few miles west of Neuve Chapelle on 11th June 1915. The Leicesters were in the front line that day but witnesses were in attendance and the

---
21 ROLLR: DE9672 Letter of J D Hills 11 December 1915

members of the court were drawn from other units.

The President of the court was Major A. G. Kemball, of the 31st Punjabis, attached to 2/8th Gurkha Rifles. Sitting with him were Capatin F. G. Kunhardt, of the 74th Punjabis, attached to the Garwhal Rifles, and a Lieutenant R. D. Sutcliffe, of the 1/3rd (City of London Regiment) Royal Fusiliers, which had joined the Garwhal Brigade in February.

Beaumont was charged with desertion, to which he pleaded not guilty. By mid-1915, it was the rule in capital cases that the only acceptable plea would be one of not guilty.[22] Beaumont did not object to any member of the court, as was his right, nor is there any suggested that he requested the assistance of an 'accused's friend'; although in 1915 this would still have been unusual. He was also given every opportunity to cross-question the witnesses.

The evidence against Private Beaumont was clear enough. Sergeant George Lomas, a South African War veteran, acting as Orderly Room Sergeant at Rouen, had encountered Beaumont walking down the city's Rue des Beufs. He had encountered Beaumont before or, at least knew something of his history: *"The accused was released from a sentence of 9 months' imprisonment which was commuted to Field punishment as far as I can remember, towards the middle of March 1915. He was handed over by the Governor of the Prison on completion of the Punishment to the Assistant Provost-Martial at Havre where he underwent the Punishment."*

A month later, Beaumont was roaming the streets of Rouen.

*"I...asked him what he was doing in Rouen. He replied that he had been sent down to the Indian Base. I asked him if he was aware that his base was Havre. He said 'No, but I will return to Havre tomorrow.' I left the accused and on meeting two Policemen I gave them an order to arrest him. They reported the next morning that they had not seen the accused and could not find him. I reported the matter officially to*

---

22 Cathryn Corns and John Hughes-Wilson *Ibid.*, p. 294. In February 1915, Private Joseph Byers of the 1st Royal Scots had been executed after pleading guilty to a charge of desertion, possibly not realising the gravity of the offence.

# "Trying to hold on"

*General Headquarters 3rd Echelon. On the 4th May I met the accused in Rue Gros Pont; he was accompanied by a woman. I told him to come along with me and handed him over to the Picquet. I am Orderly Room Sergeant at Rouen."*

ROUEN. — Rue Grand-Pont.

At some point in the trial process, certain phrases in the witness statements were underlined as significant. Perhaps most telling was that Beaumont was in female company.

The next witness was Corporal Thomas Allum.[23] Allum was in charge of a draft of reinforcements for the 2nd Leicesters which halted for the night near Locon: *"On the morning of March 14th 1915 I was with a draft from England and had arrived 'in the Field'. The draft had orders to get dressed and fall in. The Roll was called and accused was found absent. Captain Brock came to me and told me to get four men and go out as a search party for the accused. We failed to find him. I did not again see him till he was arrested."*

---
23 No. 8781 Corporal (later Sergeant) Allum was from Brackley in Northamptonshire; a pre-war regular. He was killed-in-action attacking the Quadrilateral with the 1st Battalion Leicestershire regiment on 15 September 1916 and is commemorated on the Thiepval Memorial.

# Tigers in the Trenches

The third and final witness was a Corporal T. Poole, who was with the draft mentioned by Allum, presumably returning to active service having been wounded or sick. He confirmed Allum's evidence: *"I was NCO in charge of the Guard on the Billets. Accused was put in my charge for the night. About 8 a.m. on the 14th I had orders for the draft to fall in. When the Roll was called the accused was absent."*

The record kept of the trial has many annotations. Most are under-linings of key phrases in blue ink. However, intriguingly, a red ink 'where?' also appears; beside Allum's 'in the Field' and beside Poole's 'Billets'. Although neither Allum nor Poole appeared to recall quite where the billets were that night, it was presumably close to the front line and therefore may possibly have been said to be 'in the presence of the enemy' which, of course, was an aggravating factor.

The accused was then called upon to make his statement. It was brief but effective in making the best of a bad situation: *"On the morning of the 4th March 1915 I was walking round the Billets and I seemed to lose all my wits and did not know what I was doing. I did not come to myself and realize what I was doing for three or four days. When I saw Sergeant Lomas I was going to the Indian Depot to get a pass to go back to the Regiment. I could not find the Depot and went up to Sergeant Lomas's place but he wasn't in. The second time I saw him I went and gave myself up to him. I was wearing my uniform and I had no intention whatsoever to desert. I came home with the Regiment from India."*

The statement contains some significant phrases. If Beaumont had lost his wits in March, he had regained them by June, or perhaps benefitted from some friendly advice. He had made clear that he had no intention to desert, offering retention of his uniform as evidence of this, and reminded the court that he was a regular soldier, who had been with the 2nd Battalion in India. Had the court considered substituting the lesser charge of absence for desertion, for example, here was the evidence they needed.

Beaumont also raised, in his claim to *"not know what I was doing"* some doubt as to his mental condition. The court however seems not to have

# "Trying to hold on"

been convinced and neither they, the senior officers reviewing the case, nor their legal advisors suggested that a medical examination might be called for.

Instead, Beaumont was informed that the court had no findings to announce. This was the customary procedure, which meant simply that he had been found guilty but that the court's sentence would be referred upwards for confirmation. Evidence of the prisoner's character was then heard, the adjutant of Beaumont's battalion, Captain Francis Latham (left) declaring that while he was unable to produce any documents:

*"I have known the accused for over 3 years. His character is bad. He was recently awarded imprisonment which was remitted to Field Punishment Number 1 and at the time he absented himself was rejoining from the Base Prison as a result of the remission of his sentence. His service is about six years. He is not in possession of any military decoration."*

The papers were then sent for review up the chain of command, at some point of which, the wielder of the red ink queried "which offence?" beside Captain and Adjutant Latham's report of Field Punishment No. 1.

In assessing this case we have an advantage over Captain Latham, in that his file at the National Archives contains the service records which were unavailable at the front in 1915. We know from them that Ernest Alfred Beaumont was born in the parish of St Giles in Cambridge; the son of James and Annie Beaumont. Ernest Alfred was a labourer who,

# Tigers in the Trenches

at the end of 1908 enlisted in the Special Reserve and then, on 15 June 1909, joined the regular army. He was posted to the 2nd Leicesters at Shorncliffe, then Aldershot, before sailing on the transport *Dongola* to Madras in India.

While Beaumont's medical sheet revealed only minor complaints ( gonorrhoea at Aldershot, an infected finger, inflammation of the meatus (a channel in the ear) and an abcess on the leg in India and contusion to the back 'in the field' in December 1914) his conduct was more concerning. Although somewhat water-damaged, the records show that in 1911 Beaumont had received a sentence of five days' imprisonment from the Civil Power for 'insulting language' and further imprisonment in 1914.

On the Western Front, Beaumont found life even harder. In January 1915 he was awarded ten days Field Punishment No. 1 by Major Gordon, who had recently assumed command of the battalion on Colonel Blackader's promotion, for *'reporting sick without adequate cause when for duty in the trenches'*. A month later Beaumont was tried by Field General Court Martial and sentenced to nine months imprisonment with hard labour, for 'without necessity quitting the ranks', the catch-all 'conduct to the prejudice of good order and military discipline' and 'using insubordinate language to a superior officer'. This sentence was later commuted to two months' Field Punishment No. 1. It was while returning, with a draft, from this incarceration that Beaumont went absent once again.

There is certainly no evidence that the British Army took a death sentence lightly. It had to be the unanimous finding of the court, with the most junior officer speaking first to avoid influence from above. Having found their man guilty and sentenced him to death, the court then passed the record of its proceedings up the chain of command for confirmation. Under the watchful eye of the Judge Advocate General, each officer, from battalion commander to commander-in-chief, would add their comments. In this case, the final decision lay with Field Marshal Sir John French, commander in chief of British forces on the Western Front.

Beaumont's papers went first to Lieutenant-colonel Herbert Gordon,

# "Trying to hold on"

his commanding officer. Gordon had been commissioned into the Leicestershire Regiment in 1889, seeing a decade's active service in the Sudan from 1900 until 1911, when he returned to regimental duty in India.

# Tigers in the Trenches

Gordon had no sympathy for Beaumont, noting on a 'Messages and Signals' form [previous page]: *"Character as a fighting man indifferent and very backward in going forward. Behaviour bad. He came with battalion from India and his conduct in action has been the reverse of dashing. His general attitude towards the war is one of absolute boredom and characterized by an intense and irradicable* [sic] *dislike to the trenches and in my opinion the crime was committed deliberately with the object of escaping from what he considers the unpleasant surroundings of life on active service."*

The papers were passed then to Brigadier General Charles Blackader, who had only recently left the 2nd Leicesters to assume command of the Garwhal Brigade. Mindful perhaps of his former battalion's reputation as well as that *"the object of military law is to maintain discipline"*[24], Blackader prefaced his remarks with the reassurance that *"the state of discipline in the battalion is excellent"*, adding *"though I do not consider that the state of the Battalion requires an example to be made, it appears to me from the attached report that the man himself deserves the extreme penalty."*

From Brigade Headquarters the papers passed to Lieutenant-General C. A. Anderson, commanding the Meerut Division, who recommended execution of the sentence, noting *"Although the man was in uniform he had been deliberately absent from his unit for more than a month."*

At the Indian Corps Headquarters on 17 June 1915, Lieutenant-General Sir James Willcocks agreed, passing the papers on to the 1st Army with the simple note: *"I recommend that the sentence be carried out"*. There, the following day, General Douglas Haig [above]

24 *Manual of Military Law (1914)* p. 6

# "Trying to hold on"

noted that *"the G-O-Cs of Bde, of Divn & of the Corps recommend that the extreme penalty be carried out. I concur in their opinion."* [below]

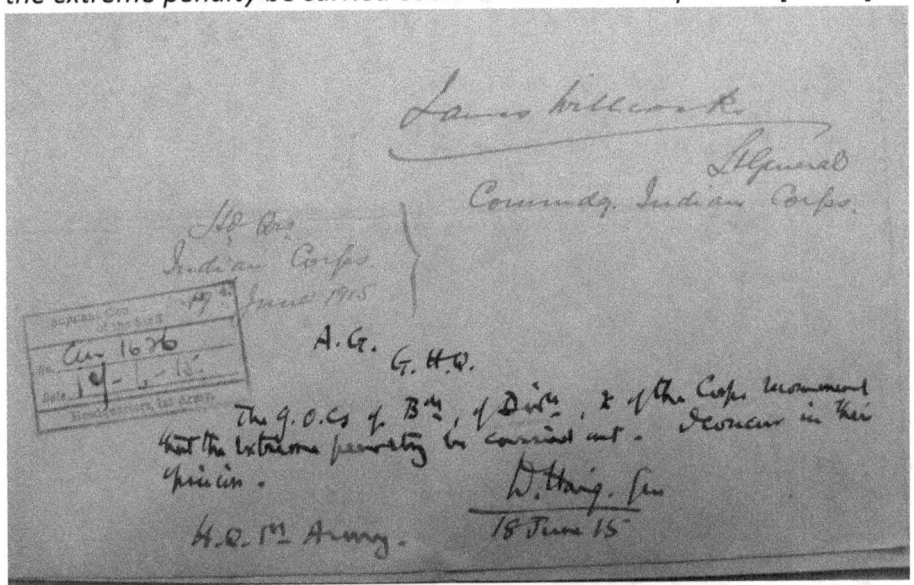

The sentence was finally 'confirmed', with that single word, by Field Marshal Sir John French on 21 June 1915. Beaumont's battalion was notified on 22 June by Captain A. M. Henderson Scott, the Deputy Assistant Adjutant General of the Indian Corps and the verdict 'promulgated' by Colonel Gordon at 4 p.m. on 23 June. The 2nd Leicesters were in Brigade Reserve, so presumably almost all were available to hear the sentence. It is not known whether Beaumont heard the decision on parade or was told quietly beforehand.

Private Beaumont was shot at one minute past four on the morning of 24 June 1915. Two days before, Lieutenant-Colonel Gordon had been notified of a *"suitable secluded spot in [an] orchard"* near to Richbourg St Vaast. Whether Beaumont was tied to a post or sat in a chair, as many did, is not recorded. Nor is his behaviour at his end. The 2nd Leicesters paused briefly in their march to 'Windy Corner' and 'Loretta Road' and Captain E. C. Deane, Royal Army Medical Corps, noted in indelible pencil on a page from his notebook: *"I certify that I witnessed the execution this day of no. 8710 Pte Beaumont E. A. 2nd Leicestershire Rgt by firing party, death being instantaneous."*

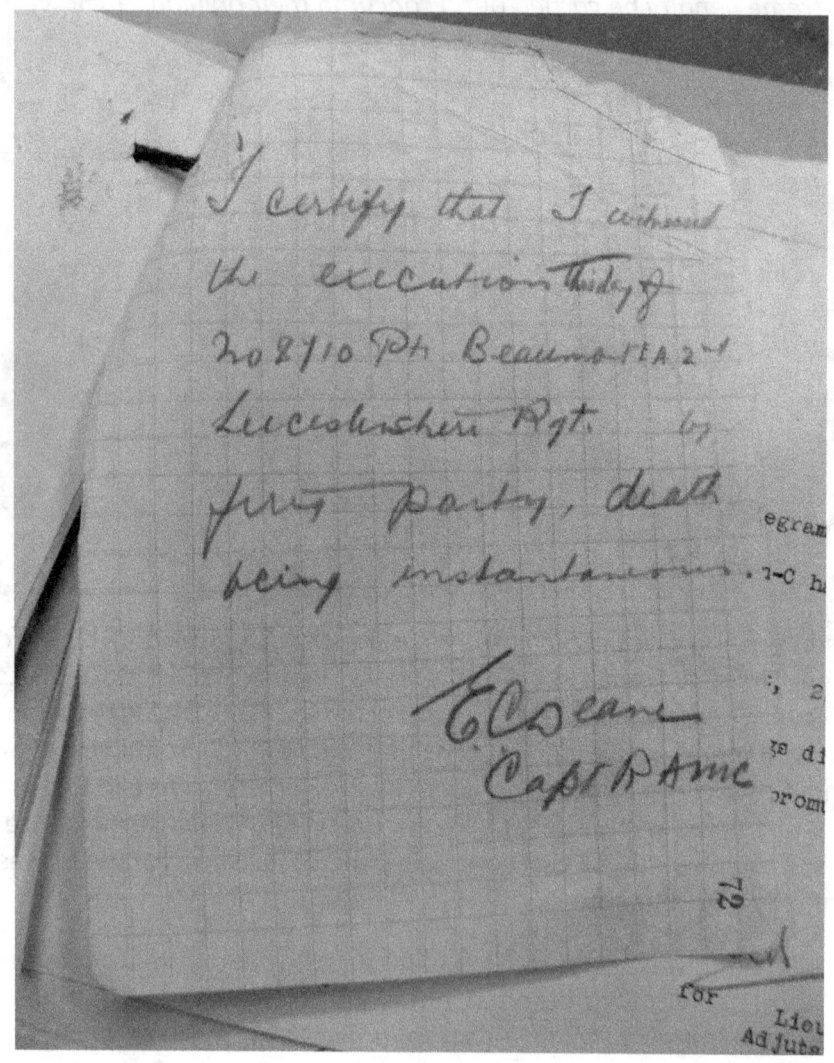

Ernest Beaumont's death certificate from his court martial file at the National Archives [ref. WO71/418]. The file includes the contemporanious record of the proceedings of his court martial. The final (top) paper is a recently inserted record of his pardon - see illustration on p. 108.

# "Trying to hold on"

*Private Beaumont's grave at St Vaast Post Military Cemetery, Richebourg-L'Avoue*

It was to be over three years before the execution of the Leicestershire Regiment's other soldier 'shot at dawn'. This time, the victim (if 'victim' is the word) was Private Joseph Nisbet of the 1st Battalion.

Nisbet was born in 1891 at Hetton Downs, in the parish of Hetton-le-Hole, near Houghton le Spring in what was then County Durham but is now Tyne and Wear. Having worked for a few years as a coalminer, Nisbet decided in October 1911 to try the life of a soldier. He enlisted in the

# Tigers in the Trenches

Durham Light Infantry but after eighty-five days, Nisbet was discharged as *"not likely to become an efficient soldier"*. This was by no means unusual, in 1897 of 38,549 recruits attested, no fewer than 4,212 were rejected by the authorities[25]; though it certainly seems inauspicious for Nisbet's future military career.

A month after the outbreak of war, on 2 September 1914, Nisbet enlisted once again; spending three weeks at the Depot and then joining 'A' Company of the newly raised 8th Battalion of the Leicesters at Bourley Camp, Aldershot. His attestation form survives, revealing that he concealed both his previous military service and his rejection from it.

Within a week of landing in France, Private Nisbet was in trouble. Tried by Field General Court Martial, Nisbet was given one month's Field Punishment No. 1, for "quitting the ranks without permission". He was, in fact, one of the two men observed by Dick Read, spreadeagled and tied to a wagon wheel as the battalion marched past.

Having spent the Autumn and Winter at Berles-au-Bois in, or resting from the front line, the 8th Battalion was withdrawn and sent for a period of rest and re-equipping near Doullens. Here, Nisbet was again in trouble. On 29 March 1916 he was tried by Court Martial on a charge of *"Disobeying in such a manner as to show a wilful defiance of authority, a lawful command given personally by his superior officer in the execution of his office."*

Sadly, the records of the court-martial do not survive but a more serious crime, coupled to a criminal record, brought a far harsher sentence. This time, Private Nisbet received three years' penal servitude, although this was soon commuted to one year's imprisonment. Joseph Nisbet was either a victimised, marked-man, an obstinately square peg in a round hole; or the thoroughly bad soldier the Durham Light Infantry had thought him five years before.

On 10 April 1916, Nisbet was before another Field General Court Martial, this time charged that *"when on active service, without urgent necessity*

---

[25] Peter S Walton (ed.) Lieut-Col. James Moncrieff Grierson *Scarlet into Khaki* (London) 1988, p.20

# "Trying to hold on"

*quitting the ranks"* and once again *"disobeying a lawful order given by his superior officer".* As before we do not know the details of Nisbet's crimes, only that on 20 April 1916, his sentence was reduced again by the Army Commander to eighty-five days' Field Punishment No. 1. As we have seen, army commanders saw little point in having fighting men languishing in cells, when by substituting the short, sharp, shock of Field Punishment there was a good chance that they could be both 'straightened-out' and returned to the firing-line.

Nisbet was not straightened-out however. A month later, on 11 May 1916, he was tried once again for the insolent disobeying of a lawful order. This time the court ran out of patience. Nisbet was found guilty and sentenced to death by shooting but, on reaching General Sir Edmund Allenby, commanding the 3rd Army, the sentence was commuted to ten years' penal servitude and on 27 June reduced to two years' imprisonment with hard labour.

The news reached Nisbet at the military prison at Blargies, half-way between Rouen and Amiens, where he had been since 4 June 1916. Even in prison, however, Nisbet failed to conform or control his temper. This is clear because, on 29 December he was tried by Field General Court Martial once again; this time for *"when on active service, offering violence to his superior officer".* It appears that when sentenced for a minor offence, Nisbet attempted to strike the prison governor, Captain George Hedley Basher. Found guilty, Private Nisbet added another four years' penal servitude to his sentence.

From Blargies, Nisbet was transferred to England on 23 January 1917, to complete his at punishment Maidstone Prison. Over a year later, on 12 April 1918, Nisbet's sentence was suspended, and that troubled and troubling soldier posted to the Leicester's 1st Battalion. Nisbet's release came the day after General Haig's 'backs to the wall' speech[26] and it can only be presumed that every able-bodied man was needed to turn back the tide of the Ludendorff offensive.

---

[26] Sir Douglas Haig had issued a stirring declaration to the effect that: *"Every position must be held to the last man: there must be no retirement. With our backs to the wall and believing in the justice of our cause each one of us must fight on to the end. The safety of our homes and the freedom of mankind alike depend upon the conduct of each one of us at this critical moment".*

# Tigers in the Trenches

If the posting to a 'regular' battalion had been made in the hope of stiffening Nisbet's resolve and ironing out his tendencies towards delinquency, those responsible can only have been disappointed by his return to form. On 27 June 1918 Nisbet was charged with disobedience of a lawful command and the catch-all *"conduct to the prejudice of good order and military discipline"*. The Field General Court Martial found him guilty and awarded two years' imprisonment with hard labour, though (presumably mindful of the need for men and the outstanding punishments) the sentence was commuted by Lieutenant-Colonel Herbert Milward, commanding the 71st Infantry Brigade, to ninety days' Field Punishment Number One.

Private Nisbet next appears in the 'official record' at 8 p.m. on 15 July 1918, in the reserve trenches near Sint Hubertushoek. He was seen there by Lance-corporal Arthur Beck, of 'D' Company, 1st Leicesters, when the section was warned by lance-corporal Passingham to prepare to move back up to the front-line at 10.45 that night.

At about eight-thirty that evening, Private Nisbet sought out the battalion's medical officer, Captain Edward. H. Granger, Royal Army Medical Corps, and reported himself sick. Granger recalled that he had carefully examined Nisbet, but could not find anything amiss. The captain therefore marked Nisbet down as *"fit to perform his duty"* but told him that he would see him at the next sick parade.

At 10.45 p.m. Sergeant Bert Hoddinott paraded the platoon and led them up the communication trenches to the front-line. Nisbet neither paraded nor appeared in the front-line. He was next seen three days' later, on 18 July 1918, at Number 4 Medical Base Depot at Beaumarais, near Calais, by the provost sergeant there, No. 7782 Sergeant D. Stewart, of the King's Own Scottish Borderers. Patrolling the trenches and dug-outs behind the Base Depot at about 11 p.m., Sergeant Stewart had disturbed Nisbet in one of the dug-outs, apparently trying to get some sleep.

Nisbet was clean and in uniform but without his rifle or equipment; which all soldiers on leave or detached duty were required to have with

# "Trying to hold on"

them. Sergeant Stewart was not satisfied with Nisbet's explanation that he belonged *"to K Depot"* and asked to examine his pay book. He then took Nisbet to the guard tent.

The inevitable result was Nisbet's return to Sint Hubertushoek and another Field General Court Martial on 8 August 1918, convened by Lieutenant-Colonel Milward. The president of the court was Major Lord Teynham[27] of 1st Battalion, The Buffs [left], assisted by Captain C. Armitage, 1st King's Shropshire Light Infantry; Lieutenant A. A. Lilley, also of the Buffs; and Captain W. A. Cummins, Chief Medical Officer to the 19th Corps. The only officers from Nisbet's battalion were the prosecutor, Captain R. N. Davis and the 'accused's friend', Lieutenant Geddes.

Captain Richard Nevill Davis, who joined the battalion near Ypres in January 1916, had been the battalion's adjutant since 1 November 1917. He had been recommended for the Military Cross as a result of his cool efficiency during the German onslaught in March 1918.[28] Lieutenant Samuel McKee Geddis had joined the 1st battalion as a second lieutenant in July 1915, being promoted to lieutenant two years later.[29]

Nisbet was charged under the Army Act, Section 12(1.a.) in that *"when on active service, deserting His Majesty's Service, in that he, near St*

---

27 Henry John Philip Sidney Roper-Curzon, 18th Baron of Teynham, 1867-1936
28 The MC was Gazetted on 16 September 1918; the citation noted Nevill's "conspicuous gallantry and devotion to duty during an enemy attack".
29 Geddis was killed in action just over a month after Nisbet's court-martial, while commanding the 1st Battalion's 'A' Company near Holnon on the River Aisne.

# Tigers in the Trenches

Hubertshoek on 15 July 1918 absented himself from his Battalion after being warned to proceed to the front line trenches, and remained absent until apprehended near Calais on 18th July 1918." Nisbet's response was to plead 'not guilty', although (as we have seen) guilty pleas were, in any case, no longer accepted in capital cases.

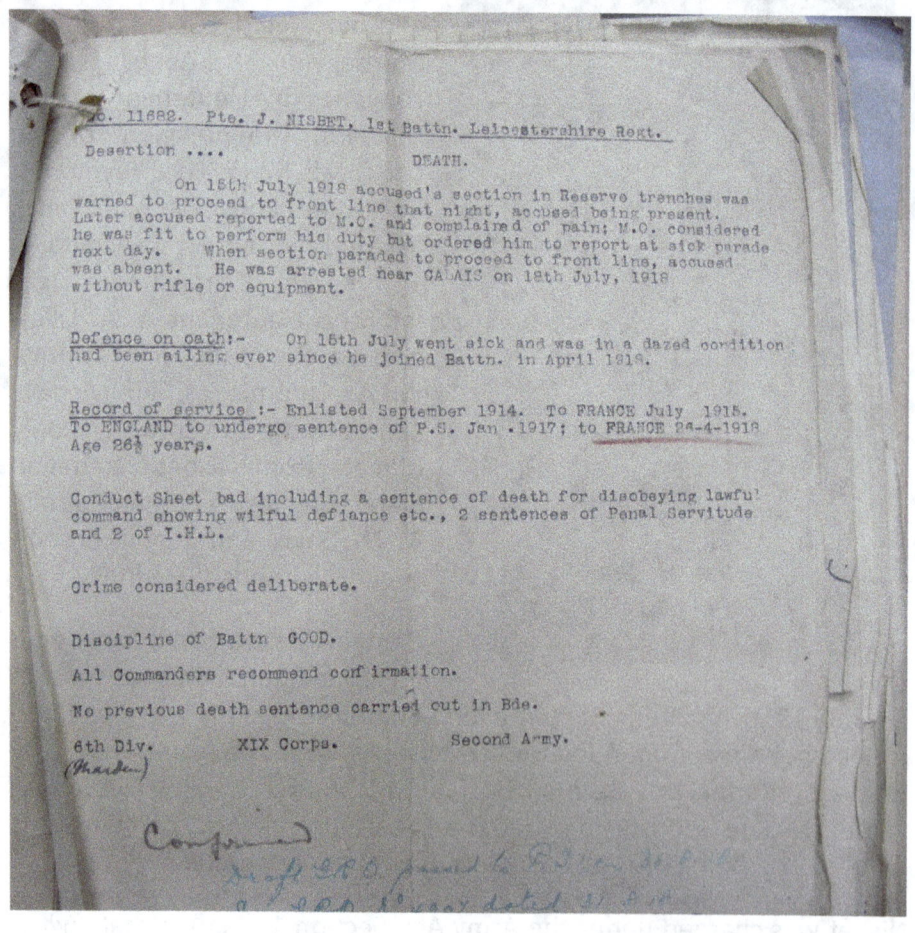

The typed record of proceedings from Joseph Nisbet's cort martial, preserved at the National Archives in Kew [WO71/663]

# "Trying to hold on"

The evidence was presented by Lance-corporal Beck, Captain Granger, and Sergeants Hoddinott and Stewart. Only Captain Granger was cross-examined, concerning the reason given by Nisbet for reporting sick. Major Lord Teynham noted on the court-martial records that *"accused complained of pain"*.

Private Nisbet, under oath, then gave his version of events, stating *"on the night in question I went sick. I was in a dazed condition. I have been ailing ever since. I came to the Battalion since 27$^{th}$ April this year."* Although Nisbet had nothing further to add, his 'friend', Lieutenant Geddis reinforced what medical defence there was, pointing out that the *"accused was certainly ill on that particular night even according to the Doctor and his statement made on oath."*

It cannot have taken long to determine a guilty verdict and sentence of death; though as both had to be confirmed by higher authority, Nisbet was simply told that no finding would be announced that day. Evidence was called of previous conduct, which revealed three suspended sentences (including one to be shot) and the Field Punishment No. 1, which the prisoner was still undergoing. As Nisbet called no evidence as to character and wished to make no further statement, the court was closed and the papers began their journey up through the hierarchy of the B.E.F.

The court-martial record reached Nisbet's battalion commander, Lieutenant-Colonel Francis Latham the following day. No doubt a busy man, Latham nonetheless filled a foolscap sheet, bearing the red Leicestershire Regiment orderly room stamp, with his small, neat, handwriting.

*"This man is not a good soldier from a fighting point of view and apart from this his character is distinctly bad. This man's Company commander considers that he has a disturbing and very bad influence on the other men in his company."*

Latham recited Nisbet's unhappy career of sentences suspended and penal servitude. He then continued:

"His Company Commander is of the opinion that this crime was DELIBERATELY committed.

I consider that the extreme penalty should be inflicted in this case, as the man has had his chance on several previous occasions of redeeming himself and evidently does not intend to soldier.

He has been sentenced to Death on a previous occasion – the sentence being subsequently commuted – and he is at present serving under three suspended sentences, and actually undergoing 90 days Field Punishment No. 1."

Latham, concluded;

"I am of the opinion that it is distinctly bad for discipline to have a man of such little value as a soldier and with such a disgraceful record moving about with men who are doing their duty. A man of this sort must have a bad effect on the morale of any men who may come into contact with him. If the death sentence be not carried out, I recommend that he should undergo any period of Penal servitude to which it may be commuted."

The view of Nisbet's battalion commander was clearly damning but not unreasonable. Nisbet, whether rogue or victim, was clearly not a good bargain as a soldier and the continuous suspensions of prison sentences simply returned a 'nuisance' to the front-line, where those required to deal with it had neither the time nor, if Nisbet's 'problem' was actually a mental one, the necessary skill to diagnose and deal with it.

Lieutenant-Colonel Milward, commanding 71$^{st}$ Brigade, concurred with Latham, adding that the 1$^{st}$ Leicesters' state of discipline was good. Considering that *"the object of military law is to maintain discipline"*, similar declarations often accompanied court-martial papers, either in defence of good battalions troubled, apparently, with one rotten egg; or to urge an execution where discipline required stiffening. Milward, however, saw this as a problem of the individual:

"I recommend that the extreme penalty should be carried out...He has been sentenced to Death before. He has not tried to redeem his character

# "Trying to hold on"

*and he has a very bad influence on any men who come in contact with him."*

Nisbet's file then passed to Major-General Thomas Owen Marden,[left] commanding the 6th Division. Marden was presented with a typescript note, declaring that Nisbet's age ('stated by himself') was twenty-six years and six months and inviting him to complete a form beginning 'I recommend...'. Having considered the attached papers, Marden added *"that the Death sentence be put into execution. Pte Nisbet is useless as a soldier, is under three suspended sentences & has had every chance."*

Within a day, on 13 August 1918, the commander of XIXth Corps, Lieutenant-General Herbert Watts had also seen the papers and noted his agreement with General Marden. The next day, General Herbert Plumer, commanding the Second Army concurred and handed the papers to Major R.C. Hills, his Deputy Assistant Adjutant General. Hills was probably the source of the blue-pencilled question-marks and under-linings on the court-martial records, which attest to the care taken by the Adjutant General's and Judge Advocate General's departments in considering such cases.

On 14 August, Hills noted that *"the particulars in the forwarding minute regarding suspended sentences are probably not technically accurate, but represent in substance his previous record."* This view was confirmed by Brigadier-General Gilbert Mellor, Deputy Judge Advocate General, on 15 August, who thought the record of Nisbet's three suspended sentences *"does not seem to be strictly true"* though as the sentences were passed and confirmed, *"it does not appear to be necessary in the* circumstances to inquire further what has become of each of them."

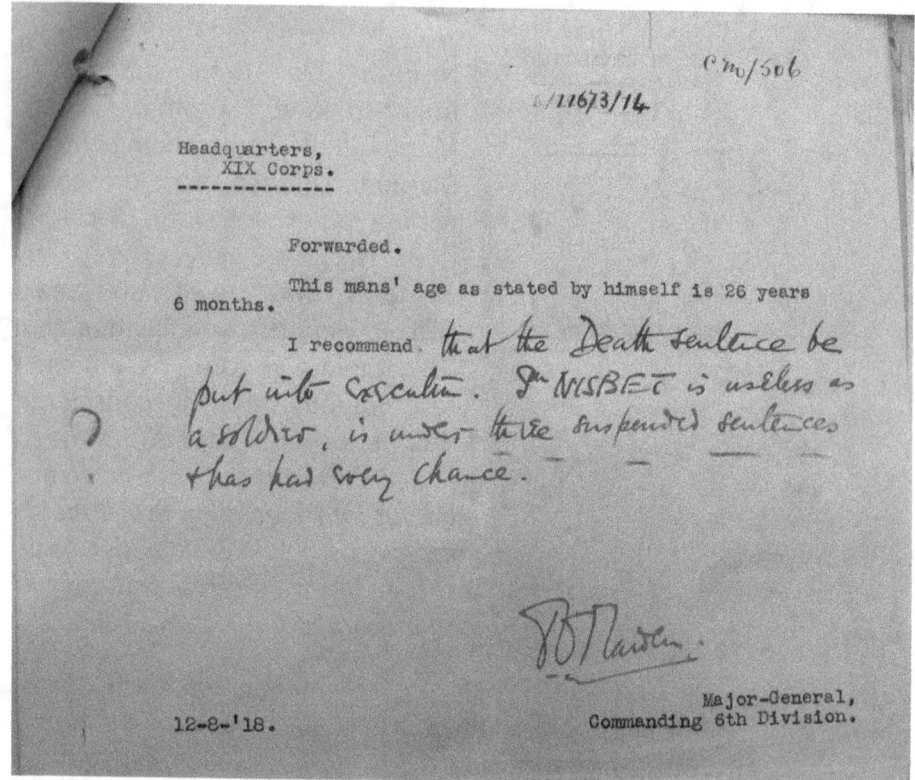

All that remained was for Nisbet's case to reach the desk of his commander-in-chief, where Field Marshal Haig confirmed the sentence on 19 August 1918. It was carried out at 5 o'clock on the morning of 23 August, at Helhoek, while Nisbet's battalion was in transit from Ouderdom to Winnezeele. Private Nisbet's death was certified by Captain A. R. Appleton Carr, of the Royal Army Medical Corps and his body interred in the Nine Elms Cemetery, a few miles west of Poperinge.

Much has been said and written about those shot at dawn. In a robust defence of military justice Gordon Corrigan criticises *"those who simply fail to understand how an army works and what the military imperatives are and were"*[30] while others make allowances for the special circumstances of active service and join him in deploring the attempt to

---
30 Gordon Corrigan *Mud, Blood and Poppycock* (London) 2003, P. 225

# "Trying to hold on"

impose modern standards and views onto the past.

It is argued that 'shell shock' or some similar mental disorder was a factor too often left unexplored by courts-martial. In neither of the Leicestershire Regiment cases is there any cogent suggestion of an undiagnosed medical condition. Nisbet had appealed to his battalion's medical officer on the eve of a return to the firing line but while this was noted (and repeated by Lieutenant Geddes) it was never developed as a defence. In fact, Nisbet seems constitutionally unfitted for a life of discipline and duty, while Beaumont, perhaps, is an example of Lord Moran's finite resource of courage[31] and what Colonel Gordon saw as *"an intense and irradicable* [sic] *dislike to the trenches"* was just a soldier at the end of his tether.

That medical science had not yet caught up with war on an industrial scale is hardly the fault of military justice however and it is certainly true that there is little evidence to suggest that those conducting trials were anything but fair and desirous of delivering a just verdict. The consideration by every tier of higher authority, frequent suspensions of sentences, and the involvement of legally qualified officers, whose blue pencil markings score many of the trial records, also suggest that the death penalty was not taken lightly.

---

[31] Moran, a medical officer during the Great War, in his *Anatomy of courage* expounded the theory of courage as a finite resource; arguing that *"Courage is will-power, whereof no man has unlimited stock; and when in war it is used up , he is finished."*

## Tigers in the Trenches

However, there is a feeling that courts-martial were seen by some as an opportunity to dispose of 'worthless' soldiers; men who failed every chance to prove themselves and eventually exhausted the patience of their commanders. Private Beaumont was, after all, *"very backward in going forward"* and Nisbet *"useless as a soldier"*. Both, undoubtedly, were ultimately nuisances, poor soldiers and bad bargains – but, from the comfort of the twenty-first century, can we ask whether such failure, or weakness, was reason enough to put them to death?

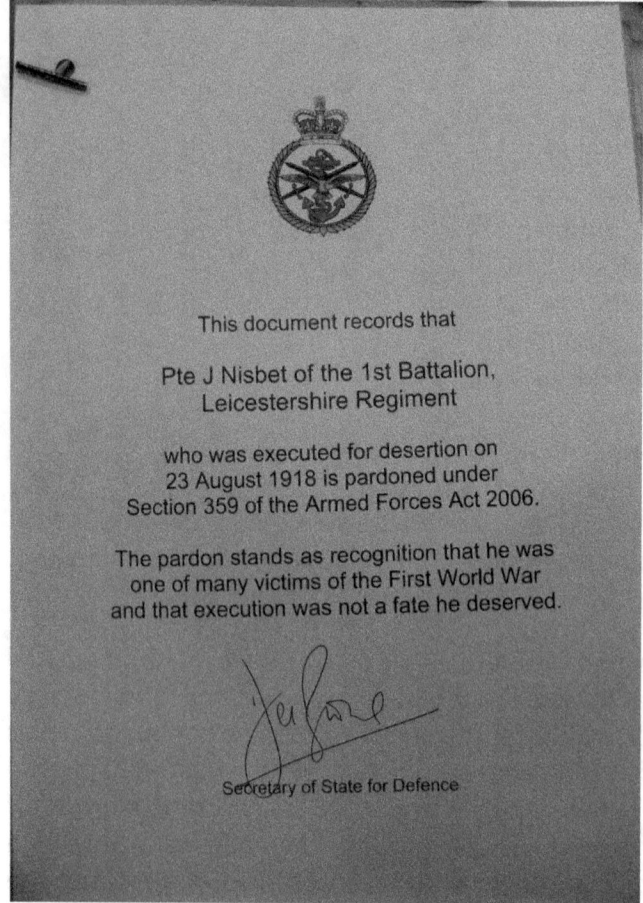

The reason usually advanced, that the occasional execution of a cowardly or disobedient soldier was a powerful tonic for flagging morale and discipline, had apparently been identified as peculiarly English as early as 1759; Voltaire's *Candide* famously containing the observation, on seeing an Admiral shot by firing squad on his own quarterdeck, that *"In this country, it is wise to kill an admiral from time to time so to encourage the others."*[32] Whether effective or not, exemplary justice was held to be

---

[32] "Dans ce pays-ci, il est bon de tuer de temps en temps un amiral pour encourager les autres." Voltaire was alluding to the execution of Admiral John Byng, whose hesitancy in attempting to relieve the garrison

# "Trying to hold on"

essential in the B.E.F. and efforts made to ensure that all executions were widely publicised.[33]

The debate will no-doubt continue. It is perhaps right to conclude, therefore, by noting that the files of all those shot-at-dawn, held at the National Archives, contain a recently inserted paper recording that the soldier concerned *"is pardoned under Section 359 of the Armed Forces Act 2006...as recognition that he was one of many victims of the First World W and that execution was not a fate he deserved."*

The Shot at dawn Memorial, erected in 2001, at the National Memorial Arboretum at Alrewas in Staffordshire.

---

of Minorca in the face of superior forces led to his execution.
33 Charles Messenger *ibid.*, p.378. GHQ's Routine Orders contained notices of all executions throughout the war and, as has been seen, both Beaumont and Nesbit's deaths were overseen by their comrades.

## Chapter Six

## *"It was a bomb business..."*

## The assault on the Hohenzollern Redoubt, 13 October 1915

On 29 September 2016, the remains of a soldier of the Leicestershire Regiment were interred, with full Military Honours, at the St Mary's Advanced Dressing Station Cemetery, near Haisnes, in the Pas de Calais. The remains had been unearthed near the town of Auchy-les-Mines by members of the Durand Group, a team researching the underground relics, the dugouts, tunnels and mines, of the Great War.[1]

Sadly, although a battered shoulder title of LEICESTER in brass remained attached to a few threads of khaki, there was nothing else to give a name to the dead man. Although a treasure trove of buttons, buckles and personal items (from a mug and spoon to coins in his pocket) were recovered, none gave any clue as to identity. There was no identity disk, no inscribed watch or cigarette case, and no personal papers could have survived a century in the wet earth.

1 The Durand Group *Report on the Recovery of a First World War British Soldier 20-21 February 2016*

## "It was a bomb business..."

The soldier, probably killed by the metal fragments which were found amongst his bones, was discovered in agricultural land north of the D39, Rue Jules Guesde, between Vermelles and Hulluch. The site was on the southern edge of an extensive German defence work known to the British as the Hohenzollern Redoubt, and to its creators as the *Hohenzollernwerk*.

To understand why a soldier of the Leicestershire regiment should be lying before the Hohenzollern Redoubt, it is necessary to go back to a series of conferences held between the British and French general staffs throughout the summer and early autumn of 1915. The year had already proved to be one of stagnation and disappointment. The stalemate of siege warfare on the all-important Western Front remained, as all attempts to pierce the superbly-sited German defences had foundered. Early promise, as at Neuve Chapelle, just as further afield at Gallipoli, had resulted in casualties out of all proportion to the territorial gains.

British hopes to postpone further offensives until 1916, when Kitchener's New Armies would be available, were brushed aside by the French commander-in-chief, General Joffre. Time was not on their side. Vast tracts of France were still in enemy hands and it was vital to relieve the pressure upon Russia, their ally in the east.

To Joffre, the area of French Flanders from La Bassee to Loos, was ideal ground for an offensive. It was where the British and French armies met, it was untouched ground and it would permit a pincer movement to link with French attacks in Champagne and Artois.

General Haig, whose First Army was to carry out the operation, recoiled from the proposed battleground. It was a flat, almost featureless prairie; its gentle slopes broken only by the occasional, dark slag heaps - or *crassiers* - of the mining region around Lens. With too few men and too little heavy artillery, Haig saw little hope of success. Even deploying the newly developed poison gas, an attack across an open plain, dominated by enemy positions well dug-in amongst the pit villages and slag heaps, was bound to end in failure and unacceptable losses.

## Tigers in the Trenches

Sir John French, commanding the B.E.F., agreed but both were overruled by the Secretary of State for War, Lord Kitchener, who put the needs of the alliance with France first: *"we must act with all energy and do our utmost to help France in their offensive, even though by doing so we may suffer very heavy losses".*[2]

FIELD-MARSHAL SIR JOHN FRENCH,
COMMANDER-IN-CHIEF
OF THE BRITISH EXPEDITIONARY FORCES.

It is important to recollect that Britain was still very much France's junior partner on the Western Front. Britain's military contribution – before the arrival of the New Armies raised in August 1914 and the start of conscription in 1916 – was still miniscule beside that of the French. Nevertheless, Haig proposed to throw at least seventeen infantry divisions forward, most massed on a narrow front; backed by two cavalry divisions, ready to exploit a breakthrough. The attack would be aided, for the first time *en masse,* by the use of poison gas.

The resulting attack, at Loos on 25 September, was not a success. The experience of the 2$^{nd}$ Battalion The Leicestershire Regiment, advancing against a German strongpoint at *Moulin du Pietre,* will serve for all. The Leicesters, climbing out of their trenches at 6 a.m, advanced swiftly over no-man's land but soon found themselves amongst their own gas – which had settled as the breeze dropped. Casualties mounted as the German fire increased. Nevertheless, the battalion pushed on, only to stall in front of the enemy lines; halted by an uncut belt of wire and deep, water-filled ditches.

Losses were heavy. The offensive cost over 40,000 killed and wounded

---

2 Brigadier-General Sir James E Edmonds History of the Great War[the Official History] 1915 Vol. 2, 1928, p.129

## "It was a bomb business..."

and while it may have relieved pressure on hard-pressed allies, it gained precious little ground. Most troubling was a salient, or bulge, left in the enemy lines where the Germans still clung grimly on.

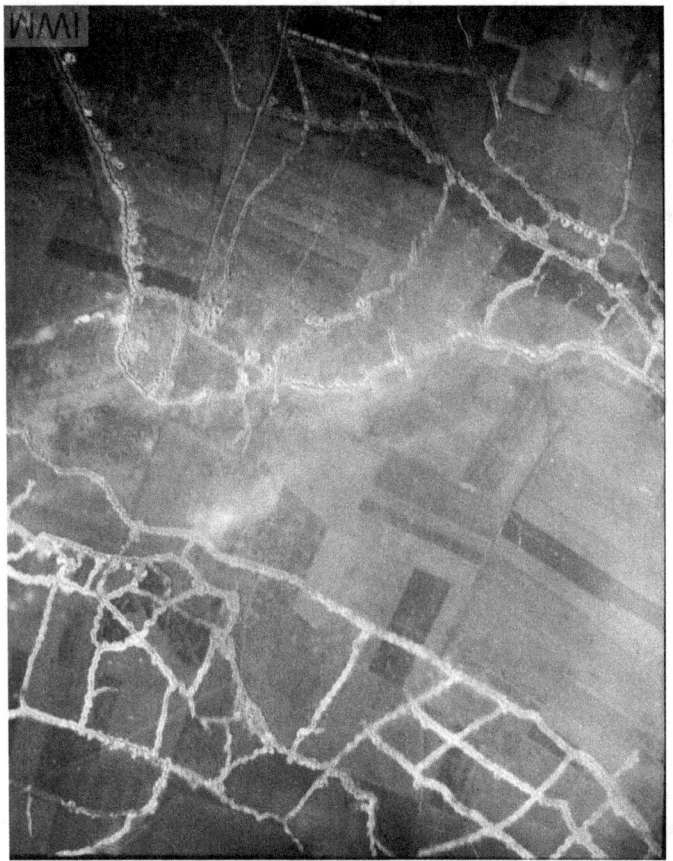

*The 'bulge' of the Hohenzollern Redoubt clearly outlined in chalk on this Imperial War Museum aerial photograph (Box 60/1437)*

At the tip of this bulge was the Hohenzollern Redoubt. As an old boy of Leicester's Bridge Road School (who saw it) wrote home: *"Don't think that the redoubt named after the German dynasty was a great fortress in the sense generally used. It was really an array of trenches dug on*

## Tigers in the Trenches

*a ridge, and of course strongly protected by wire and machine guns."*[3] The redoubt had been linked to the main German line by well-defended trenches; known to the British (presumably in honour of the Kaiser and Crown Prince respectively) as Big and Little Willie. Following an earlier assault, Big Willie, to the south of the redoubt, was partly in British hands.

Although hidden from the British trenches; on aerial photographs the chalky soil shows the redoubt traced in white - an intricate network of front-line and communication trenches, studded with machine-gun nests. The position was further strengthened behind by *The Dump*, a flattened slag heap criss-crossed with trenches on one side, and, on the other, terraces of shell-battered miners' cottages (or *'corons'*) characterised by stout cellars impervious to shellfire and ideal for defence. Further defensive fire came from *Fosse 8*, a pit head from which German observers could monitor every British move and correct any inaccuracy of their artillery.

The Redoubt had to be taken and the bulge of its salient flattened out. The front-line would be shortened, with a great saving in manpower, and the Germans' advantages for observation eliminated. A further attack required fresh troops however and so the 46th (North Midland) Division was brought down from Ypres.

These were Territorials from the Leicestershire, Lincolnshire, Sherwood Foresters, and North and South Staffordshire Regiments. In many ways these Territorials – the 'Terriers', or even 'Terrors' to the local newspapers – were the cream of local youth. They were the adventurous, likely lads who found clerical or factory work unfulfilling and fancied the comradeship and free holidays of the army's summer camps. The new estates and suburbs of Leicester (Clarendon Park, Aylestone Park, Evington, Humberstone and even as far out as Wigston) had filled the ranks of the 4th Battalion of the Leicestershire Regiment; while the county completed the 5th Battalion with hosiery hands from Hinckley, miners from Ashby and office and shop-floor men from Market Harborough.

---

3 *Leicester Daily Post*, 28 October 1915

## "It was a bomb business..."

As we have seen, they were swiftly mobilised in August 1914 and marched to Belper, then Luton for training. Having opted, almost to a man, for overseas service, their 46th Division was one of the first to arrive in France at the end of February, 1915. Though keen as mustard, the territorial divisions were weaker numerically than their regular counterparts and in many cases equipped with out-dated rifles and artillery.[4]

The two Leicestershire battalions of the 46th Division arrived at Hesdigneul-les-Béthune, a dozen or so miles behind the lines, on 7 October 1915 and immediately began preparations for the assault. Parties of officers and NCOs slithered and slipped up the muddy communication trenches to gaze through periscopes across a no-man's land, still littered with the dead of previous attacks, at the Redoubt and *The Dump* beyond, while the men spent days practising with the new Mills bombs.[5] A German counter-attack had recently been driven off, almost solely using these new hand-grenades, and supplies were rapidly sought and promised.

The then Lieutenant J. D. Hills, commanding 'D' Company of the 1/5th Leicesters, though shortly to be detached for intelligence work, noted the daunting nature of the task ahead: *"...the redoubt alone was a very strong point. It formed a salient in the enemy's line and both the Northern area, 'Little Willie,' and the southern 'Big Willie,' were deep, well-fortified trenches, with several machine gun positions. Behind these...two more deep trenches...thought to be used for communication purposes only, and leading back to 'Fosse' and 'Dump' trenches near the slag heap...the redoubt and its approach from our line were well covered by machine gun posts, for, on the North, 'Mad Point' overlooked our present front line and No-Man's Land, while 'Madagascar' Cottages and the Slag-heap commanded all the rest of the country."*[6]

Having been delayed by a German counter-attack, it was not until the

---

4 It is worth noting that a Long Magazine Lee Enfield rifle, predating the SMLEs (Short Magazine Lee Enfield) normally issued to regular units, was found close to the soldier excavated by the Durand Group in 2016.

5 The 1/4th Battalion War Diary records several days practice with " 'live' Mills No. 5 Grenades" and, on 11 October, a visit from the G.O.C. to watch the training.

6 Captain J. D. Hills *The Fifth Leicestershire* (Loughborough) 1919, pp. 71-2. Though not an inappropriate name in itself, 'Mad Point' was an abbreviation of Madagascar – the name of a nearby mining community.

# Tigers in the Trenches

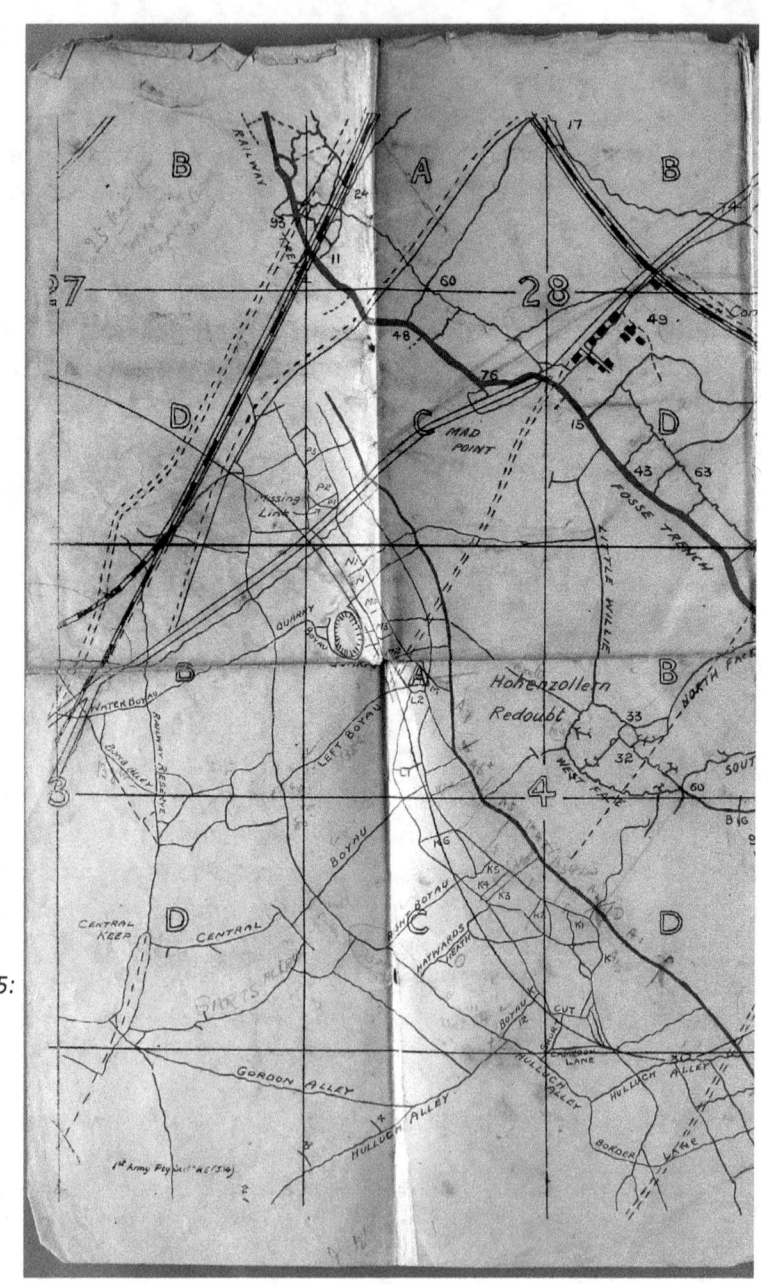

Trench map, October 1915: ROLLR DE5891/15

# "It was a bomb business…"

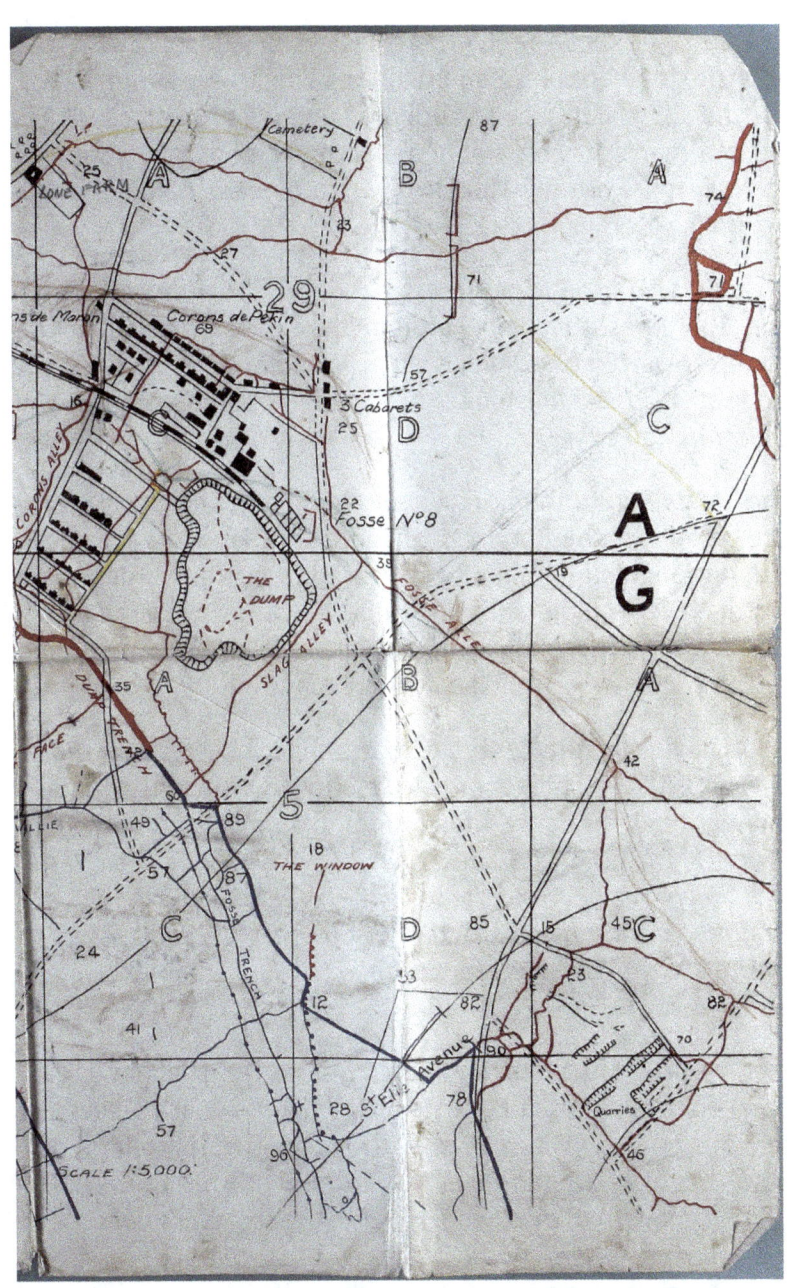

night of 12th October that the 1/4th Leicesters began to occupy the front-line opposite the Redoubt. Behind them, filling the communication trenches was the 1/5th Battalion in support - every man with sandbags and every fourth man carrying a shovel - to make good any captured trenches. To their left were the Lincolns, with a pioneer battalion from Monmouthshire in reserve.

The two brigades of the 46th Division, 137th and 138th, were to attack together; the 137th was advancing around the southern edge of *the Dump* slag heap to seize *Fosse Alley* trench, while 138th Brigade swept over the redoubt itself, establishing a new defensive line amongst the ruins of the *Corons de Pekin*.

The Leicesters' march up to the firing line proved tiring and frustratingly slow, despite good weather and an encouraging send off from the brigade band. Although equipment was reduced to 'fighting order', with rolled greatcoats, every soldier was encumbered with six sandbags and a shovel between three; which was no easy matter when the cramped and slippery communication trenches were reached.

Private W. Hutchinson of the 1/4th Leicesters described his battalion's arrival, after some twelve miles, in a letter home. Hutchinson finally halted at midnight having paused for food and to pick up bombs and other equipment. *"The firing line,"* he recalled, *"was very quiet, very little firing, and not much was heard of the big guns on either side. We did our usual sentry duties during the night, and also during the morning: and then we were told a tremendous bombardment would commence at 20 minutes past eleven..."*[7]

It was, in fact, to be another forty minutes before the shelling began. Lance-Corporal Harry Pexton, a Leicester lad with the 1/4th Leicesters clearly noted the time (which agrees with that in the battalion *War Diary*): *"On the stroke of 12 mid-day...the big guns started to roar, and the shriek of the heavy shells overhead, was like the ceaseless passage of a thousand electric cars. I ensconced myself in the artillery observation station and watched the progress of the shelling...It was a horrible sight*

---
7 *Leicester Daily Post*, 28 October 1915.

## "It was a bomb business..."

*which I had to watch, the two lines of trenches (German and English) were almost obscured by the clouds of thick oily black or yellow smoke from the bursting shells. A scream and a roar and then a huge cloud of smoke, a cascade of earth and stones, of sandbags and rifles, and of men and pieces of men – and then the rattling, splitting crash of exploding lyddite. Over and over again it is repeated up and down both lines...We could plainly see the poor devils in the enemy trenches being blown a hundred yards high, turning fantastic Catherine wheels as they fell - it was horrible!*

The bombardment of the Redoubt (IWM Q29002)

*At 1pm the heavy guns quietened down, and were succeeded by lighter pieces, simultaneously there arose from our line a low, rising whitish cloud of vapour. Slowly, slowly it eddied and curled upwards and outwards, spreading but always advancing until the German trenches were wholly enveloped in a cloud of death."[8]*

Once again, the British had released poison gas in an effort to neutralize the devastating fire attacking troops would have to face. According to

---
8 *Leicester Daily Post,* 4 November 1915.

the *Official History*, the gas was either in insufficient quantity or the wind too light, as most appeared to settle in the shell holes and old trenches which scarred no-man's land.[9]

However, *Hauptmann* Ludwig Wolff, whose 1st Battalion of the Infantry Regiment No. 104 held the *Dump* and its neighbouring trenches, found the gas effective enough: *"At 2.00 pm precisely, the enemy suddenly lifted their fire to the rear. Almost simultaneously the sentries reported that the enemy was releasing gas. From a southwesterly direction, the dense white clouds rolled threateningly along the ground towards us. We instantly took gas precautions. The simple masks...were donned and the ointment smeared on the eyelids. Fires of wood and straw were lit on the parapets, so that the heat would drive the gas upwards. Despite all...the fighters in the trenches suffered badly from the gas. Their faces turned blue and red as they almost suffocated and coughed incessantly and painfully. Their eyes swelled, turned bright red, burning, hurting and streaming with tears."*[10]

The shifting bombardment gave the German artillery warning to commence their own retaliatory fire and the British front-line was battered by heavy shell-fire in an effort to destroy or disrupt the gas cylinders. In three places the 1/4th Leicesters' front-line trenches were filled with their own chlorine gas. *Hauptmann* Wolff himself observed the flickering of small fires along the opposing front-line, mirroring his men's efforts to disperse the gas. At 1.50 pm the mortar fire of gas and smoke bombs ceased, allowing much of the firing-line to clear.[11]

Harry Pexton recalled the last few minutes before the attack at two o'clock: *"A small ration of rum was handed round, and then a message: 'The C.O. wishes God-speed and good luck to all his men'. Officers stood, watch in hand, counting the crawling seconds. 'Five minutes to two. Four! Three! Two! One! – then 'Over you go with best of luck.' Brave lads, up they climbed at intervals of a yard apart, liberating a heavy mist of smoke as they went. A few seconds and the next line followed, and we*

---
9 *Official History 1915 Vol. 2*, p. 384
10 Jack Sheldon *the German Army on the Western Front 1915* (Barnsley) 2022, p. 238. The German Army's time was an hour ahead of the British; the bombardment commencing for the latter at 1pm.
11 Hills *Ibid.*, p. 76

## "It was a bomb business..."

*advanced straight to our front through the smoke and suddenly came out into the light of day – and Hell."*[12]

A young Territorial, whose letter home was printed in the *Leicester Daily Post*, joined the advancing line of 'tommies', all four companies of the 1/4th battalion in line abreast, cheering as they went, with gas helmets rolled on the top of their heads. He also experienced Lance-Corporal Pexton's 'Hell':

*"The parapet was swept by machine guns as we started...We were simply mowed down by rifle and machine gun fire...The men on the left were a little better off, as a rise in the ground shielded them a little from the machine guns...The men were simply magnificent. They went over the parapet as one man. Not one hesitated a moment, when men were falling all around."*[13]

Amongst the first to fall was the battalion's commanding officer, Lieutenant-Colonel R. E. Martin, (left) who was brought down with a bullet through his left leg, yet remained, exposed to enemy fire throughout the action, on the parapet of the front-line trench. Martin could not have been prouder of his men:

*"I wish you could have seen them go. There was nothing wrong with them then, I can tell you. And it wasn't any blooming practice either. The machine gun and rifle fire was very heavy...the Huns must have put their machine guns into deep dugouts while our guns were firing and brought them up when*

---

12 *Leicester Daily Post*, 28 October 1915.
13 *Leicester Daily Post*, 22 October 1915.

# Tigers in the Trenches

*they lifted."*[14]

*Bombers of the North Midland division advance across no-man's land in this dramatic lantern-slide recreation. ROLLR:LS6318*

Despite their many fallen comrades, the Leicestershire 'Terrors' swept on, into an increasingly devastating flanking fire from a German machine post at 'Mad Point' to their north. Private W. Hutchinson, a North Evington man with the 1/4th Leicesters described (with forgivable exaggeration as far as its source is concerned) the German fire as *"murderous; there were thousands of Germans firing rapid, and as soon as we got over they turned about eighty machine guns on us, each of which was firing 600 shots a minute, so you can give a slight guess of what it was like. Our fellows were dropping in dozens...I may tell you I had to pray; it seemed to come natural. It was awful to see your comrades falling...but this*

14 Record Office for Leicestershire, Leicester & Rutland (ROLLR): 22D63/411

## "It was a bomb business..."

position had got to be taken at any cost, and so we had to keep going forward."[15]

The advance crashed through the enemy wire and overran the frontline of the Hohenzollern Redoubt. Harry Pexton was there: *"The spit and phut of the rifles and machine gun bullets was incessant, incredible, but the boys never wavered. Men fell and lay where they fell but the long thin line went forward determined and strong. We reached the German first line to find nearly all the enemy dead – we disposed of the live ones and passed onwards to the second line. Now we came into a veritable inferno of flying death, shrapnel and bombs, high explosives and grenades, and more and more machine gun fire. We kept on until we came to the third line where the German reserve who had been hurried up made a most determined stand. However, with rifle and bomb and bayonet we disposed of them and went on till we nearly reached the fourth line. Here we were hemmed in by a broken village and a ruined colliery shaft..."*

The Leicesters had been halted by fire from *The Dump* and the virtually impregnable cellars of the *corons*, the ruined miners' cottages which lay beyond the Redoubt. The Germans, ever masters of defence, now threw in their reserves; supported by a devastating bombardment to cut the attackers off from their own.

Private Hutchinson reached the third line of German trenches: *"we had to keep going forward...we captured their first line of trenches, and then we pushed on and did likewise to their second line; then on again. But we did not manage to hold their third line, although we entered it. Their bombing was tremendous and there were thousands of them firing at us..."*

German troops still occupying portions of what the British called 'Little Willie' trench found themselves both overrun and encircled, forced to fire over the *parados*, or rear of the trench, while others even leapt from cover to have clearer shots at their enemies.[16] The battle amongst the network of trenches and ruined miners' cottages became a bitter fight

---
15 *Leicester Daily Post,* 28 October 1915.
16 Sheldon *Ibid.*, p. 239. *Hauptmann* Wolff described how one of his 2nd Company's machine-guns was operated in the open until its crew was destroyed.

of bayonet and hand-grenade. As our Bridge Road schoolboy observed: "it was a bomb business...and some splendid work was done in this line".

Some of this work was done by Drummer Gaton, of the 1/4th Leicesters, whose blood was clearly up: "*One bomb thrown properly will kill outright a dozen or fifteen men besides wounding many more. And the thing itself is not much larger than an egg, and much the same in shape. A man can carry fifty of them in the two bags with which we were provided for the purpose. I had one bag of twenty, and I threw eight before I was wounded. Of course, we were all a little shaky for a start, but as soon as I saw my pals falling round me all the fear seemed to go from me, and my one desire was to avenge them and kill some of the gray figures whom we could see opposite us hurling bombs as fast as they could.*"[17]

An hour after the assault began, the county men of the 1/5th Leicesters began to move up in support of the Leicester battalion. Private Fred Williamson, a Coalville man, described how he crossed no-man's land in their wake to join the battle for the pit village: "*It was a walk over the first line, but the second proved a bit harder. Well, after bombing and bayoneting what was there we took it, and went for the next, which, of course, proved harder still. But we took the third line. This time we took several prisoners, but not many....We had a go for a village behind. Some of my company got in the village, but could not get much further. All this time the Germans were pouring hundreds of shells into us. After holding on for about four hours, somehow or other, the order came to retire...*"

By 5 o'clock barely an officer of the 1/4th Battalion remained unhurt and increasingly desperate messages were arriving from the shambles of the Redoubt appealing for bombs and officers. By this time the Leicestershire Territorials were holding grimly on in the front lines of the Hohenzollern Redoubt; its second and third lines untenable by either side. As Captain John Milne recorded in his history of the 1/4th Battalion: "*The attack has been carried out with the greatest dash, courage and precision, but the odds are too great, the machine-gun fire from Fosse 8 has been devastating. No man's land is a shambles.*"[18]

---

17 *Leicester Daily Post*, 27 October 1915
18 Captain John Milne *Footprints of the 1/4th Leicestershire Regiment* (Leicester) 1935, p. 56

## "It was a bomb business..."

*An attempt to convey the drama of an attack under cover of gas, from H W Wilson's Great War magazine (1915)*

By three o'clock the redoubt had been captured but heavy machine-gun fire from the flanks and rifle fire from Fosse and Dump Trenches, as well as the resistance of insolent German pockets in both Little and Big Willie, made it impossible to advance further. The 5th Leicesters had moved up in support and a party, led by Lieutenant C.H.F. Wollaston was slowly bombing its way up Little Willie. Only a shortage of hand grenades prevented the capture of the entire trench but by six o'clock strong counter-attacks had driven the British back to the front face of the redoubt.[19]

With a horrific number of casualties, particularly of officers, there was little hope of doing more than holding onto the nearest edge of the Redoubt - and even this required reinforcements and fresh supplies of bombs and ammunition which were slow in arriving across open

---
[19] Hills *Ibid.*, p. 80. Jack Sheldon refers to the determination of the defenders to prevent any portion of a strongpoint bearing the name of the German imperial family falling into enemy hands and that its recapture became a matter of honour. Sheldon *Ibid.*, p. 239-40

ground, still swept by enemy machine-guns and bombardment with high explosive and gas shells.

*A portrait of Leicester writer Eric Pochin whilst on leave in 1915, which captures well the spirit of the Territorials. Note his long Lee Enfield rifle, typical of the slightly out-moded weapons issued to the 46th Division. (ROLLR: DE3620).*

The fallen soldier, whose skeletal remains were finally laid to rest a century later, in September 2016, is likely to have been mortally wounded at about this time; hastening across no-man's land with his gas helmet rolled on his head and a sandbag of at least thirteen Mills bombs in his hand. Knocked aside by shrapnel, the Leicestershire 'terrier' had rolled

## "It was a bomb business..."

into a shallow trench where he lay, curled-up, face to the sky, awaiting rescue or death.

On the evening of 14th October, the two Leicestershire battalions (or what remained of them) were relieved. The 1/1$^{st}$ Monmouthshires, the divisional pioneer battalion, hastily digging a new trench, The Chord, which would be the new front-line and, to a limited extent, straighten-out the salient of the *Hohenzollernwerk*.

At fearful cost, the Territorials had seized the Hohenzollern Redoubt and held grimly on to its western edge. Private Claude Alexander declared in a letter home to his parents in Leicester: *"No doubt by now you have read in the papers about the taking of the Hohenzollern Redoubt and the main German trench. Well, you can feel proud to know that [the] 4$^{th}$ Leicesters took them, and I was amongst the first to get there...We got as far as the third German lines, but they were too strong for us, for their trench was absolutely packed with men waiting for us. We had to pay the price for it though. We went in the trench 659 strong and came out 181 strong having nearly 500 casualties."*[20]

Private Alexander's estimate wasn't far from the truth. One hundred and eighty eight men answered the roll-call; representing losses in the 1/4th Leicesters of 20 officers and 453 Other Ranks. Even in support, the 1/5th Battalion lost 12 officers and 175 men.

Could more have been done? Perhaps – if reinforcements or more bombs had come sooner; if there had been more artillery; or a stronger breeze to carry the gas. Claude Alexander felt *"we could not get reinforcements up fast enough"*[21] while Captain J. D. Hills criticised the failure to supply the promised Mills bombs with which his men had trained so assiduously: *"Then came the cruellest blow of fortune, for many of the bags and boxes of bombs sent up during the afternoon were found to contain bombs without detonators, many others were filled with types of grenades we had never seen."*[22]

---
20 ROLLR: DE5767 (printed with amendments in the *Leicester Daily Post*, 21 October 1915).
21 A phrase omitted in the printed version of his letter.
22 Hills *Ibid., p. 84*

# Tigers in the Trenches

Colonel Martin, who remained in the front line all day, directing operations despite a serious wound to his leg, felt his men had done their best: *"To every body of troops comes their day...Let us be thankful that when ours came the men went forwards with a good heart and did a fair share of what they were asked to do...The main thing is to be satisfied...that the battalion...has not gone out for nothing."*[23]

The tenacity of the Territorials in taking and holding on to part of the Redoubt was widely noted. Private Hutchinson felt *"we have got a feather in our caps"*[24] while another of the 4th Leicesters reported *"every man heaps praises on every other man, but every one is a hero."*[25] If there had been doubts about the territorial divisions, the attack on the Hohenzollern redoubt seems to have dispelled them. Private Claude Alexander concluded; *"We have made a name for the 'Terriers' of Leicester. Some of the Coldstream Guards who watched us go for them said they had seen 14 or 15 charges with the bayonet but never had they seen one like ours. Instead of going mad when we got over, we went for them cool and collected as could be. We simply walked across to them..."*[26]

The casualty figures were truly appalling. Despite the local newspapers' emphasis upon *"the Famous Charge"* and *"Terrific Struggle"*[27] there was no disguising the horrific human cost of the attack. The news fell upon Leicester like a thunder clap. The Territorial Forces Association offices were besieged, newspapers sold out on the street corners and hardly a street of town or county did not dread the arrival of the telegram boy. Even the Petty Sessions halted in its work to acknowledge the catastrophic losses. The chairman, J B Everard (opposite), begged the pardon of the court *"to refer to the grief that has fallen on the town and county...it is a grief that has affected all classes...We...have to mourn with some of our colleagues the loss they have sustained. We also have to mourn the loss of friends...they were given work to do, and they did*

---

23 (ROLLR): 22D63/411
24 *Leicester Daily Post*, 28 October 1915
25 Letter of a 'well-known Wigston man', *Leicester Daily Post*, 1 November 1915
26 (ROLLR): DE5767
27 *Leicester Daily Post*, 9 November and 25 October 1915 (amongst many other examples).

## "It was a bomb business..."

*it...and they have won a name which we shall not willingly let die."*[28]

From 20 October the newspapers printed long lists of the dead, wounded and missing. On 21 October photographs of ten of the officers, killed or missing, appeared; their names reading like a directory of Leicester's best known businesses: Faire, Russell, Corah and so on. Those Leicestershire war memorials which bear a place or date of death, are rich in Hohenzollern Redoubts and the 13 October 1915.

The 46th Division, as a whole, had suffered a loss of no fewer than 180 officers and 3,583 other ranks. Most, as the *Official History* observed, *"in the first ten minutes of the attacks"*.[29] The 4th Leicesters alone had lost 20 officers and 453 men. Captain Milne's account of the attack, in his history of the battalion, concludes with a description of the withdrawal to billets behind the lines on 15th October. Every officer of the battalion was killed, wounded or missing, save for the two whose duties kept them from the front line. Milne wrote: *"The quartermaster and the transport officer mess together alone, but they dare not look at each other."*[30]

The 5th Leicesters, who had been spared the initial assault, nevertheless saw 12 of their officers and 175 men killed, wounded or missing. It would mean a long period of recovery and retraining. Captain J. D. Hills, who had led 'D' Company of the 5th Leicesters into the attack and miraculously escaped unscathed, noted:

---

28 *Leicester Daily Post,* 25 October 1915
29 *Official History, 1915 Vol 2,* p. 387.
30 Captain John Milne *Footprints of the 1/4th Leicestershire Regiment* (Leicester) 1935, p. 57

# Tigers in the Trenches

*"The 5th were in support & so suffered least. Col. Martin of the 4th was wounded in the knee early on in the assault & stayed for twelve hours directing operations...None of his Officers have escaped unwounded... Thank goodness our C.O. is alright tho' Toller has concussion. Hastings & Langdale are both killed - Petch, Lawton, Thomson, Wynne, Marriot, Moss, are wounded. Williams was hit but after being dressed he returned to work. Wollaston, though wounded in the back & arm rallied weary men, & collecting a few enthusiasts led a successful bombing party, working on for four hours after his wound. I escaped without a scratch; why I don't quite know."*[31]

*Wounded from the attack are helped to awaiting ambulances in the village of Vermelles. Imperial War Museum Q29005*

The Hohenzollern Redoubt remained a bloody bone of contention throughout the war. Assaulted and mined, captured and lost, its grim reputation grew. As General Jack later noted in his diary: *"Part of our lines are in the famous Hohenzollern Redoubt...it is a disgusting sector*

---

31 ROLLR: DE9672 Letter of J D Hills 14 October 1915

# "It was a bomb business..."

with the parapets full of bodies, debris and rats."³²

For the Official Historian of the Great War, Sir James Edmonds, writing in the 1920s, the assault on the Redoubt *"brought nothing but useless slaughter of infantry"* and the near ruin of a promising division. The human cost was certainly great and there is no shortage of poignant testimony to that fact.

At the County Record Office in Wigston (a town which had been rich recruiting ground for the 4th Leicesters) are a number of eyewitness accounts and letters, including that of Colonel Martin himself, relating to the attack on the Hohenzollern Redoubt. Few are as telling, as dignified, or as tragic as a brief note from Mrs Mogridge, the wife of the vicar of Scalford and mother of Second-lieutenant Basil Mogridge of the 4th Leicesters, however.

*"I have been advised by the War Office to appeal to you...for some particulars regarding the death of my son, 2nd Lieutenant B. F. W. Mogridge...at the attack on the Hohenzollern Redoubt. I should be so glad to know how he died, whether instantaneously, or if he had to lie a long time, wounded and suffering, before found. Is there any possibility of a mistake having been made, and that he might be missing and a prisoner?"*³³

Lieutenant Mogridge's name appears on no fewer than four memorials, at Scalford, in the church and churchyard.

The Royal Leicestershire Regiment has no shortage of Battle Honours. The old regulars are justly proud of their 'Hindoostan' scroll (which was omitted from the Territorials' cap badge) and each year they commemorate the gallant Defence of Ladysmith. For the Territorials, however, it is the Hohenzollern Redoubt which is remembered.

The *Leicester Mail,* even in the thick of a war filled with seemingly senseless slaughter, had it right. On 13 October 1917 the *Mail* editorial recalled: *"At two o'clock in the afternoon of October 13th, 1915,*

---

32 John Terraine *General Jack's Diary 1914-1918* (London) 1964, p. 156
33 ROLLR: DE8145/37/1

# Tigers in the Trenches

the Leicesters and Lincolns went 'over the top' in their assault on the Hohenzollern fortress...The Leicesters conducted that attack as though they were on the parade ground and with a coolness which called forth a shower of compliments from all who saw them...Since that memorable day the Leicesters have taken part in many battles...None of their subsequent feats has, however, outshone the Hohenzollern...In this assurance Leicester will always cherish October 13th as a day on which memories of pride can be intermingled with those of sorrow."

We remember and honour them still....[34]

*One of the memorials to 2/Lieut. Mogridge in the parish church at Scalford, Leics.*

[34] This chapter is adapted from a talk given by the author at Leicester Cathedral on the centenary of the battle, 13 October 2015.

# "The Tigers' Bloodiest Day"

## Chapter Seven

# "The Tigers' Bloodiest Day"
## The Assault on Bazentin Wood, 14 July 1916

> *"Woods have always had an attraction for me. As a boy a spinney always invited inspection...But a wood has now quite a different meaning to me...You can imagine what a difficult matter it would be to clear an obstinate force in occupation of a well-timbered wood, but where, in addition to Nature's dense growth, you have to push against trenches, barbed wire, man traps and heavy batteries..."[1]*

Everyone knows something of the Somme. From its first day and the heaviest casualties ever experienced by a British army, the campaign earned a reputation for profligacy. Fought over the last six months of 1916, the campaign absorbed men and *matériel* at an unprecedented rate; the casualty figures, though subject to much debate, undoubtedly far exceeding half a million men on both sides.

That the battle was fought in the valley of the Somme, from July 1916, was due to two simple coincidences that Spring. Firstly, that the British Expeditionary Force was, at last, with the arrival of Kitchener's New Armies, strong enough to contemplate a major offensive and, secondly, that there, along the River Somme, was a hitherto largely untouched sector of the Western Front where the British and French armies abutted and could therefore easily co-operate in an attack.

The plans of General Haig and his 4th Army commander, Sir Henry Rawlinson, in concert with the French, were intended to leave little to chance. The offensive, 'The Big Push', was to be on a twelve mile front, deploying 400,000 men. The extensive German defences were to be pulverised by a bombardment that would dwarf all others; 1.7 million shells were to be fired by 1 field gun to every 20 yards of the front and 1 heavy gun or howitzer to every 58 yards. In addition nineteen mines had

---
1 An Old Boy of Bridge Road School, printed in the *Leicester Daily Post*, 28 July 1916.

# Tigers in the Trenches

been dug under the enemy lines, to destroy strong-points and so blast a way through to the German headquarters and rail and road centre at Bapaume.

The first day of the Somme is rightly notorious for the horrific casualties inflicted, particularly upon the attacking British divisions, and for the gulf it revealed between aspiration and reality. The Leicestershire Regiment offered up its share of the 57,470[2] casualties suffered by the British Army that day, though, curiously they were not on the Somme battlefield but at Gommecourt, a few miles to the north.

*Tigers at rest before the opening of the Somme campaign*

There, the Leicestershire territorials of the 46th (North Midland) Division, in concert with the Londoners of the 56th Division, were once again to assault a salient in the enemy line (in fact the most westerly point held by the entire German army) which followed the boundary of the local, landed estate.[3]

2 Martin Middlebrook *The First Day on the Somme (London)* 1984, p. 263
3 See chapter six for an account of the attack on the Hohenzollern redoubt salient.

# "The Tigers' Bloodiest Day"

Though it seems harsh to say it, what happened at Gommecourt on 1st July 1916 did not matter. It mattered, of course, to those who fought and died there - and the massive build-up of troops and supplies, the practice attacks and training all had a purpose - but once the attack began further south on the Somme, Gommecourt had served that purpose. The attack was simply a diversion to draw enemy troops from the main offensive and by 7.30 a.m. on 1st July, any German battery or infantry division which might have been diverted north from the Somme was long gone. The Gommecourt attack went ahead, but its object - to straighten-out that bulge in the German line - was secondary, almost incidental, to the 'Big Push'.

*A modern view of the German lines at Gommecourt, showing the open ground across which the Tigers attacked.*

The result, alas, was catastrophic. While the 56th Division, attacking from the south, managed to fight their way into the German defences in Gommecourt Park, the South and North Staffords and Sherwood Foresters of the North Midland Division ran into heavy machine-gun fire from two strongpoints which jutted out from the German lines to the north - the 'Z' and 'Little Z'; enabling a devastating enfilade fire. As Captain J D Hills, of the 1/5th Leicesters, remarked:

# Tigers in the Trenches

*Map of the German position, showing in red the density of wire and trenches.*

# "The Tigers' Bloodiest Day"

*"Gommecourt was naturally strong, and this addition to the garrison [of German troops from the Somme] made it doubly so, while the Artillery found it very difficult to destroy the wire which was thick along the whole front. The trees in the wood were all wired, and there were strong belts in front of every trench..."*[4]

Worse, after half an hour the smoke screen dispersed, leaving the first waves of the attack to be pinned down. A thorough German artillery barrage also fell, with horrific force, along the British trenches - cutting off reinforcements and supplies and catching support troops as they gathered in the front-line.

It was at this time that the 1/5th Leicesters were ordered forward. One company went over the top, to occupy the ruins of a *sucrerie* where they began to dig in. The other companies were bringing up fresh ammunition and supplies, contending with blown-in trenches, turned into sucking quagmires by rain and high explosive. Many troops took to the ground above, climbing out of the trenches to get forward and to avoid hindering the stretcher-bearers in their grim work.

Lieutenant Aubrey Moore of the 1/5th Leicesters recalled the scene: *"I never before or after saw such appalling slaughter. Needless to say we only reached No Man's Land and <u>some</u> of us got back. I took in with me three officers who had hardly heard a shell burst. One, in the line for the first time, was killed very early, together with my CSM, and one officer was wounded...The idea was that we and the 56th Division would attack the village of Gommecourt from two sides and pinch out the pronounced salient round the west side of the village. Excellent idea - on paper. For some reason nobody ever knew, the 37th division on our left made no feint or demonstration of any kind. As soon as the Boche realised this all those guns and machine guns were turned on us with the result that the 139 brigade, Notts and Derby, were almost wiped out by enfilade fire. Of course all the front attacking troops were caught in this crossfire. That was why the slaughter was so heavy. But for this we might have reached our objective. Certainly casualties would not have been so heavy."*[5]

---

4 Hills *Ibid., p.136*
5 Aubrey Moore *A Son of the Rectory* (Gloucester) 1982, p. 136-137

# Tigers in the Trenches

By mid-afternoon it was clear that the man of the hour was Lieutenant-Colonel Charles Herbert Jones [right]. Before the war Jones had been a Military Member of the Leicestershire and Rutland Territorial Forces Association, whilst earning his living as House Master and leading light of the O.T.C. at Uppingham - with a brief interlude spent fighting the Boers in South Africa. He had commanded the 5th Leicesters since 1913 and so, as senior colonel of the brigade, found himself, on 1st July 1916, with its fate in his hands.

With the trenches blocked with mud, stores and wounded, and little chance either to gather information, or communicate it to the few remaining senior officers, Jones realised there was no hope of organising another attack. The decision to call a halt to the attacks was undoubtedly the right one. It certainly seemed so to one anonymous chronicler of the 'Tigers':

*"The new attack was to start at 3.30. Our artillery opened fire. We started to move forward. The Staffords stayed put. They had not been told when to start. What a bloody mess. Trenches clogged with men. It was hopeless but we are ready to go. Colonel Jones gets new orders, cancel the attack. Saved; the mass slaughter will not happen today..."*[6]

---

6 *The Pork Pie Crunchers* (MS account of 'C' Company, 1/5th Battalion, The Leicestershire Regiment)

# "The Tigers' Bloodiest Day"

Nothing could help the Londoners of the 56th Division and they were slowly driven out of Gommecourt Park and back to their starting point. The 46th Division was withdrawn, bruised and battered, to hold a quiet sector of the front-line around Monchy-au-Bois, where they might rest and gradually recuperate. Despite the congratulations of their Corps Commander, Lt. General D'Oyly Snow [below] *"for the manner in which they fought and endured"*, the division was to sense a bitter and unjustified taint of failure and accusations of a *"lack of offensive spirit"* for many months.

Further south, on the Somme proper, the attack on 1st July had fared little better. All along the front line, at 7.30 a.m. the infantry climbed out of their trenches and began to walk across no-man's land towards the German lines. Almost everywhere the experience was the same. The barbed wire was imperfectly cut and, far from having been swept away, the German machine-gunners, though dazed, rushed up from their deep dugouts to open a deadly fire upon the advancing Tommies.

The regulars of the 1st Battalion, The Leicestershire Regiment, mercifully, were in reserve that day. Their duty was safer but sadder. As Private Harold Startin recalled:

*"We had to bury the Newfoundlanders at Beaumont Hamel. If they were face downwards it wasn't too bad but if they were lying with their faces up, and the sun had been shining on them, the faces were smothered in flies and blue bottles and it was enough to make you sick. There were no graves dug for them – they were put into shallows. You might get three, four, five, or six into the crater and then you shovel down earth with a spade, and cover the bodies up. There were no crosses put there. We had*

# Tigers in the Trenches

no wood, we had no nails, we had no hammer. So they were just covered up and left."[7]

The 1st Newfoundland Battalion had lost 26 officers and 684 men within minutes of leaving their trenches. Only 68 men remained to answer the roll.

Only on the south of the Somme front, was there anything approaching success. The terrain there was less advantageous to the defenders and the French techniques of artillery and infantry cooperation were more sophisticated. Mametz fell and Fricourt was abandoned by the Germans.

*The Dragon memorial to the Welsh Division with Mametz Wood beyond*

The attention of Haig and Rawlinson was now on the southern part of the Somme valley, where the greatest gains had been made. The next attack was on Mametz Wood, which fell to the 38th Welsh Divison after five days of horrific fighting and a loss of nearly 4,000 officers and men. In support and ready for the next move, against the Germans' second line

7 Quoted in Joshua Levine *Forgotten Voices of the Somme* (Ebury Press) 2009, p.122

# "The Tigers' Bloodiest Day"

of defence, were the Leicestershire Regiment's four service battalions of the 110th Brigade, which had just been hurried south, to replace the badly mauled 63rd Brigade in the 21st Division.[8]

Eager to press on, Rawlinson hastily planned a new attack on a broad front from Bazentin-le Petit to Longueval. It was to punch through the German second line of defence, seizing Bazentin Wood and the villages along Bazentin Ridge. Cavalry was even in attendance to exploit the anticipated breakthrough to Bapaume.

Despite the initial scepticism of the commander in chief, Rawlinson's plan was finally adopted. It was certainly a new departure and seemed to break all the rules. The initial advance was to be made at night, the first assault waves would assemble in no-man's land (not the British trenches) and the preliminary artillery bombardment, though devastating, would be very brief and then shift to keep pace with the attack, preceding the advancing waves of infantry.

Most worrying of all, the attack was also almost entirely to be carried out by comparatively untried New Army units; such that in the headquarters of the neighbouring French commander, General Maurice Balfourier [right], the whole notion of a night advance, followed by hours of silent waiting, was scathingly dismissed as an *"an attack organised for amateurs by amateurs"*.[9]

On 13 July 1916, those amateurs, the Service Battalions of the Leicestershire Regiment moved forward to Mametz Wood

---

8 The 6th, 7th, 8th and 9th Battalions had been raised in response to Lord Kitchener's appeal in 1914. They had been on the western Front for nearly a year, occupying quiet sectors of the front line in France and Belgium.
9 A. H. Farrar_Hockley *The Somme* (London) 1971, p. 180. The scepticism of Haig and Balfourier seems to have given rise to ever greater determination on the part of the attackers, General Archibald Montgomery-Massingberd declaring to Balfourier that he would eat his hat if his men were not on Longueval Ridge by 8 the following morning (Hugh Sebag-Montefiore *Somme Into the Breach* (London) 2017, p. 249).

in preparation for the assault on Bazentin Wood; which anchored the German second line of defence to Bazentin Ridge. These were the men who had answered Kitchener's call in 1914 and had been formed into a New Army, distinct from the Regulars and the Territorials, yet preserving the traditions and badges of their parent regiments. What they may have lacked in experience, the Service Battalions easily made up in spirit and determination.

Lieutenant A. C. N. de Lisle [left], supervising a party from the 9th Leicesters, had spent the entire day in Mametz Wood, hauling 80,000 hand grenades to create bomb dumps just behind the firing line. De Lisle had also taken in the sights, from four abandoned 9.2 inch howitzers, still in position (but without their breech-blocks), to the profusion of unburied Welsh dead:

*"...everywhere the whole wood resembled a charnel house. Up both of the outside edges of the wood it seemed that a whole British firing-line had been knocked out by some poisonous gas for death had overcome them in their little holes made with their entrenching tools..."*

The busy lieutenant also encountered a lieutenant-general reconnoitring the north-western corner of the wood; a meeting which de Lisle recorded *"to show that our Generals go right up on the field of battle...I told him we were establishing forward bomb-dumps...I also told him that I did not consider we should have much difficulty in an attack on the morrow; in fact, I thought it would be a walk-over. He replied: 'do not be too optimistic'."*[10]

---

10 A. C. N. de Lisle *History of my Company in the Great Push n.d. [c. 1916]* (ROLLR: DE8145/38) pp. 19-20 & 23

# "The Tigers' Bloodiest Day"

*A general and staff officers photographed in Mametz Wood; Imperial War Museum Q868.*

Shortly after midnight on 14 July, the Leicestershire brigade began to move through Mametz Wood towards its starting positions for the attack. The silent advance through the moonlit wood, still showing every sign of the carnage of 7 July, would have tried the nerves of the most hardened veteran. Captain D. V. Kelly, on the staff of the Leicestershire Brigade, recalled the ghastly sights, revealed in the distorting light of flares and exploding shells:

"The wood was everywhere smashed by shell-fire and littered with dead – a German sniper hung over a branch horribly resembling a scarecrow, but half the trees had had their branches shot away, leaving fantastic jagged stumps...Along the west edge ran a trench, from the side of which in place protruded the arms and legs of carelessly buried man, and as our men moved up to attack, dozens of them shook hands with these

# Tigers in the Trenches

*ghastly relics...over all hung the overwhelming smell of corpses, turned up earth, and lachrimatory gas."*[11]

Heavily laden with additional ammunition, bombs and entrenching equipment,[12] the Leicesters threaded their way through the tangled undergrowth and hampering debris of battle, slipping into shell holes hidden by rotting branches, and always assailed with the stench of the unburied dead – *"the worst ever experienced during the war"* according to D. A. Bacon, Quartermaster Sergeant of the 9th Battalion.[13]

*The view today, with Mametz Wood on the left and Bazentin Wood to the right.*

The line of a German trench railway, which actually continued northwards along the Western edge of Bazentin Wood, offered an easier route from the centre of the wood but from 2 a.m., the area was subjected to a heavy enemy bombardment. The 7th Leicesters were badly hit, a platoon of the battalion's 'C' Company losing half its number and their commanding officer, Lieutenant-Colonel Drysdale being wounded by shrapnel. His place was taken by the adjutant, Captain A. A. Aldworth.

---

11 D. V. Kelly, *39 Months with the Tigers* (London) 1930, pp. 28-29
12 The battalion War Diaries and Brigade Orders record that each man carried 220 rounds of rifle ammunition, two hand grenades and two sandbags. Specialists, such as 'Battalion Raiders' and platoon grenade groups took an extra 20 grenades and picks and shovels were issued, twenty each, to every company.
13 D. A. Bacon typescript memoirs; ROLLR: 22D63/146, p. 57

# "The Tigers' Bloodiest Day"

Nevertheless, the deployment continued; the battalions emerging from Mametz Wood and taking up their positions which extended north of the wood into no-man's land, where they either occupied abandoned German trenches or began to scrape their own hasty cover.

On the far left, their right flanks resting on the German railway, were two companies of the 8th Leicesters, supported by the brigade's heavy machine guns. The 7th Battalion occupied the centre and the 6th the right of the line; each in two lines of two platoons. The line, according to the War Diary of the 8th Battalion, finally halted some 200 yards beyond the cover of Mametz Wood, ready for the advance. Tapes had been laid out by Royal Engineers the night before to mark position. Behind, in reserve, were the other two companies of the 8th Leicesters, and the 9th Battalion, which reached the front line only as the British bombardment began.

The attack had been carefully planned and explained to the troops before they moved off that morning.[14] Six waves of infantry would advance, sixteen platoons from each battalion in the first two waves, with about thirty yards between them. The next four waves, of four platoons per battalion, would follow in support. Here, co-ordination with the artillery was of paramount importance. Each stage of the advance would be covered by a dense barrage, carefully timed and lifting periodically to remain ahead of the troops, paralysing the defence by keeping the enemy in their dugouts until the very last moment and then rolling forward in stages; the blanket of high explosive and shrapnel catching reserves as they advanced and survivors in flight.

The artillery bombardment, which broke upon the German lines at 2 a.m., was devastating. For the last ten minutes an unprecedented weight of shells fell across the front of Bazentin Ridge; a far greater concentration than had heralded the attack on 1 July 1916.[15] Quartermaster Sergeant D. A. Bacon noted *"one continual roar of Guns and of shells whistling and*

---
14 De Lisle, p. 21

15 Peter Hart *The Somme* (London) 2005, p.263. In ten minutes, 189 field guns and 311 heavy howitzers fired, respectively, 33,072 and 14, 928 shells; thereafter slackening to a rate of fire of two 18 pounder and 1 howitzer rounds per minute. The preliminary bombardment, from 11 July, had used up a further half a million shells – all directed at a front line about 6,000 yards long. The bombardment prior to 1 July had employed more guns but their firepower had been spread over a front of 22,000 yards and several lines of defences (which the Germans had not had time to build on 14 July).

# Tigers in the Trenches

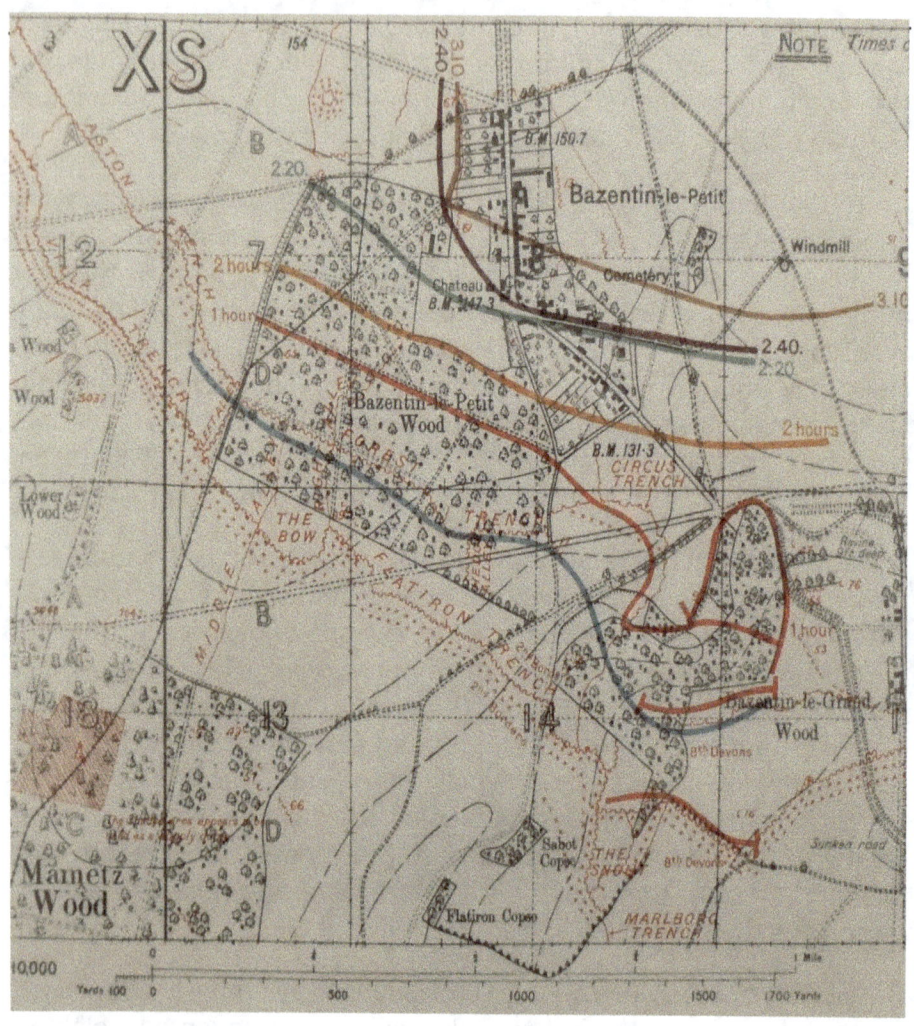

20th Infantry Brigade Operations Order map of 13 July 1916, showing in different colours, the shifting artillery bombardment; the times at which each stage would lift and move on are given at the ends of each coloured line. The Leicesters began their attack from a position just ahead of Mametz Wood.

# "The Tigers' Bloodiest Day"

down for the benefit of the 110th Infantry Brigade".[16]

Giles Eyre,[right] of the King's Royal Rifle Corps, who had been transferred to bolster the 110th Brigade's trained bombers, watched the *"all-devouring storm of shells"* from trenches occupied by the 8th Leicesters until called from the fire-step to sup a rum ration doled out with a spoon:

*"I swallowed mine eagerly and a pleasant glow warmed me. Everybody became keyed up, and excitement pervaded the ranks. The Leicesters kept jabbering and fiddling about, jumping on the fire-steps looking over at that awful flail of fire that raked the German lines like a searing lash, slashing and whipping at their defences, leaving furrows of tumbled earth and riven, mangled bodies."*[17]

At 3.25 a.m. the British guns shifted their aim from the German front line and all along the front of Mamtez Wood whistles blew for the advance[18]. Two lines of 'tommies' rose and raced for the enemy lines. Almost everywhere the attack was successful, though at varying cost.

On the left, where the 8th Leicesters were to storm the portions of *Villa Trench* and *Aston Trench* beyond the tramway, 'raiders' had squirmed ahead into no-man's land, and, despite heavy losses, were able to bomb many dug-outs and block the trenches to prevent counter-attacks from the flank. Even so machine-gun fire from the flank tore into the advancing waves of 'D' Company, cutting down every officer and many of the men.

16 D. A. Bacon *Ibid.*
17 Giles E. M. Eyre *Somme Harvest* (London) 1991, p. 149. Signaller W. R. Carter (writing to his parents in Enderby) recalled *"a good hot cup of tea, and the usual drop of rum"* Leicester Daily Post, 15 August 1916.
18 Private Jack Horner's platoon officer (6th Leicesters) simply pointed forwards and shouted 'Go!' [Quoted in Edward Hancock *Bazentin Ridge* (Barnsley) 2001, p. 100

# Tigers in the Trenches

The 7th Leicesters, advancing in the centre, also met with varied success. On the right, the battalion's 'A' Company swept across no-man's land and into *Flat Iron Trench*. The centre companies, 'B' and 'C' however, were temporarily pinned down by machine-gun fire from *The Bow*, a small bulge in the front-line trench where a party of Germans stubbornly held on until outflanked.

The southern edge of Bazentin Wood. The position of the German trench known as 'The Bow', is still marked by the lighter soil.

The German machine-guns were almost certainly the three surviving maxims of the 106th Machine-gun Company commanded by Reserve Lieutenant Borelli. His men, alerted by the *crescendo* of the bombardment, had waited in the entrances of their dugouts:

*"Just before 4.00 a.m. I realised that the enemy was lifting his fire rather more to the rear. The sentry fired a flare and in the same second bawled, 'Get out, here come the British!' Everyone took up position in the shell craters. The enemy had advanced to within twenty to thirty metres of our position...The enemy assaulted in about six waves. These were not dressed lines of infantry; rather they were concentrated groups of soldiers. My machine gun crews suffered heavy casualties because the British, who were sheltering in the craters directly to our front, could*

## "The Tigers' Bloodiest Day"

*not be brought under fire and so were able to throw grenades with impunity..."*[19]

By 4 a.m. the advance had reached *Forest Trench*, two hundred yards inside Bazentin Wood. On the far right, the 6th Leicesters had taken some thirty prisoners in the German front line; the battalion's third and fourth attacking waves sweeping on to capture a pair of heavy machine-guns in the wood's south-eastern corner. In the centre the Germans fled before the 7th Battalion, while on the left, the Lewis gunners of the 8th Leicesters emptied their magazines into the fleeing Germans and the *Villa* and *Aston* trenches were blocked to prevent flank attacks. Everywhere, consolidation of the trenches, converting the parados to a parapet, to render them defensible against a counter-attack proved difficult due to the devastation caused by the British artillery.[20]

Rifleman Giles Eyre's party, throwing their grenades at the forefront of the attack, destroyed a machine-gun nest but then halted:

*"The Leicesters are attacking the line of the wood on our left, but seem to be hung up, for all of a sudden a wave of rapid fire breaks out from them. We move forward again now, but very carefully, and plunge into the tangle of trees and scrub...The Lewis opens fire quickly and we make another rush, only to crash against a barrier of barbed wire stretched and tangled between the trees...Somehow we get over the wire, our clothes tearing and the barbs scratching and pulling at our bodies and equipment, and we run slap-bang into another gun just behind. Germans jump up and come at us. For a moment there is a flurry of figures, half-seen, hazy faces loom in front of me. I push forward my rifle and let go, working the bolt automatically, and then, as I empty my magazine, slash forward with my bayonet...Short, sharp bursts of fire and a crowd of the Leicesters break through...We are now drunk with it all and have become utterly reckless. With cries and whoops we dash on again, breaking through wire and obstacles."*[21]

---

19 Quoted in Jack Sheldon *The German Army on the Somme* (Barnsley) 2012, p. 193. See also Christopher Duffy *Through German Eyes* (London) 2006, p. 177. The Germans, of course, operated an hour in advance of the B.E.F.'s time.

21 Giles E. M. Eyre *Ibid., pp. 154-55*

# Tigers in the Trenches

One of the Leicesters' bombers also plunged into the hand-to-hand fighting; as he wrote home to his old headmaster, at Bridge Road school in Leicester:

*"It was our first platoon's job to take the first line, ours being the second... The first got theirs all right, as the Boches had all retired to the second line, except one or two left to work the machine-guns, and they played havoc till they were sent 'West'...We got to the second line and found it strongly held, but four of us, all bombers, got a footing in the trench and set to work with our bombs and bayonets. I got at it well[with] one fellow well over six feet, and I can tell you it wasn't all going my way. He cut my left eye, and my ribs seemed as if they were broken, when one of my chums who had finished his man shouted to me and the Boche just turned for a second, but I had finished it. Then came the work of clearing them out of the dugouts. After we had put one or two bombs down them, the Boche would come up with his hands up, "Mercy, Kamerad" and looking scared to death. Some we took prisoners."*[22]

The fate of prisoners seems all too often to have been a matter of good or bad luck; of circumstances and military necessity. Private F. N. Burchmore, of the 8th Leicesters' 'C' Company, found himself guarding 127 dazed and demoralized Germans captured in *Villa Trench*:

*"Just before moving a shell landed killing some of the guards...We dug a trench in the wood in case of counter attack. Some poor devils lost track moving across and were blown to pieces. The stink was awful then the dirty devils used gas shells. It was awful. What to do with the prisoners [?] All we chaps could do seventeen of us was to shoot and we shot them down like rats. They had no arms all we did was to pump lead into them and we did, poor devils. I found dozens of helmets took a badge off one no way of carrying a helmet..."*[23]

Burchmore's account is typical of many similar 'atrocity' stories from

---
22 *Leicester Daily Post*, 1 August 1916
23 Record Office for Leicestershire, Leicester and Rutland (ROLLR): DE8145/36 Photocopy of transcript of the diary of No. 17574 Private Frederick Norman Burchmore. There is even a suggestion that a veiled 'no prisoners' order had been issued from GHQ: see Matthew Richardson *Fighting Tigers* (Barnsley) 2002, p.83.

# "The Tigers' Bloodiest Day"

Bazentin Wood and most other battles on the Western Front. Clearly confusion reigned, no officers were present (having been killed or wounded) and the inexperienced troops faced the stress of battle – the shelling, dead comrades, gas, and the ever-present threat of death or maiming. Prisoners were taken however and immediately pressed into service, as Lieutenant de Lisle noted:

*"30 Hun prisoners trooped out like a flock of cowed sheep. This was a most welcome capture, for we had quite a number of wounded with no stretcher-bearers to send with them to the rear. So we made these prisoners carry all our wounded to the rear on waterproof sheets or improvised stretchers. The less seriously wounded acted as escort with rifle and fixed bayonet. These prisoners were most awfully good about it, and took great pains; possibly the glint of the escort's ready bayonet was the incentive – an argument not to be scoffed at! For in an attack, feeling runs very high, and it does not need much provocation from a prisoner for him to sign his own death warrant."*[24]

*German prisoners receive friendly treatment at the hands of 'Tigers' on 14 July 1916. [IWM Q809]*

---

24 A. C. N. de Lisle *Ibid.*, p. 32

# Tigers in the Trenches

By 4.45 a.m., 'C' Company of the 8th Leicesters had reached the northern edge of Bazentin Wood. On their right, the 7th Battalion also continued to advance, despite heavy losses (including all but two officers in three of the battalion's companies) and having to despatch a party under a company sergeant major (CSM Geary of 'B' Company) to mop up *"a number of the enemy who had been passed over in the rush"*.[25] Although no real resistance was met with in reaching their final objective at the edge of the wood, both the remaining officers, Captain A. A. Clarke and Lieutenant Wakeford, were hit by sniper or machine-gun fire from the flank, leaving the battalion without officers.

*The site of the German second line in Bazentin Wood (2013).*

At about the same time, the first platoons of the Leicesters' 9th Battalion also entered Bazentin Wood bringing up valuable supplies of water[26] and ammunition and pushing on through the tangle of undergrowth and smashed timber. Lieutenant A. C. N. de Lisle observed the methodical

---
25 War Diary
26 I. L. Read, with the 8th Leicesters recalled the foul taste of the water, badly contaminated with petrol. *Of those we love*, p. 154

## "The Tigers' Bloodiest Day"

advance, waves of infantrymen waiting while the artillery pounded the German defences ahead and then pushing forward as soon as the barrage lifted and moved on.

"Behind the German first line...ran the great wood, Bazentin-le-Petit, which itself was spanned at intervals by three successive lines of trenches, each with its separate wire protection. Between these lines were short lengths of trench, so it was a veritable maze. These fell into our hands, one after the other...The wood was so dense, so choked with fallen timber, so full of shell holes that it was all climbing, jumping, scrambling and sprawling..."[27]

While some Germans fled back into the wood, others fought on; often in isolated groups fighting to the last. Snipers, too, took their toll on the advancing 'Tigers'. Near Bazentin-le-Petit village 'Dick' Read and his chum, 'Jackie' Johnson, were driven to take cover by a sniper:

"Jackie and I spotted our man in the same instant, sitting in a tree barely a 130 yards away...having had ample time to aim, we both fired. The German toppled over backwards and fell to the ground, his steel helmet following his descent through the branches. We both rushed to the spot, as one does after potting a rabbit. He was quite dead."[28]

Shortly after 6 a.m. the 6th Leicesters, with support from the 9th Battalion, had overrun the chateau and straggling street of houses and outbuildings which constituted the village of Bazentin-le-Petit. With the village, the two battalion's took 3 officers and some 200 men prisoners; including *Oberstleutnant* Kumme, the sector commander, the headquarters staff of both Kumme's Lehr Infantry Regiment and 3rd Battalion, Bavarian Infantry Regiment No. 16, and a field hospital.[29]

Conditions in the wood and around the desolated chateau were desperate and confused. A fierce German counter-attack was driven back and trenches hastily dug for shelter and defence. Pockets of Germans still resisted or moved warily back through the wood, clashing bloodily

---

27 A. C. N. de Lisle *Ibid.*, pp. 24-25
28 I. L. Read *Ibid.*, p. 154
29 The 9th Battalion's War Diary claims the honour of Kumme's capture for its 'D' Company.

with the advancing 'Tigers'. Water was in short supply as the village wells were choked or had been blocked by the artillery bombardment. The air was foul with the fumes of battle and German gas shells.

By 8 a.m. only the North west corner of the wood (above) and a few of the village houses remained in German hands. Private W. R. Carter, a signaller with (presumably) the 8th Battalion, recalled being 'held up' at the edge of the wood:

*"Nevertheless, we were able to get into the village...where we found the enemy hiding in cellars. These men we took prisoners, and they were escorted back to our lines, where they were employed carrying our wounded to the dressing station, a job they seemed to relish a great deal more than the one they had just left. After having obtained our objective - with the exception of the corner of the wood – we got busy with our entrenching tools, and dug ourselves in a little, for protection against the shrapnel, which was coming thick and fast."*[30]

Although the wood was by this time largely in British hands, an enemy strongpoint at the North West corner clung grimly on and German artillery

---
30 *Leicester Daily Post*, 15 August 1916.

# "The Tigers' Bloodiest Day"

continued to cause casualties and disrupt communication. Fierce attacks on the western and northern edges of the wood were driven off, though at heavy cost. On the West, where *Aston* and *Villa Trenches* were held by 'C' Company of the 8th Leicesters, both the company commander, Second-lieutenant J. Alexander, and battalion commander, Lieutenant-colonel J. G. Mignon were killed in a flurry of bombs and rifle grenades.

*A Mills bomb, probably dropped by a soldier of the 8th Leicesters, unearthed by ploughing on the western side of the wood in 2013.*

At about 10 a.m. another fierce and prolonged assault was made by the Germans on the northern edge of Bazentin Wood. For several hours shellfire was interspersed with attacks by bayonet or bomb, while the 'Tigers', frantically digging-in or blazing-away with Lewis guns and rifles, maintained a precarious position. By 11 a.m. eight platoons of the East Yorkshire Regiment had arrived from Mametz Wood and the Leicesters' 6th Battalion had linked-up with troops of the 7th Division advancing to the East past Bazentin-le-Grand.

Despite the continued German shelling of Bazentin Wood and its approaches, the afternoon of 14 July was spent in securing the position and in consolidation; deepening and repairing trenches, removing wounded, and replenishing supplies of both water and ammunition. Like the other battalions, with most officers dead or wounded, the 7th Leicesters were *"considerably mixed up"*[31] while Captain C. A. B . Elliott noted, in correspondence with the Official Historian after the war: *"I am doubtful if the wood was entirely cleared on July 14th, as I encountered a small enemy party on the N.E. edge on the afternoon of July 15th which was dug in and not dislodged till July 16th, when a Stokes Gun was brought up."*[32]

Late that afternoon the brigadier[33] arrived at the 9th Battalion's headquarters and determined that the N.W. corner of the wood would have to be cleared *"that evening at all costs".*[34] Without fresh troops, it was decided that every available officer and man, including the brigadier, colonel and headquarters staff, would be hurled at the enemy strongpoint. This force included the battalion's Quartermaster Sergeant D. A. Bacon:

*"Our Artillery opened with a heavy barage [sic] on the enemy's position which was immediately answered by the enemy who fired promiscuously with Machine Guns and Trench Mortars from three directions; the din thus created was awful, bullets whistled and cracked at all elevations and angles...At a given signal rapid Rifle fire was directed on the enemy for two minutes and then a Charge was ordered; every man who got up was knocked down, wounded or killed immediately. Some minutes later this was repeated with the same result; it was Hellish – the men dropped like stricken sheep. The enemy were not in large force, but were concealed behind the brushwood and a bank, and well supplied with Machine Guns...it was then decided that stealth would have to be employed. To this end certain of the men were ordered to crawl within a few yards of the enemy and then rush him; this succeeded w[h]ere bolder methods failed, but our casualties were exceedingly heavy."*[35]

---

31 War Diary
32 ROLLR: DE8402
33 Brigadier General William Francis Hessey (1868-1939)
34 D. A. Bacon *Ibid.* p. 58
35 Ibid., p.59

# "The Tigers' Bloodiest Day"

Attempts to push on beyond the edge of the wood were thwarted by nightfall, a determined German resistance and *"a Hellish Barrage of trench mortars"*[36] and the enemy were left to establish a line of scrapes and shell-holes about thirty yards beyond, from which they kept up a constant machine-gun fire and barrage of grenades.

*German machine guns in action [IWM Q61039]*

Darkness brought some respite. During the night an attempt to push further north from the ruined village of Bazentin-le-Petit, by parties of the 6th Leicesters and Yorkshire Regiment were driven back. The crushing losses of the 110th Brigade were only just being realised. The 6th Leicesters had seven officers killed and twenty wounded with 500 Other Ranks killed, wounded or missing. So round a figure as 500 clearly indicates the confused nature of the fighting and inability to gather troops for a more precise roll call.

The 7th Battalion's War Diary records the battalion occupying 150 yards of trench on the northern edge of the wood, after *"about 100 men answered the Roll"*. Later, about 2p.m. on 15th July forty men were

36 Ibid., p.59. The 7th Battalion's War Diary had already noted *"the bushes and trees were very thick round this part which necessarily made progress slow"*.

detached to support another attempt by the 8th and 9th battalions on the N.W. edge of the wood, where a German counter-attack was believed to have (briefly) retaken a small corner of blood-soaked, shell-blasted brushwood. The 7th Leicesters had lost 18 officers and 535 men killed and wounded; including their colonel, William Drysdale, and their captain and adjutant, A. A. Aldworth, who succeeded him.

The 8th Battalion also lost their commander, Lieutenant-colonel J. G. Mignon, as well as four officers killed or mortally wounded and a dozen more wounded. The Other ranks' losses were 415 in total; 66 killed or mortally wounded, 310 wounded and 39 missing. The 9th Battalion, despite its role in support of the attack, played a full part in securing Bazentin Wood, losing a further eighteen officers and 394 Other ranks (or just over sixty percent of the battalion's original strength of 25 officers and 650 men[37]).

*Tea for the wounded on the road from Mametz Wood, July 1916. [IWM Q3973]*

---

37 The figures are QMS Bacon's; from his memoir (p. 61). German losses are not known as units became hopelessly intermingled as reinforcements were fed into the fighting and at least two regimental headquarters were overrun. The British *Official History* asserts that the three battalions of the 16th Bavarians, alone, lost 2,300 officers and men.

# "The Tigers' Bloodiest Day"

The scale of the losses was not lost on the men of the Leicester Brigade. Ian Leonard 'Dick' Read [below] and his chums, noting the arrival of *"bulging sandbags"* of now superfluous rations on the evening of 14 July, could not help but run through *"the names of our mates we knew*  *already to be killed, wounded, or missing. Both of us had lost all our best pals, and we sat there with leaden hearts, lost in our thoughts. Eventually Jackie broke the silence. 'Plenty of rations tonight, Dick!' nodding towards the pile. 'Enough food for the whole battalion, eh? About six times too many.' He added bitterly, 'Christ, there'll be hell to pay in Leicester and Loughborough...and Coalville...and Melton... and Uppingham...when they know about this. The Leicester Brigade, eh? Bloody well wiped out!' And he trailed off into silence again..."*[38]

The drama was still not quite over, however. Shortly after 5 a.m. on 15 July the four battalion headquarters in Bazentin Wood were surprised to receive orders to abandon their positions and, as Captain C. A. B. Elliott of the 8th battalion, put it: *"concentrate as a brigade by [the] S.E. corner of Mametz Wood...with a view to preparing for a further attack."*[39] Having assisted in gathering together his battalion's widely dispersed platoons and reached Mametz Wood, Elliott then conferred with Captain H. L. Beardsley, now commanding his battalion, only to be told by the brigadier *"to go straight back..."*[40]

'Dick' Read was a witness to this final mystery of the battle, pausing in the excavation of a mass grave, to gaze across to Mametz Wood *"where groups of men from the battalions of our brigade had appeared at several points. As we watched, our mounted, red-tabbed brigade major galloped across our trench towards them, closely followed by the staff captain, gesticulating frantically and shouting, 'go back – go back!' to the now – halted men...A few minutes later an artillery driver came up,*

---

38 I. L. 'Dick' Read *Of those we Loved* (Barnsley) 2013, p. 159
39 Captain C. A. B. Elliott (ROLLR: DE8402/54)
40 Diary of Captain C. A. B. Elliott (ROLLR: DE8402/2)

# Tigers in the Trenches

*inquiring about his horse. Was the officer coming back? Apparently the brigade major seeing the incredible situation then developing, had borrowed it..."*

By a miracle the withdrawal was reversed and Bazentin Wood again occupied, apparently with little intervention from the enemy. Captain Elliott was later told by Brigadier General Hessey that " *'it was all a mistake'. I found out afterwards that it was not his, but he never said so.*"[41]

How History would judge the assault on Bazentin Ridge without the intervention of the 'hero on a stolen horse' is a matter for conjecture of course. As it is, the attack, though the bloodiest in Leicestershire Regimental history, was a model of dash and courage and led the way for a new approach to trench warfare on the Somme. It was a soldiers' battle too, fought with bomb and bayonet; with N.C.O.s leading companies and lance-corporals platoons.[42]

*A German Christmas card "picked up in Bazentin July 1916" and kept as a souvenir.*
*[ROLLR: 22D63]*

---

41 ROLLR: DE8402/54
42 Many awards for gallantry were made. The 8th Battalion's War Diary alone records thirteen recommendations: to Captain Beardsley, sergeants Parsons, Stafford and Jeffs, Corporal Lings, Lance-corporals Benington, Robinson and Black and to privates Dale, Toon, Warden and Pitt.

# "The Tigers' Bloodiest Day"

All along Bazentin Ridge the British attackers drove back the Germans. The two Bazentin villages fell, as did the adjacent Longueval and Trones Wood. Private W. R. Carter, the 8th Battalion signaller, actually watched cavalry manoeuvre in anticipation of the breakthrough: *"Towards night we had a feast for the eyes. Our cavalry! Cavalry coming up for a charge! You read about it in the papers. We saw them..."*[43]

For a moment it seemed as though Bapaume really was within reach. However, the Germans - always masters of defence - threw in their reserves and the front was stabilised. Along the ridge, woods which seemed British for the taking, became bloody battlegrounds. High Wood and Delville Wood became charnel houses; their names still by-words for slaughter.

For a moment however, the Generals and Press marvelled at what had been achieved and what might have been. For Sir Douglas Haig, the Commander-in-Chief, the attack reflected the *"highest credit on the Commanders and staffs who planned and arranged it and on the troops of all ranks who executed it with such vigour and bravery...It was a very fine feat of arms..."*

To the French the attack was a sign of hope, that 'amateurs' might, after all, achieve something. News of the attack's success was telephoned to General Balfourier's headquarters, where his liaison officer, Capitaine Sérot, observed with satisfaction: *"Ils ont osé; ils ont réussi"* ("They dared; they succeeded" or perhaps, more idiomatically, "Who dares, wins". [44]

Few of the 'Tigers' were in a position to assess the advantages of the attack against its cost. Late on 15 July 1916, Lieutenant H. W. H. Tyler, one of the few remaining officers with the 7th Battalion, The Leicestershire Regiment, had barely energy enough to write home:

*"We have had hell for six days in the great attack; yesterday we did wonders. There are thousands of stories to be told, but oh, it is awful. The fighting was terrific; we took four lines of trenches, but we had to*

43 *Leicester Daily Post,* 15 August 1916
44 *Official History, p.82*

# Tigers in the Trenches

*pay for it; so did the Boche...I have been lucky, but nearly exhausted. Have not been to bed for six nights, neither have I had my boots off, but we have cheered up tonight. I pray I shall never have to go through this again. I nearly broke down this morning and was on the point of going to the M.O., but I decided to stick it.*

*Everything is quiet this morning, and the Boche is fairly cowed."*[45]

*A crucifix from a village shrine between Bazentin Wood and High Wood, the next British objective, still bears the marks of battle.*

---

45 *Leicester Daily Post,* 21 July 1916

"Come on the Tigers!"

Chapter Eight

## "Come on the Tigers!"

## The Leicester Brigade at Polygon Wood, 1 October 1917

Although the Somme campaign had petered out at the end of 1916, much had happened in the following few months. One by one Britain's allies faltered and appealed for any distraction that might relieve the weight from their enemies. Unrest in Russia had caused the abdication of the Tsar in March 1917 and though the succeeding Provisional Government resolved to continue the war, there was much concern amongst the Allies at the prospect of diminishing pressure upon the Germans in the East.

In April a confident new commander-in-chief, Robert Nivelle [right], had launched a major French offensive on the Aisne. Within ten days the attack had ground to a halt, with more than 130,000 casualties.[1] The French army, already weakened by the blood-letting at Verdun, collapsed into a state of shock; some units openly defying their officers, others holding their trenches but sullenly declining to attack. Only the replacement of Nivelle with Pétain, the hero of Verdun, and a drastic scaling-down of the offensives saved France from disaster. By a miracle, the scale of France's agony was not realised by Germany.

GÉNÉRAL NIVELLE

---

1 The French Sixth and Tenth Armies lost 30,000 killed, 100,000 wounded and 4,000 missing between 16 and 25 April 1917. Ian Sumner *They Shall Not Pass* (Barnsley) 2012, p. 156.

# Tigers in the Trenches

The Spring of 1917 did not only bring ill tidings however. On 6 April the United States had declared war on Germany. Three days later the British launched their own offensive from Arras. Caught unawares and near blinded by sleet and snow, the German defenders were driven back and up to three and a half miles of territory, including Vimy Ridge, was lost in the first two days. Early success soon turned to disappointment however and the end of the battle, in mid-May, left the British little further forward, with casualties of over 150,000.

South of Arras, the Germans had, in fact, already withdrawn to their newly prepared Siegfried Stellung, or (to the British) the Hindenburg Line. Following in their wake, the wary vanguard of the 110th (Leicester) Brigade could only marvel at the devastation left by their enemy. Captain D. V. Kelly, on the brigade staff, recalled the *"thorough destruction"* through which they advanced, and the loss of many horses denied clean water.[2]

To the Hanoverian Fusilier officer, Ernst Jünger [right], laying waste to what was about to become enemy territory was a military necessity:

*"Every village up to the Siegfried line was a rubbish-heap. Every tree felled, every road mined, every well fouled, every watercourse damned, every cellar blown up or made into a death-trap with concealed bombs, all supplies or metal sent back, all rails ripped up, all telephone wire rolled up, everything burnable burned. In short, the country over which the enemy were to advance had been turned into an utter desolation."*[3]

---

2 D. V. Kelly 39 Months with the 'Tigers' (London) 1930, p. 60
3 Ernst Jünger The Storm of Steel (London) 1929 p.126. The choice of the name 'Unternehmen Alberich', or Operation Alberich, for the destructive withdrawal, is suggestive – Alberich being the malign, or mischievous, chief of the Nibelungen.

## "Come on the Tigers!"

The Hindenburg Line was, if anything, an even more daunting prospect. Dick Read, now a sergeant with the 8th Leicesters, saw through the mist *"a dark brown band many yards in depth, threading its way as far as we could see...belts of rusty wire defences of terrific strength...piles of sandbags and turned up earth of a trench system."*[4]

*Methodical German destruction - trees felled to block the road at Peronne [IWM Q5014]*

Captain Kelly also marvelled at the *"two great parallel trenches...each protected by dense masses of V-shaped wire entanglements, with lanes purposely arranged to be swept by concentrated machine-gun fire. The trenches were elaborately built with regular symmetrical traverses, numerous concrete 'pillboxes'...and saps for machine-gun posts."*[5]

Admiration for the engineering skills of the enemy grew when the Leicesters moved up into 'Tunnel Trench' in preparation for a renewed attack in May 1917. The trench was in fact a tiny bite taken out of the Hindenburg Line, originally the German front-line, named after <u>an immense </u>underground complex which stretched for miles in a

4 I. L. 'Dick' Read Of those we loved (Barnsley) 2013, p.254
5 Kelly, Ibid., p. 61

continuous line beneath the firing trench, to which it was linked with regular shafts and stairways. As 'Tunnel Trench' was still held by German troops at either end, both the trench and tunnel beneath were blocked and guarded at either end.

*Trench map of the german defences around Fontaine les Croisilles, showing the Hindenburg Line and tunnel beneath.*

The 2nd Royal Welch Fusiliers had occupied the tunnel earlier in April, their chronicler noting: "The Hindenburg Line was a truly wonderful piece of engineering...Tunnel trench was on the reverse slope; it was of the same construction, but the wire and much of the fittings were incomplete... All these surface works had been considerably knocked about by our heavy guns. Beneath the support trench, at a depth of about 40 feet, was a huge dug-out or tunnel some 6 feet 6 inches high, and said to be two miles long in this portion. It was fitted down the middle with tiers

# "Come on the Tigers!"

of bunks, and small living-rooms and store rooms opened off it.; it was wired throughout for electric lighting, but current had not been laid on. There were entrances of solid joiner-work every forty to fifty yards, and wide timber-cased stairways alternated with inclined planes for stores."[6]

The Leicester Brigade was to take part in the renewed offensive, a second attempt by Sir Hubert Gough's 5th Army to break through the German lines on a broad front around Bullecourt. Although popular with Haig as an aggressive, 'thrusting' commander, Gough [left] was careless in preparation and his apparent willingness to trade lives for speed, only lowered his reputation with the troops. The ten thousand casualties suffered by the Australians in the two attacks on Bullecourt did much to create an impression of British military incompetence and callousness which persists to this day.[7]

On 3 May 1917, the 8th and 9th Battalions of the Leicestershire Regiment, supported by the 6th and 7th, had joined the attack on the Hindenburg Line just north of the village of Fontaine-les-Croisilles. The first wave, of two lines about ten paces apart, went over the top at 3.45 a.m., closely following a creeping barrage intended to keep the German defenders' heads down until the assault was upon them. Sixty yards behind was another wave, followed by 'moppers-up', who would deal with any pockets of the enemy left behind by the advance. Two tanks were allocated in support of the brigade.

Almost immediately the plan went awry. The War Diary of the 8th Leicesters makes clear the difficulties they faced:

6 Captain J. C. Dunn (ed.) The War the Infantry Knew (London) 1987, pp. 328-9. Frank Richards, also of the Royal Welch Fusiliers, considered the Tunnel "a marvellous piece of work" with handrails on the entrances and "a concrete floor with boarded sides and roof...tiers of wire-netting beds...[and] sufficient room to carry a man on a stretcher." Old Soldiers Never Die, London, n.d., p. 226
7 The influential film Gallipoli is an example. Blundering and blinkered British staff officers and a willingness to save British lives at the expense of Australian are but two of the themes common in Australian films of the Great War.

# Tigers in the Trenches

*"The morning was very dark – sunrise was not until 5.23 a.m. (summer time), the dust and smoke from our own barrage and that of the enemy which opened simultaneously, making it impossible to see more than a few yards ahead."*

The battalions, squeezed by the 18th Division to their left, veered to the right and found themselves under heavy artillery fire and pinned down in what appeared to them to be a line of shell-holes but which was more likely a battered communication trench, the Mecklenberg-Schweriner Weg, and in danger of being cut off. German machine-guns well placed in a sunken road on the approaches to the village had effectively halted the attack.

The sole tank to appear in support was driven back by two machine-guns, ordered up by Officer-Deputy Klann, of the Reserve Infantry Regiment 226 and which were firing *SmK* armour piercing rounds.[8] Altogether, the German defence had been stout and pugnacious, as well as superbly supported by their artillery.[9]

The Royal Artillery's counter-battery fire, for once, proved inadequate; the German shelling compounding the confusion of darkness, dust and smoke. Communication with the neighbouring brigades also failed, as telephone wires were constantly cut by shellfire, and runners to and from headquarters took hours to get through, if they managed to do so at all. Lieutenant-colonel Bent, commanding the 9th Leicesters, recorded in his battalion's war diary the arrival of one vital message, carried by Lance-corporal Labbet: *"This runner had been 4 hours getting to the Hd. Qrs. As he had to move from shell hole to shell hole owing to enemy fire..."*

The attack is now largely forgotten, although it cost the two attacking battalions of the Leicester brigade twenty-seven officers and nearly six hundred other ranks killed, wounded or missing. Many of the missing had been taken prisoner; victims of the confused fighting and disorientating

---
8 War Diary, 9th Battalion The Leicestershire Regiment
9 Jack Sheldon *The German Army in the Spring Offensives 1917* (Barnsley) 2015, pp.287-8. SM-K (Spitzgeschoss mit Kern – or 'pointed tip with [steel] core') bullets had been developed to pierce the steel shields used by snipers in trench warfare.

## "Come on the Tigers!"

smoke. In recapturing the Mecklenberg-Schweriner Weg alone, two companies of the R.I.R. 226 captured three officers, eighty other ranks and five Lewis guns.[10]

To Captain Kelly [left], the reasons for what he called *"a tragic failure"*, were not hard to find: *"Delivered in pitch darkness, so that touch between units was rapidly lost, it was on too wide a front...and over too deep an area – one thousand yards of Nomansland had to be crossed before reaching the enemy. The ground had been imperfectly studied, so that several unexpected trenches were encountered in which many who had lost touch with their neighbours settled down. Finally, the enemy seemed well aware of our intentions...Nevertheless, some hundreds got right up to the enemy and kept up an isolated fight through the morning till they were rounded up by them or crawled back from shell-hole to shell-hole."*[11]

Several miles back from those shell-holes, army staffs on both sides were constantly evaluating and developing new strategies to cope with the apparent near stalemate of trench warfare. German experts, like Friedrich von Lossberg, were moving from a strong, single line of wire and trenches studded with concrete emplacements, to a looser, deeper defensive front, rich in machine-guns, supported by a strong, mobile reserve which could be called in to retake any lost ground. These Eingreif or 'Intervention' divisions, well supported by artillery, would overwhelm any attacking force just before the consolidation of any battlefield gains, at the moment of its greatest disorganisation and dislocation.

On the British side, army staffs debated the relative merits of small-scale, meticulously planned and resourced 'bite-and-hold' offensives against

---
10 Ibid., p. 288
11 Kelly, Ibid., p. 67

the increasingly unrealistic prospect of massive onslaughts, intended to puncture the German line on as wide a front as possible, before flooding through into open country with cavalry. Sadly, while lengthy preparation could deliver a devastating coup, there was no means of following up with sufficient strength to turn a breach into a breakthrough.

In June 1917, Sir Herbert Plumer's Second Army had demonstrated the value of 'bite and hold' by seizing the Messines Ridge, which overlooked and dominated approaches southwards from Ypres, after months of careful preparation. Embracing the Vauban principle of spadework to save lives, nineteen vast mines had been dug beneath the German lines. Their detonation, plus a bombardment of three and a half million shells, annihilated the defences of the ridge and nearly ten thousand of its garrison.

The choice of the Ypres salient once more as the main theatre of operations for the B.E.F., had some advantages. Ypres itself, a constant drain on resources, would be relieved and a break-out eastwards offered the prospect of capturing the rail-hub at Roulers and even depriving the Germans of their U-boat bases on the Belgian coast. The disadvantages of fighting in Flanders were well known: the ground was a bog, susceptible to bad weather and with a delicate drainage system easily destroyed by shelling and any attack was, literally, an uphill struggle against a succession of ever-higher ridges which gave the defender every advantage.

Despite official designation as the Third Battle of Ypres, the name of one village in West Flanders, Passchendaele, with its religious overtones of unbearable suffering, has become a short hand for the attempts, from July to November 1917, to seize that dominant, higher ground south and east of Ypres. The word Passchendaele itself stands almost as a metaphor for the popular perception of the Great War: the stinking, glutinous mud; the trenches and barbed wire; floundering tanks, men and pack horses; the gas and devastating bombardments. The seemingly heartbreaking, grinding futility of it all.

The Leicestershire Regiment's territorial battalions, 2/4$^{th}$ and 2/5$^{th}$, had

# "Come on the Tigers!"

arrived in the Ypres North sector on 24 September and were immediately thrown into the fighting to capture the German strongholds of Hills 37 and 35 and Elmtree Corner on the Menin Road ridge. The line was taken and held but at a cost of eighteen officers killed or wounded and 89 Other Ranks killed and 356 wounded or missing. The 11th Leicesters, the Midland Pioneers, had been in the salient much longer, since August suffering a constant trickle of casualties from shelling and air attack, while working on railways south of Poperinghe and between Ypres and Zillebeke.

*Men of the Midland Pioneers relaxing near Zillebeke, August 1917 [ROLLR: DE6262]*

The 110th (Leicester) Brigade, having spent some weeks in reserve, finally moved up to the front line at the end of September 1917. After fierce fighting the Australians of the 1st ANZAC Corps had overrun German defences in Polygon Wood; once a Belgian cavalry training ground but by 1917 a wasteland of mud, shell-craters and concrete pill-boxes. Only the stumps of trees remained in a landscape so cratered that in aerial photographs it resembles the skin of an orange.

Trench map of the Polygon Wood. By 1917 British maps usually omitted 'friendly' positions, marking enemy trenches and wire in red. The profusion of red here showing the density of german defences toi be overcome.

"The route", recalled Sergeant Douglas Bacon of the 9th Leicesters, "led by a much broken road to Hooge Crater...thence across the Ypres-Menin Road, where a sleeper track was encountered. This track was laid, or rather embedded, in mud ranging from three to six feet deep, and pursued its course through Glencourse Wood to a point in the morass known as Clapham Junction, from whence the track, now narrowed to one of 18 inches in width, continued via Black Watch Corner to Polygon

## "Come on the Tigers!"

*Wood...The night was very dark and the track broken in many places... and the enemy...continually concentrated their shelling thereon, with the consequence that portions would be blown up, leaving intervals of unadulterated mud."*[12]

Although generally regarded as over, save for consolidation, by 26 September[13], this is a verdict on the battle for Polygon Wood which would have surprised the officers and men of the Leicestershire Regiment's service battalions.

The 'Tigers' had relieved the 30th Australian Infantry shortly before midnight on the night of 30 September; the 8th and 9th battalions hastily consolidating a front line of shell-holes and *"isolated portions of trenches"* with company headquarters in a *"line of concrete shelters"* just behind[14]. The 7th and 6th Battalions lay further back, respectively in support and reserve. The night was unusually quiet, the relief being carried out without a single casualty.

At 5.25 a.m. on 1 October German artillery opened fire, deluging 'A' Company of the 9th Leicesters and the wood behind with high explosive and shrapnel shells, followed soon after by smoke. It was *"the heaviest enemy shelling I had ever encountered"* Captain D. V. Kelly recalled.[15] Sergeant D. A. Bacon was also impressed by the ferocity of the attack:

*"...we were rudely awakened by a terrific barrage, supplied by the enemy, and which was later proved to cover the whole immediate front to a depth of approximately 1000 yards...shells burst as thick as a hailstorm, and the din was awful. Tree stumps, mud and everything that happened to be about, was going up in all directions...At 5.15 a.m. enemy 'planes*

---

12 D. A. Bacon typescript memoirs; ROLLR: 22D63/146. Frank Richards, serving with the 2nd Royal Welch Fusiliers viewed the wood a few days earlier: "I expected to find a wood but it was undulating land with a tree dotted here and there and little banks running in different directions. About half a mile in front of us was a ridge of trees, and a few concrete pillboxes of different sizes." Old soldiers never die (London) n.d., p.247. This was, of course, before the worst of the enemy bombardment.
13 Charles Bean, author of The Australian Imperial Force in France, 1917, Vol. IV (1941) for example concluding his account of Polygon Wood on that day, with "The whole objective of the British attack was secured" (p. 831).
14 9th Battalion War Diary
15 Kelly, Ibid., p. 78. The Official History (1917 Vol. 2, p. 302) describes the bombardment "smothering with shell the whole area back to a thousand yards".

# Tigers in the Trenches

*flew low over our lines, so low in fact that the occupants could be seen quite plainly, [firing]...drum after drum of Machine-gun bullets into the troops."*[16]

In the next five minutes, two waves of German infantry burst through the smoke screen but were driven back with rifle and Lewis gun fire. Captain Lee, commanding 'A' Company, was killed and enemy troops began to infiltrate their right flank. On the left the 8th Leicesters also came under heavy shellfire and both battalions sent up S.O.S. flares, which brought a 'friendly' barrage down across the attackers' front.

The assault came from regiments of two fresh German divisions, the 8th and 45th (Reserve), though the cutting edge of the attack was provided by a dozen sections of specially trained units from the Fourth Army's Sturmbataillon. Their orders were to retake all the ground and concrete defences lost on 26 September.[17]

At 5.40 a.m., with the front-line beginning to buckle and S.O.S. flares sent up all along the line, the 9th Leicesters' commanding officer, Lieutenant-colonel P. E. Bent [left], led 'B' and two platoons of 'D' Company in a desperate counter-attack from his command post – a pill-box on the west side of Polygon Wood. Bent, according to D. V. Kelly, who had it from eye-witnesses, said " '...we'd better get on'...and went forward with his headquarter personnel. Collecting the reserve company and everyone available, the Colonel led a counter-attack, and, struck down in the moment of victory, was last seen – for his body, doubtless blown to pieces, was not found – waving his pipe and calling, 'Go on, Tigers!'*[18]

16 D A Bacon Ibid.
17 Official History (1917 Vol. 2, p. 302)
18 Ibid., p. 79. D. A. Bacon recalled: "the Colonel lead the charge shouting "Come on the Tigers" and reports that Bent was shot through the temple.

# "Come on the Tigers!"

*The view from a captured German pillbox under bombardment, near Polygon Wood, 27 September 1917. [IWM Q2901].*

The respite won by Bent's charge was significant but all too brief. Lieutenant Burn, commanding 'B' Company, was killed leading another counter-attack and a growing breach in the line was detected as increasing numbers of Germans were detected infiltrating between the 8th and 9th Leicesters. On the left, the 8th Battalion was attacked at about 6.30 a.m. by enemy infantry "moving by short rushes towards our right front line company and threatening to turn the right flank of the Battalion."[19] The incursion was eventually halted with heavy Lewis Gun and rifle fire and no further German progress noted in that area.

Shortly before 7 a.m. the supporting fire from British artillery, which had done much to halt the enemy attacks, ceased and for the next three or more hours wave after wave of German infantry attacked the 8th Leicesters' open flank. To their right the 9th Battalion had been driven back about one hundred yards but the new line held firm, supported by

19 7th Battalion War Diary

increasing numbers of reinforcements from the 7th Leicesters.

*War Office copy of the telegram sent to Bent's mother deeply regretting his death in action [National Archives WO339/3608]*

A further threat came from the *"very aggressive"* German aircraft, one of which swept low across the 9th battalion's front, until brought down by Corporal Outhwaite; landing in no-man's land where it was eventually destroyed by shell fire.[20] By mid-morning the 7th Leicester's commanding officer, Major Howitt[21] had arrived at the eastern edge of Polygon wood where he took command of the leaderless 9th Battalion.

Although several German prisoners warned of further assaults, well-timed artillery barrages proved deterrent enough and overnight the line was further strengthened and reinforced from the 6th Battalion. Shortly after 8 p.m. an assault had been made on the Royal Welsh Fusiliers, dug-in to the left of the 8th Leicesters, but S.O.S. rockets brought down an

---
20 9th Battalion War Diary
21 Major Thomas Cecil Howitt DSO was a well known architect in his native Nottingham, for both Boots and the City Council, for whom he built the Council House and Processional way.

## "Come on the Tigers!"

hour's bombardment which disrupted the attack enough to prevent any progress by the enemy.

The following day, 2 October 1917, brought relative calm again to Polygon Wood. Stretcher bearers were able to evacuate all of the 9th Battalion's wounded and only the activities of a sniper, who *"caused a few casualties"* disrupted a *"fairly quiet"* morning and afternoon. At 6.30 p.m. German artillery fire provoked retaliation and for nearly two hours the edge of Polygon Wood was rocked by *"an intense artillery duel"*.[22] The 8th Battalion's war diary noted the arrival of a new commander, Major H. E. C. Anderson, to relieve the wounded Lieut-Colonel Utterson but otherwise observed that *"with the exception of desultory shelling of POLYGON WOOD during the morning, the day passed quietly, the situation remain [sic] unchanged and the enemy made no attempt to carry out any further attack."*

That night the Leicester Brigade was withdrawn for rest and reorganisation. Casualties were heavy; the brigade as a whole losing some forty officers killed and wounded and 255 Other Ranks killed and 428 wounded.[23] For the two front-line battalions on 1st October, this resulted in a temporary amalgamation, from 4 to 12 October, as the 8/9th Battalion; each of the former battalions providing two new companies under the command of Major R. N. Yalland of the 6th Battalion.

This was not, however, the brigade's last experience of Polygon Wood. On 8 October the three battalions were deployed for four days to the east of the wood, holding a line of concrete pill boxes linked by barely discernable trenches and shell holes. Although an anticipated infantry assault did not materialise, German artillery was persistent and effective; the 8th Battalion War Diary recording three officers and fifty-three men killed and wounded in three days.

---

22 7th Battalion War Diary. The casualties included a Second-lieutenant Dowell, who had crawled out to engage him the sniper but was shot through the shoulder whilst firing at him.
23 Figures are derived from the War Diaries of the four battalions, which are inconsistent in their methods of recording. The 9th battalions total is for the whole month of October for example, while the 7th Battalion, interestingly, breaks down its wounded into wounded (115), gassed (7) and shell shock (13). The losses by battalion are: 6th battalion – 4 ORs killed and 81 wounded; 7th battalion – 2 officers killed and 5 wounded and 26 ORs killed and 115 wounded; 8th Battalion - 11 officers and 175 ORs killed and wounded; and 9th Battalion - 5 officers and 50 ORs killed, 8 officers and 213 ORs wounded and 38 ORs missing.

# Tigers in the Trenches

In addition, the notorious Flanders weather had once again turned treacherous and *"during the whole of the time was extremely wet, and the men suffered severely in the open trenches & shell holes, which in many cases were full of water."*[24] That the campaign was to continue, despite persistently awful weather in a terrain so devastatingly affected by both continuous rain and destructive shelling, for another month and a half, remains both a testimony to the stolid courage of the front-line soldiers as well as an indictment of their higher command.

As one of those 'Tigers' of October 1917 observed, just a dozen years later:

*"Time scatters the poppies of oblivion over most things, but the lapse of twelve years has not effaced the impressions of sordid horror and melancholy which this period of the War engraved on the mind. The general setting was inconceivably dreary and miserable, death or frightful mutilation by shell-fire were ever at hand…and the effort and sacrifice demanded of our Army – and willingly made – is scarcely credible….When one compares the results with the dogged tenacity of infantry, gunners and transport men under loathsome nerve-wracking conditions and the utterly prodigal expenditure of munitions and technical resources of every kind, one feels resentful of the doctrinaire fanaticism which kept the machine driving on at top-pressure, month after month, as though the gain of each few yards of water-logged craters was worth any sacrifice."*[25]

The Australians' and New Zealanders' capture of Polygon Wood at the end of September 1917 is rightly part of what might almost be called the 'folklore' of the campaign of Passchendaele or the third Battle of Ypres. The part played by the Leicestershire Regiment in clinging on to the Wood in the face of the Eingreif divisions' counter-attacks would, however, no doubt be largely forgotten but for the subsequent award of the Victoria Cross, posthumously, to Lieut-Colonel Philip Bent for his part in rallying the defence in the first, crucial minutes of the attack on 1 October.

---
24 8th Battalion War Diary
25 D. V. Kelly 39 Months with the 'Tigers' (London) 1930, pp. 74-5

## "Come on the Tigers!"

As the London Gazette recorded: *"The coolness and magnificent example shown to all ranks by Lt.-Col. Bent resulted in the securing of a portion of the line which was of essential importance for subsequent operations. This very gallant officer was killed whilst leading a charge which he inspired with the call of 'Come on the Tigers'."* [26]

Men of the 1st Leicesters pause to investigate 'Hyacinth', a ditched Mark IV 'male' tank on the Hindenburg Line, a mile west of Ribecourt on 20 November 1917.

[IWM Q6432]

---

26 London Gazette, 30471, January 1918 pp 722-723

## Chapter Nine

# "Bored to tears and covered in mud"
# Trench Warfare – in and out of the line

*"Nothing I could say would describe the awful desolation as one approaches the trenches...gaunt trees killed by gases, some torn up by shells, and farm houses mere ruined walls...There are thousands of troops in dug-outs, with here and there a path three feet wide to walk on , and as all one's domestic affairs, washing etc., have to be done on this promenade you can imagine the difficulty, which is equally great, in going up the communication trenches , especially as the trenches are apt to get blown in."*[1]

On 14 July 1916, the letter of Second-lieutenant C Stanley Hagon, a Leicester officer at the Front, was printed in the *Leicester Daily Post*. Hagon was eager to show off to his parents his grasp of the latest slang as well as to reassure them that he was safe and well:

*"Gee! But I'm O.K. and having one grand time, bored to tears and covered in mud. Oh, Yes! This is some life. But, joking apart, up to the time of going to press everything has been absolutely 'cushy', to use the vernacular, which being interpreted means comfortable and absolutely top hole."*

Hagon had discovered, as many others had before him, that war is often "months of boredom punctuated by moments of terror". This was certainly true of the trench warfare which dominated the Western Front from the end of 1914 until the autumn of 1918. There were many 'quiet' sectors of the front-line and even where no-man's land was actively contested, as much as half of each battalion might be in 'reserve' or 'support' some distance back.

---
[1] Letter from a 'Soldier in a Leicester Battalion', Leicester Daily Post, 28 July 1916

# "Bored to tears and covered in mud"

This certainly applied to the 1/4th Leicesters, sent a few miles back from Lens to 'rest' at Petit Sains Fosse 10. As Captain John Milne observed: *"Life at Fosse 10 was not unpleasant. Certainly the place was shelled occasionally, but no one seemed to mind unless they were hit."*[2] Life in 'reserve', or 'support', remained hazardous – from enemy shell-fire – but life-expectancy extended with every footstep away from the front-line.

*A typical trench scene, at Givenchy in January 1918. One 'Tiger' keeps watch through a trench periscope, while others eat or view the photographer warily. [ROLLR: DE6262]*

Experiences of trench living varied enormously of course. Few relished the prospect of a move to Ypres, while living *alfresco* in summer is a different prospect to the dark and cold of winter. As Charles Carrington recalled *"in quiet trenches, in good weather, the men on duty in the front line might have a rather easy time. In the mild autumn of 1915 tales were told of men crawling out into the long grass of No Man's Land,*

2 John Milne *Footprints of the 1/4th Leicestershire Regiment* (Leicester) 1935 p. 102

# Tigers in the Trenches

*when off duty, to smoke and read their home letters undisturbed."*[3]

A 1st battalion trench at Rue de Bois in 1915. While one man snipes at the enemy, his sergeant prepares breakfast. Just visible to the left is Sergeant Cunningham who (according to a note on the original photograph) was killed by shrapnel shortly afterwards.

---
3 Charles Carrington *Soldier from the Wars returning* (Barnsley) p. 88

# "Bored to tears and covered in mud"

Horace Charles Slater, a regular with the 2nd Leicesters swiftly became disenchanted with both strict discipline and grim conditions of the 'new' warfare. Writing from his dug-out, Slater complained bitterly to his brother about conditions in a front-line held by too few men: *"we are still like slaves in this regiment, we are on from Reveille until lights out, on guard every three nights…the African war was a pick nick to this…you say you would like to exchange places, but you would soon want to get out of it as it is murder…they are only 150 yards in front of us…so you can g[u]ess how it is here and roll on when they pack in…"*[4] Like many soldiers, Slater took solace in tobacco, writing *"I smoke all day long to pass the time away…"*[5] He was one of twenty-two men of the battalion killed at Neuve Chapelle on 15 May 1915.

As we have seen at Christmas 1914, enemies could be induced to forget their differences when cooperation was beneficial. In his diary from November 1917, the Quartermaster Sergeant of the 2/5th Leicesters described an example of what has been termed 'the live and let live system':

*"…the line the Battalion was in was rather a weird place. Men are pushed out in little posts of an N.C.O. and 6 men; here in an old trench, there in the ruins of a house. Some of the posts were in Avions village. In one place one of our posts was in a cellar, a double sentry stood half up the steps, but had to keep themselves concealed as a German post was only 25 yards away in the cellar of another ruined house. Before we came in to relieve the Staffords, both the Germans and British in one spot used to draw their water from the same well; but at different times of course. The Staffords blued this arrangement for they captured the whole of the German water party which came that night. After that the well became unhealthy for both, and a fresh water supply had to be found by each."*[6]

Many accounts of trench warfare record instances of enemies turning a blind eye for mutual benefit. One example comes from the Ypres salient where troops on both sides, driven from the cover of their trenches by

---
4 ROLLR: DE9103/3
5 ROLLR: DE9103/6
6 ROLLR: DE5970/70 (13 November 1917). For an examination of the 'live and let live system' see Tony Ashworth *Trench Warfare 1914-1918* (London) 2000.

# Tigers in the Trenches

flood-water, refrained from opening fire. Another, subtly different is the often repeated tale of trench dwellers' resentment of itinerant trench mortar teams whose arrival in the front-line, to launch a few bombs at the enemy, brings a vicious response shortly *after* their departure.

*Territorials of the 4th Leicesters repair their trench in the Ypres Salient in 1917. The high water table and heavy rain necessitated constant repairs and the use of sandbags piled high above wooden 'A' frames.*

Some stretches of the front-line were known to be grim, dangerous places; others enjoyed a sunnier reputation. Edmund Blunden even

## "Bored to tears and covered in mud"

recalled one as a 'rest-cure sector' and considered *"the observance of the 'Live and Let Live' principle, one of the soundest elements in trench war"*.[7] Much, in such a quiet sector, depended upon an obliging enemy. I. L. Read, serving with the 8th Leicesters near Berles au Bois in September 1915, even recalled that *"The snipers were no worry in those deep trenches. In fact, we became bored and played a lot of solo, pontoon and brag when off duty."*[8] A month later, Corporal C. Murray of 'C' Company, 1/4th Leicesters, wrote home to his grandmother with a full description of life in the Ypres salient:

*"We are settling down nicely to the trench conditions, which mean plenty of work, hot days, cold nights, very little sleep, and cave dwelling. Our day generally starts at 'Stand to', at sunset, this being a favourite time for the Germans attack. After 'Stand down' we have sentries on in the trench, and the remainder sleep in the bays of the trench if they are not too cold. No one is allowed in the dugouts at night, as gas attacks would be fatal to anyone sleeping there. At dawn we have another hour of 'stand to' and alertness, and after that the lucky ones can get to sleep in the dugouts until 7.30 - breakfast time.*

*After that we are liable to any amount of fatigues – trench repairing, fetching rations, water etc., work at night repairing parapets, and fetching water and rations, so you see sleep is uncertain. Our dugout is quite "comfy" for a Tommy, but, of course you would think it simply awful. It is a square hole dug in the ground, at the rear of the trench, about five feet deep, and 20 feet by seven feet; and connected with the support trench by a narrow trench each end. There are logs of timber covered with a thick layer of soil for the roof. Each end are two bunks, which each hold two men, whilst in the middle of the floor...is sleeping room for about five more men. We lie on straw and have rats and mice for company."*[9]

The rats, in particular, were a constant source of irritation and disgust. One 'Tiger', writing to his old headmaster at Bridge Road School,

---
7 Edmund Blunden *Undertones of War* (London) 2010, pp.95 and 118.
8 I. L. 'Dick' Read *Of Those We Loved* (Barnsley) p. 50
9 *Leicester Daily Post*, 2 October 1915

# Tigers in the Trenches

Leicester, declared: *"I must not forget the rats. They come out in full parade, and sometimes in 'mass formation'."*[10]

*'L' is for Lousy; from* An Alphabet from the Trenches *written and illustrated by two officers of the Leicestershire Regiment [ROLLR: 22D63]*

Lice, too, attracted their fair share of denunciation in memoirs and letters home. As Captain Milne noted, his battalion *"was very lousy. The 'Chat,' as the species of louse was called, was no respecter of persons. He paid his respects to the Colonel, visited the adjutant; called on the company commanders; became attached to the platoon sergeants for rations, but not discipline; and fraternised only too frequently with the rank and file. In some dug outs men itched as soon as they sat down."*[11]

Writing to his wife in Blaby, Lieutenant George Buckle-Pickett of the 9th

10 *Ibid.*, 21 August 1916
11 Milne *Ibid.*, p. 47

# "Bored to tears and covered in mud"

Leicesters (and later 110th Trench Mortar Battery) followed a well-worn path: *"I shall be glad if you will send me a small box of Keatings Insect Powder as soon as possible. I made an interesting discovery this morning viz. that I am keeping company that I can very well do without, owing no doubt to the filthy hole in which I was sleeping about a fortnight ago."*[12]

Despite a feeling, prevalent long after any reasonable expectation, that trench warfare was a temporary phase, soon to be replaced with a return to fighting in open country, official efforts were made to ensure that 'filthy holes' were as rare as possible. In May 1915 the 138th Brigade, including the 1/4th and 1/5th Leicesters, issued 'Standing Orders' for trench duty.

Cleanliness was clearly close to the heart of the brigade staff, the orders stipulating that food was to be kept "carefully covered up at all times" against flies, and that "on no account must any water be drunk except that obtained from the water cart or recognised Battalion Supply." The role of tidiness in sanitation was also clearly recognised, the Orders requiring that "a few empty tins or other receptacles should be distributed about the trench and any miscellaneous refuse, such as pieces of paper, rags, etc., deposited therein."

The disposal of *"dirty water, tea, or other liquids"* was also controlled, with regular changes of 'soak aways'. Urine was also recognised as a source of infections and consequently it was ordered that the vessels used for it should be checked for leaks and, when emptied, care taken to avoid spillage. As for the latrines proper, it was ordered that "a supply of dry earth will be kept near each latrine box and...sprinkled over all the excreta & paper whenever the latrines are used".[13]

Many trenches and the no-man's land between them, especially those dug in haste where the fighting in open country ceased in 1914, were littered with the decaying corpses of the earlier battles. A South Wigston private, of the 1/4th Battalion, wrote home in April 1915: *"there are bodies, many of which lie just where they fell..."*[14]

12 Letter of GB-P, 21 October 1917 Imperial War Museum 8611
13 ROLLR: 22D63/177/22
14 *Leicester Daily Post*, 20 April 1915.

# Tigers in the Trenches

Many soldiers would scarcely refrain from rifling the pockets of a dead enemy for a watch or cigarette case and others, like 'Dick' Read were alive to the possibilities of warmer clothing or better boots. At Bazentin Wood in July 1916, Read and his mates had made good use of German groundsheets *"which, incidentally, were much better affairs than ours in every respect. Examining them more thoroughly, we selected one each from the kits of dead Germans lying nearby, for keeping out the night chill; also a greatcoat from a dead officer, beautifully lined with lamb's wool, for a blanket."*[15]

While tales of the protruding hands of carelessly buried corpses being shaken for good luck or in grim humour seem to abound[16], wiser counsel is to be found in 138th Brigade Orders: *"men must be warned against the danger of disease arising from examining or handling dead bodies that may be found. No corpse will be handled except by orders of an Officer."* On a cold night, orders (like Hamlet's customs) were understandably 'more honour'd in the breach, than the observance'.

The 1/4th and 1/5th battalions were holding the line at Lindenhoek, beside Mont Kemmel, south-west of Ypres. Shelling was sporadic and mining and counter-mining a drain on both men and nerves. It is unlikely that the Standing Orders' counsel of perfection could have been observed to the letter, though they remain an interesting acknowledgement of problems to be solved.

More informal arrangements also existed for happy co-existence in the front-line, as well as effective defence. Lieutenant C.A. B. Elliott, serving with the 8th Leicesters, copied into his 1915 pocket diary a helpful note, full of advice born of experience:

*"Taking over trenches – find out where everything is, especially ammunition gas sp...,[17] bombs, tip for latrines, picks, shovels and boots.*

---

[15] I. L. Read *Ibid.*, pp. 158-9
[16] For an excellent example see Nigel Atter *With Valour and Distinction* (Warwick) 2019, p.26. Donald Weir, serving with the 2nd Leicesters at Neuve Chapelle observed his men shaking the protruding hands of dead Gurkhas and remarking 'Good luck to yer', 'cheer-oh old sport' and the like.
[17] Presumably Elliott here refers to anti-gas Vermorel Sprayers, likened by Edmund Blunden to "simple machines such as were used in Kent to wash cherry-trees with insect-killer" see *Undertones of War* (London) 2010, p.13.

# "Bored to tears and covered in mud"

*See that guides go very slowly and halt at intervals. In moving in and out as a platoon as quickly as possible and meet at a given spot even if at some distance. If fairly close go straight back to billets by platoons. Each platoon drops a man to report to Co[mpan]y Commander when relief is completed."*[18]

Men of the 4th Leicesters covering their newly issued steel helmets with sacking, 1916.

---

18 ROLLR: DE8402/1

# Tigers in the Trenches

Movement in and out of the line – and even beyond where enemy artillery was active – was always hazardous and stories of delayed reliefs and of bodies of troops lost in a featureless terrain or utter darkness are legion. As a clearly irritated Lieutenant Buckle-Pickett confided to his wife:

*"...the whole country is pitted with shell holes and intersected with trenches and I was told to go 'over there' to the tents allotted to officers, so I went but it happened to be the wrong 'over there'. It was pitch dark and I went head first into several shell holes and trenches but as I was wearing a 'tin hat' I was not hurt...I found a man of the Black Watch who tried to help me out but it was not much good as it only meant two people falling into shell holes instead of one."*[19]

Life in the trenches was in large part a matter of repair and maintenance. Even without enemy action, few earthworks will last long without constant remedial work. The winter of 1915-16 proved a trying time for 'Dick' Read and his comrades of the 8th Leicesters: *Every now and then, huge slices of trench sides slipped down to the bottom, loosened by the alternate frosts, rains and thaws...the thaws had flooded the trench floor, and in places the duckboard sump covers had floated off. Where earth from the sides had fallen, we unsuspecting unfortunates blundered in up to the waist."*[20]

As the soldier, whose letter opened this chapter, recalled on the return of his company to the first-line trenches after a period of rest in billets:

*"Our work now begins. We climb to the parapets and start filling in sand-bags, and building up trench sides, when, swish! comes machine-gun fire. We all drop down (I never thought that at my age I should get flat so smartly). Up again, and this time a light goes up and we stand perfectly still. The whole place is as light as day. This goes on all night, until morning, about one o'clock. We then start back, with the same programme as when coming, and breakfast at eleven a.m. But this does not end our troubles. About 250 yards away our big guns start firing*

---

19 Letter of GB-P, 11 October 1917 Imperial War Museum 8611
20 I. L. Read *Ibid.*, pp. 90-91

## "Bored to tears and covered in mud"

*about four in the morning, and they keep on sending over about 20 shots at a time. Then the gunners go back to their safe dug-outs, while the Boche replies. The shells come screaming over our heads, and as we can hear them coming for some seconds before they arrive you can imagine the suspense. After that the Boche planes come and try to spot where our guns are hidden. They also chance their aim and drop a few bombs. The thing happens over again about four in the afternoon, when we are again resting, and our people retaliate. It's all retaliation here, but above all stands out the marvellous fact that so few people get hit. Men get shovels knocked out of their hands, dents in their steel helmets, holes through their clothing. One shell dropped near a party of thirty of our men., but it was a 'dud'."*[21]

Not all aspects of trench-life were the occasion for griping or complaint. Captain J. D. Hills, in his account of the 1/5th Battalion The Leicestershire Regiment, made clear his appreciation of newly learned or invented techniques which made trench-living safer or more comfortable. The 'A' frame, which "some genius invented", is lauded as a "really wonderful labour saving device" while the fact that their brigadier was originally a sapper is seen as not without its positive side:

*"we were soon instructed in the mysteries of sump-holes, 'berms' and 'batters,' interlocking trench floor boards, and the correct angles for the sloping sides of a trench, while anyone who dared to undercut a parapet for any purpose had better not be present the next time that the General appeared."*[22]

Many officers' dugouts, especially in one of the relatively quiet sectors, achieved something approaching homeliness. Lieutenant A. P. Marsh, of the 1/5th Leicesters, writing home to his fiancé, was perhaps careful to paint a comforting domestic picture:

*"Our new trench is quite a good one & will be much better when we have raised part of the parados to shut out a nasty fire we get from the back in one part. I've made myself quite an excellent dug out & just now Charity*

---
21 Letter from a 'Soldier in a Leicester Battalion', *Leicester Daily Post,* 28 July 1916
22 J D Hills *The Fifth Leicestershire* (Loughborough) 1919 p. 155.

# Tigers in the Trenches

*Men of 6th Leicesters enjoying their rations, on the Somme in 1916. [ROLLR: DE6262]*

# "Bored to tears and covered in mud"

## Tigers in the Trenches

*has brought in a bunch of roses he has gathered in the garden of a ruin just behind our lines. So now it looks quite cheerful. It is just high enough for me to sit up straight in. Not quite long enough for me to lie straight out in. One side is taken up by a table below ground level & about 1 foot of sand bags. The walls are hung with sand bags split open & the floor well covered with sand bags. The roof is made of 6 poles covered with canvas & then has three thicknesses of bags on top of that to make it shell proof (of course you can't make it proof against a high explosive). I've fixed up a shelf at one end & pegs to hang kit up all round. It does not sport a window & the door is only a waterproof sheet. The bed is an extra thickness of sandbags on the floor & my air pillow."*[23]

Food was, inevitably, at the forefront of most minds; especially in an area comparatively untroubled by the enemy. A letter written by an officer (presumably the Quartermaster) of the 4th Leicesters to Mr Williams of the well-known Leicester provision merchant Simpkin and James, not surprisingly touched on the means of supply:

*"The system of rationing the men in the trenches is simple, but it entails a little thought, and plenty of work, and I am constantly on the go. I have the number of men in each trench, which is numbered or lettered, and we make their food up in sand bags for each trench, and at a stated time they go up to the rear of the trenches at night and men are sent to carry them in. they have braziers and burn coke and charcoal, and are able to have warm tea and bully and biscuits or bread. The bacon is boiled, and they have it cold. Last night I forwarded each man one of the packets of chocolate which the 'Leicester Daily Mercury' Fund sent..."*[24]

In support trenches or out of the front-line, the supply of food was easier and more reliable. 'Dick' Read's fond recollections of 'Tante's cottage' or Émilienne's at Berles au Bois are too well known to require repetition. Each soldier found his own source of food and comfort for a brief respite from the discomforts and dangers of war. One soldier of the Leicesters, writing home to his mother – Mrs Harbutt, of Evington Drive –described life in December 1915:

---
23 ROLLR: DE3695/67
24 *Leicester Daily Post* 22 April 1915

# "Bored to tears and covered in mud"

*"When in billets over the fire many recipes of doubtful origin are cooked. Our favourite is toast, cheese and jam – don't smile. A fellow from South America introduced it. The peasants supply us with milk and eggs and many's the billy tin of cocoa and hot milk that is made..."*[25]

Private M. S. Holden, of the 1/4th Leicesters considered *"bully beef and biscuit and plenty of it"* to be his chief food, *"and sometimes bacon for breakfast"*. He added that newspapers were hard to come by and *"milk is very difficult to get"* and that flash-lights were useful due to a shortage of matches. Not all food was legally obtained, of course, Private A. Derry of the 2nd Leicesters 'D' Company confessing that, when on signalling duty, *"I used to track off to the old farmhouse just half a mile back behind the trenches. I used to be up the chicken run after the eggs, and at the time shot a few chickens for the pot..."*[26]

Out of the line, un-rationed food was always attractive for both its variety and quantity. Troops at leisure often sought out the nearest surviving settlements for food and drink but also recreation and souvenirs. Captain J. D. Hills recalled how many of his battalion, officers and men, would walk or ride two miles into Bailleul *"to call on 'Tina,' buy lace, or have hot baths (a great luxury) at the Lunatic Asylum."*[27]

The Army itself often provided entertainment for troops fresh from the line (who were fortunate enough to escape the many demands for construction and supply work which often made 'rest' anything but restful. A letter home from the 1/4th Leicesters in March 1916 illustrates the point. Even church parade had been abandoned in favour of snow-clearing when relief arrived in the form of a musical diversion:

*"The splendid band of the Royal Artillery paid a visit and gave us a programme of music, but it was given under the worst possible conditions. It was snowing and blowing, in fact quite a blizzard. They stood under the lee side of a barn. Officers and men stood in the road and got nearly frozen, and I am inclined to think that they clapped their hands more to*

---

25 *Ibid.*, 18 December 1915
26 *Ibid.*, 10 February 1915.
27 J D Hills *Ibid.*, p. 38.

*keep warm than for the sake of applause..."*[28]

*A military band prepares for a performance. [IWM Q52062]*

Private A. Simms, of the 6th Leicesters, agreed. He enjoyed football competitions and reading the Leicester 'papers sent from home but, he observed: *"if there is one thing more than another that cheers us up it is our brigade band, which plays every night when we are out of the trenches...We had an excellent concert party and band with us the other night, known as the 'Wissbangs' and I have never enjoyed a turn at the music halls better that I enjoyed hearing those men. The whole performance was delightful and helped to take away the thoughts of trench life for over two hours."*[29]

Attitudes to the local population varied greatly – as, no doubt, did the locals themselves. Lieutenant C. A. B. Elliott, of the 8th Leicesters recorded

---

28 *Leicester Daily Post,* 8 March 1916.
29 *Leicester Daily Post,* 5 August 1916.

# "Bored to tears and covered in mud"

a mixed reception in his diary. On 5 August 1915 he noted: *"bivouacked in field of farm. Farm very dirty and owner who talked Flemish very fast inclined to be inhospitable. We could hear the guns quite clearly in the evening."*[30] This was at Eecke, south-west of Poperinge, and just a couple of miles into France.

Elsewhere, the French proved more friendly and also curious. On 24 August Elliott recorded that at Baileul *"the school mistress asked H.W.S and self to have coffee and gave us a very good meal"* while on 2 September, despite sleeping on the *"very hard and mousy"* floor of an estaminet, their reception had, at least, not been hostile: *"French people on the way had not seen English before and were quite excited."*

Good relations were established, too, with the Belgians. A territorial of the 1/4th Leicesters wrote home the day after Elliott encountered the inhospitable farmer of Eecke with evidence of the cultural exchanges that war made inevitable: *"We have a little Belgian boy here, quite a linguist. He has just walked up smoking a cigarette. He is about eleven years old, and speaks English well, and the Indians taught him quite a lot of Hindustani. He reads the English papers...and he is also fond of our jam ration."*[31]

*Exhausted 'tommies' at rest in Athies, Spring 1917 [IWM Q1980]*

---
30 Diary of Lieut. C A B Elliott (8th Leicesters) 1915. ROLLR: DE8402/1
31 *Leicester Daily Post,* 6 August 1915.

# Tigers in the Trenches

Trench warfare, as we have seen, was a life of welcome reliefs and short spells out of the line, before orders to return to the front-line were received; signalling the recommencement of discomfort and danger. Such was the fate of the 14th Leicesters on 15 September 1918, when orders reached battalion headquarters to relieve the 18th Scottish Rifles in the notorious *Hohenzollern* sub section, near Auchy. Quarry Trench, Fosse 8 and Clifford crater were all to be occupied; each man to carry 50 rounds of small arms ammunition as well as a shovel each for those in the rifle platoons of 'A' and 'B' companies. Gas rattles and fans were to be taken.

If, at times, the order to relieve a unit occupying one of the grimmer sectors of the front was the cause of resentment or dismay, it is hardly surprising. Was it war-weariness, momentary impatience or merely the desire for a suitably opaque code-word which caused Captain & Adjutant H. G. Oxley to conclude the orders as he did?

*"RELIEF COMPLETE will be notified by code word 'BUGGER' "*[32]

---

[32] War Diary 14th Battalion. The Leicesters' 14th (Service) Battalion had been formed at Aldeburgh in June 1918, in large part from men of the 2/4th battalion which had been reduced to a cadre. They moved to France at the end of July 1918 and joined the 47th Brigade (16th Division). Captain Harold Gordon Oxley had risen from the ranks, having begun the war as No. 2783 Private Oxley. See Royal Tigers Association website.

"Kudos if it succeeds..."

## Chapter Ten

# "Kudos if it succeeds, silence if it does not, but a hell of a lot of casualties either way."

## Trench Raids and Listening Patrols

In Leicester, the New Year of 1915 was enlivened by the display of a pair of German machine-guns (above), which had been repaired and repainted at the Glen Parva Depot. Carried on the back of a motor lorry and escorted by eight, fully armed soldiers of the 2nd Battalion, on sick leave from the front, the two *Maschinengewehr* 08s proved a popular feature of several recruiting rallies and parades: *"These death dealing weapons looked innocent enough in their new paint, and it was difficult to realise that they had probably taken the lives*

# Tigers in the Trenches

*of hundreds of England's brave sons..."*[1]

The machine-guns were trophies captured from the Germans in a raid on their trenches at Richebourg l'Avoué just a few weeks before on 19 December. Trench raids were a new feature of the war and had been pioneered, in part, by the 2/39th Garhwal Rifles; a sister battalion of the 2nd Leicesters in the Garhwal Brigade. Although the Black Watch had raided German lines near La Bassée to silence a troublesome machine-gun on 9 November 1914, according to Anthony Saunders *"the Garhwali raid of 9-10 November 1914 is usually considered to be the first trench raid of the war. There is no doubt that it set the pattern of future raiding operations as it was undertaken under cover of darkness, was intended to surprise the enemy, damage his defences and inflict casualties, without taking and holding ground except on a temporary basis necessary to carry out the operation."*[2]

*A commercial stereoscopic photograph of an obviously staged trench raid, c. 1917. Two 'tommies' remove epaulettes and insignia from a 'captured' German.*

---

1 *Leicester Daily Post*, 11 January 1915. For further reports and a photograph see also 5, 6 and 7 January 1915.
2 Anthony Saunders Raiding on the Western Front (Barnsley) 2012, p.1

# "Kudos if it succeeds..."

The role of raids and counter raids was really no newer than any other feature of the siege warfare which characterized the Western Front from the end of 1914 onwards. Raiding was no more a novelty than tunnelling or artillery bombardment but it had many attractions for the staffs and commanders of brigades, divisions and corps behind the lines. Raids maintained front-line troops at peak efficiency, gathered intelligence through the capture of prisoners, papers and maps, or even epaulettes from enemy uniforms (which identified the opposing units) and they demonstrated a fancied dominance over the enemy; that the enemy was 'on the defensive' and that no-man's land was 'ours'.

On 19 December 1914 the 2$^{nd}$ Leicesters, supported by a half battalion of Gurkha Rifles and a company of pioneers, were pushed forward in an effort to capture a section of the German front line. To judge from the battalion's war diary, planning and preparation were limited and rudimentary; the diary simply noting *"informed ½ B[attalio]n Gurkha rifles to relieve us at once as the Bn was going to take part in capturing some of the enemy's trenches."*[3]

The war diary's account of the raid, written by Colonel C. G. Blackader [above] who played a key part in it, is vivid and detailed enough to have been reproduced at length in the battalion history.[4] Having crept into no-man's land, where they lay quietly until 3.30 a.m., three companies of the Leicesters were to storm the German trenches behind a bombing party.

*"The bombing party...jumped over the barricade, cut the wire, advanced to the*

---
3 War Diary: 18 December 1914
4 Colonel H. C. Wylly *History of the 1$^{st}$ and 2$^{nd}$ Battalions The Leicestershire Regiment* (Aldershot) 1928, pp. 113-115.

enemy's barricade and bombed it. The left company had barely gone twenty yards when a maxim opened on their right, then twenty more yards and they were stopped by a hedge with barbed wire in the ditch...they got through and immediately a second Maxim opened. The Company then entered the trench under the fire of two Maxims and captured it and the guns."

These were the guns so proudly displayed in Leicester a month later. The attack had achieved some success, though the German defenders of the trench had escaped due to delays in breaking through a hedge and wire, leaving only one man behind. An attempt to advance was halted by machine-gun fire from both flanks and it was decided to consolidate what ground had been taken. Blackader caught up with the leading company soon after its capture of a German support trench:

"...as it could be seen that a main enemy's trench flanked its right, I ordered it to be made into a fire trench as well as to be traversed...It was not long before the enemy started on it with heavy bombs from mortars and bringing a maxim up the trench blew the barricade down. We were steadily pushed back along it, until finally we only held 30 yards of it."

The situation of Blackader's leading company and its accompanying Pioneers steadily worsened. The Germans counter-attacked, threatening to overwhelm the Leicesters' hastily built barricades.

"The conclusion was now being forced on me that unless an attack was initiated on the right and the enemy's trench in that direction held the position was untenable...The retirement was well carried out without loss. Finally, the net profits were 2 Maxim guns, 4 prisoners, and I personally saw 5 dead Germans, but my officers report many more than this wounded and I consider more were killed. One of the killed was an officer, but it was impossible to get to him."

Although frustrated in their effort to retrieve whatever lay in the dead German

## "Kudos if it succeeds…"

officer's pockets, the Leicesters had nevertheless demonstrated an energetic and courageous command of the disputed trenches. The good work of the battalion was noted; the Indian Army Corps commander making special mention of several 'brave Leicester officers and men', including 'Colonel Blackader, who led his battalion and withdrew it skilfully'.[5]

As the techniques of trench raiding developed, their scale generally diminished. Swift, small-scale raids became far more normal rather than major, multi-company affairs with co-ordinated artillery fire and co-operation between units. It was, after all, often easier and far less costly if anything went wrong for an officer and half a dozen men to seize a prisoner or papers.

By 1915, the more enterprising battalions of the B.E.F. were constantly patrolling no-man's land, listening to enemy activity or interrupting work on saps or wire. On 10 April 1915, Private James Richmond, of the 1/4th Leicesters, wrote home to his parents in Thurnby with a description of the new type of warfare;

*"it comes to us to go on a listening patrol, which is as follows: five men and an officer went out at the end of a trench, bent down for a little distance, then get down, and gradually crawled under fire nearer and nearer to the German trenches, to within only a few yards if possible. It's a nervy job…"*[6]

Curiously, another account of, presumably, the same patrol was penned by Private F. W. Preston of the 1/4th Leicesters. He also wrote home to his parents: *"a bit of excitement came my way. I was told off with five others and the sergeant-major to go out on a listening patrol, a bit of a weird job, and only carried out on dark nights when we cannot see what is happening across the other side…we set out from our trench, the S.M. leading. Star shells were frequently sent up, and as soon as you see them go down you have to get as flat as you can, and stay perfectly still, then up again when they die down and*

---
5 Wylly Ibid., p. 115
6 Leicester Daily Post, 16 April 1915.

# Tigers in the Trenches

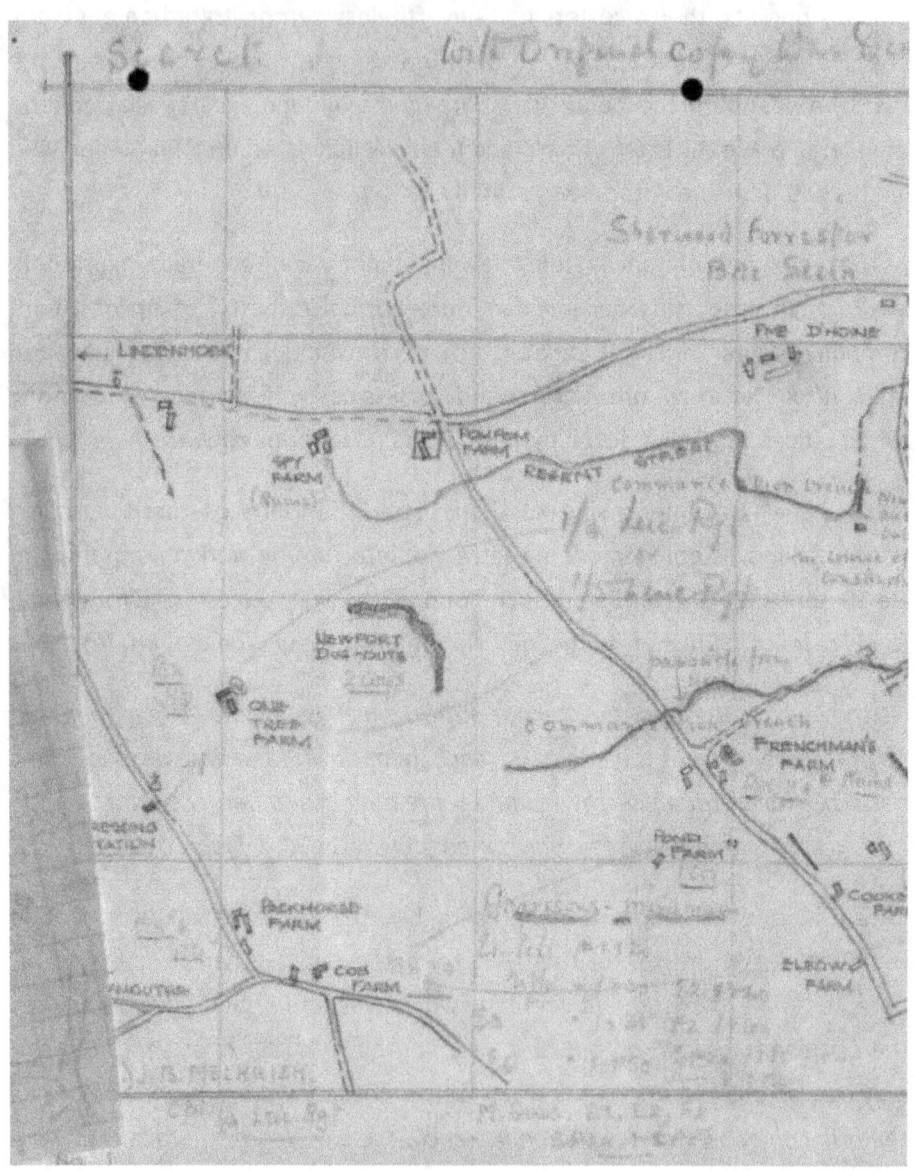

*A map from the War diary of the 1/4th Leicesters, showing the area held by the battalion in April 1915. Trench E1, the scene of the German raid, is directly south of the*

## "Kudos if it succeeds..."

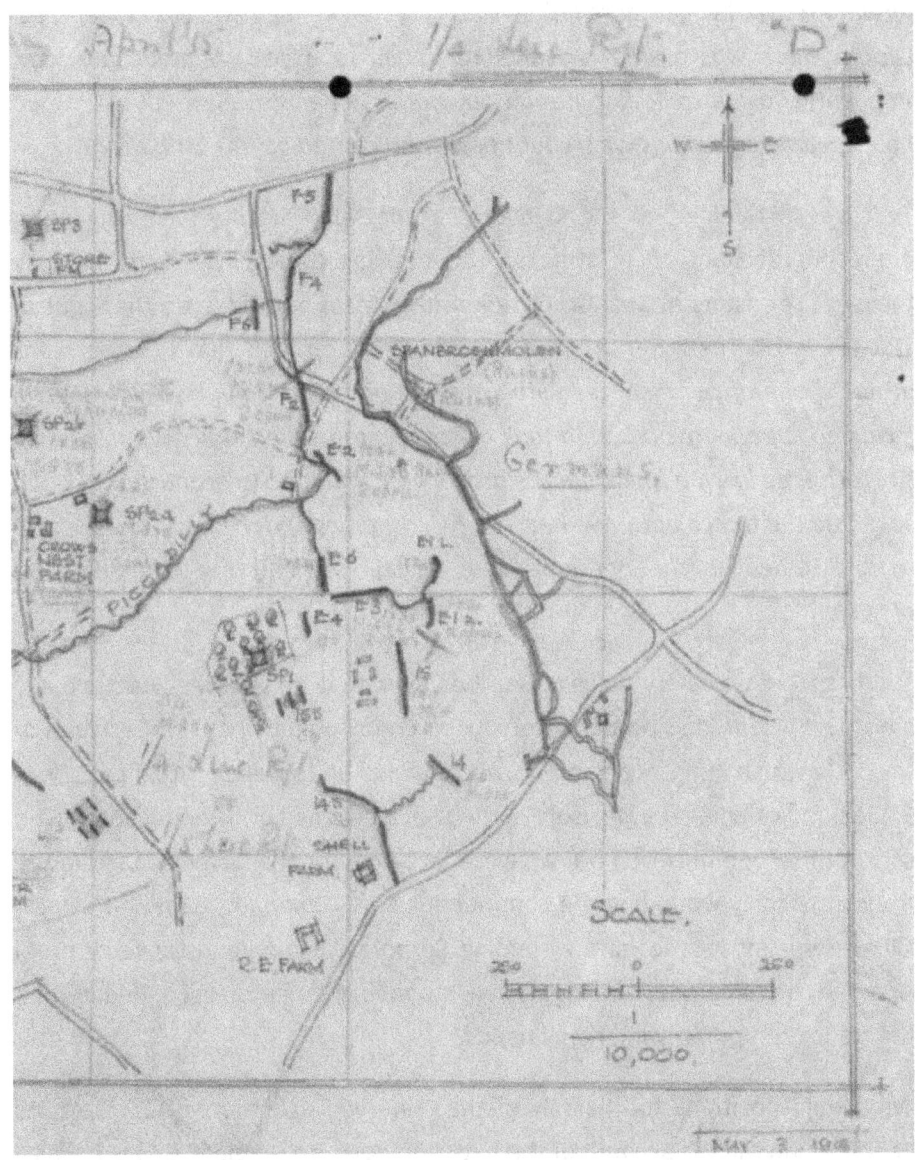

village of SPANBROEKMOLEN (ruins).[National Archives: WO95]

## Tigers in the Trenches

*forward to what cover there happens to be between the two lines of trenches. Luckily, there was a small hastily-dug trench to which we made our way, frequently having to lie flat in mud and water...After staying in all about two hours between the lines we trudges back, and carried on as usual..."[7]*

That trench raiding was by no means a one-sided activity is shown by an interesting account of an attack on an outlying trench, 'E.1. Left', held by the 1/4th Leicesters at Spanbroekmolen near Messines Ridge on the night of 10 May 1915. The letter, from 'a Leicester lad' reported that *"the Germans attacked one of our trenches with bombs soon after midnight, killed several including captain Haylock, and took the trench for a short time. We rushed up support; fired like madmen, got the artillery on, and made a counter-attack and soon had the trench back. We had several casualties and the Germans are said to have 50 dead in front of the trenches, including an officer with half his head blown off."[8]*

The battalion war diary makes clear, however, that this incident was actually a highly efficient (and probably very lucky) trench raid by half a dozen men of the 5th Bavarian Infantry Regiment, who crawled up to trench E.1 Left at about 11.30 p.m.; catching the garrison "somewhat weakened by listening posts, who saw nothing". Some seven bombs were thrown, two of which exploded in the trench, mortally wounding the commander of 'C' Company, Captain Haylock, killing Sergeant Jacques and wounding Corporal Reading and Lance-corporal Goadby. The remainder of the garrison, stunned and demoralised, fled leaving the trench temporarily in enemy hands.

We should not think too harshly of the unnerved defenders of E.1. Left. As Captain John Milne's account of the battalion's war makes clear, E.1. Left was a vile and dangerously exposed hole, characterized by *"gruesomeness...noisome atmosphere and...unutterable filth"*; a position *"built on dead bodies of both*

---
7 Ibid., 26 April 1915.
8 Leicester Daily Post, 14 May 1915

# "Kudos if it succeeds…"

French and British, which had been partially smothered with filth and chloride of lime…about 15 yards in length and about 30 yards from the German lines and slightly below them."[9]

Milne's account of the raid confirms that the body of a German officer, a six foot three giant of a man, was indeed also left behind by the attackers. Captain Milne also notes that the morning's roll-call revealed that one man, whom the war diary identifies as No. 2444 Private Iliffe, a bookbinder from Belgrave in Leicester, was also missing; perhaps seized and carried off by the raiders. The battalion war diary records that he *"was never seen after 11.10 p.m. at which time he was resting in E.1.L. from fatigue."*

Iliffe's surviving service record in fact confirms what was suspected, that despite serious wounds, he was carried back to the German lines for interrogation. He died there that night. On Iliffe's 'Casualty Form', on 20 July 1915, a bold hand recorded *"Extract from a German Document. Wounded & Captured by the 5th Bavarian Regt. Died of wounds in the German Lines 11/5/15."* Arthur Iliffe is remembered on the Menin Gate in Ypres.

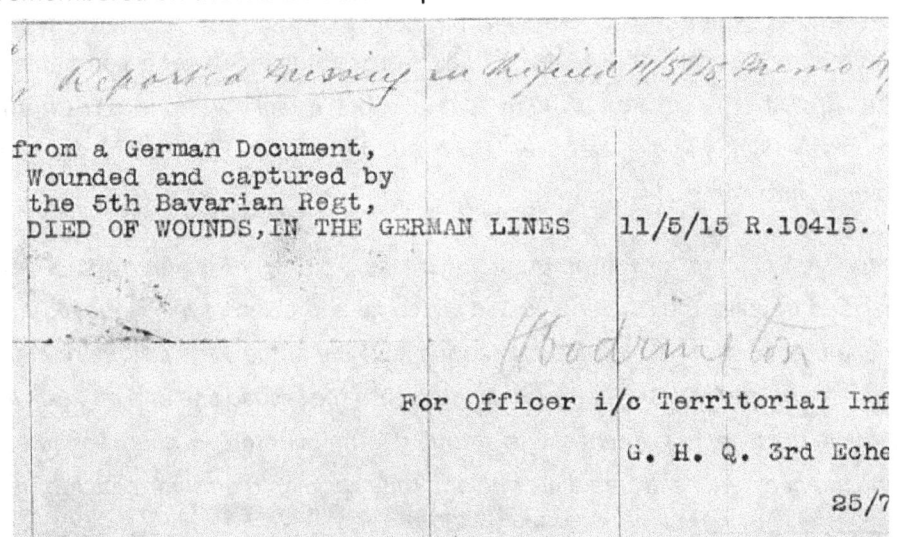

[9] John Milne Footprints of the 1/4th Leicestershire Regiment (Leicester) 1935, p. 25

# Tigers in the Trenches

In a war characterized by innovation, it is hardly surprising that the techniques and methods of trench raiding were subject to constant appraisal and change. What had been a fairly impromptu business early in 1915 had become, by 1916, a matter for careful preparation and coordination.

Indeed, on the eve of the Somme campaign, the 7th Leicesters were experimenting with what their war diary terms a "Minor Enterprise Company consisting of 4 officers – 70 men and 9 R[oyal] E[ngineers]." These men were, according to one of the officers, *"trained very highly and ...as hard as nails."*[10] They had been *"specially selected* [and] *struck off all company duties and fatigues"* for a six week period of intensive training *"in Bayonet fighting, Physical training (including running) and bombing."*[11]

The company was equipped for raiding, mingling trench fighters armed with rifle and bayonet and bombs (hand grenades) with support troops, including six Royal Engineers, with their dug-out destroying torpedoes, ladders, wire, mallets and 'lachrymose' bombs. There were also stretcher bearers and telephonist signallers.

Lieutenant Herbert Tyler MC, the 7th Leicesters' bombing officer accompanied the raid: *"At 4 our smoke started to float over, and it really was one of the most impressive sights I have ever seen. On about a five mile front the line seemed to burst into flame..."*

German S.O.S. rockets prompted a damaging artillery response, so Tyler decided to leave the listening post in which he had taken cover: *"I moved my men out, and struck on a compass bearing, arriving at the German wire right in front of the gap at 4.30...our guns all lifted onto the second line and at 4.30 we were in the trenches. A sentry was standing firing over the parapet...I shouted and jumped, and he dropped his rifle and ran. Our men then swarmed into the*

---
10 Letter of Lieut. H. W. H. Tyler, Leicester Daily Post, 10 July 1916.
11 National Archives WO95/2164/2 War Diary, 7th Battalion The Leicestershire Regiment, 29 June 1916.

## "Kudos if it succeeds..."

trench, keeping in perfect order. P. Clarke's (B) squad went in first, and wheeled to the right, and Mason's (A) to the left, Hollis (C)...cutting across the back...I went down to the left with them, and made a block with wire while we brought over, and 'tear' bombs. Meanwhile B were having a great fight on the right with the bayonet...they killed every Boche in the trench for 50 yards, and then made a block. I sent the R.E. up with their torpedoes, and each dug-out was systematically blown up...At 4.40 things were getting warm. The Boches had started shelling...so I sounded my klaxon for the withdrawal...we counted 30 dead Boche in their lines...and a conservative estimate was 30 killed and buried by the torpedoes..."[12]

The raiders lost one officer, Lieutenant Alan E. G. Mason, died of wounds, and two killed, one of whom was from the Royal Engineers. Three other soldiers were seriously and twenty-five slightly wounded. Only the body of No. 15656 Private Harry Cross, the one 'Tiger' killed, was left behind in the German trench. The battalion diary does not record whether prisoners or intelligence were also brought back.

The trench raid carried out by the 7th Leicesters in June 1916 had been carefully planned; using a specially prepared 'Minor Enterprise Company' and a schedule of training and battle tactics which occupied three pages or more of the battalion's war diary. A year later, on the night of 16-17 August 1917, the 1/5th Leicesters were to carry out a raid which was to occupy the entire battalion in practice attacks and generate a set of instructions so large and meticulous that they occupied eleven closely-typed foolscap pages.

The newly arrived commanding officer of the 1/5th battalion, Lieut-Colonel J.B.O. Trimble M.C. was not a man to leave anything to chance. His operational orders were, according to one of his officers, *"so lucid one could not go wrong"* and the same officer retained a set issued for an attack on a colliery site near Lens as a model for what such orders should be and for eventual deposit in the

12 Ibid.

regimental museum.[13]

The task in hand was a raid by the entire 1/5th Battalion on three hundred yards of the German frontline in front of the devastated mining village of Hulluch, just a few miles south-east of the infamous Hohenzollern Redoubt. Colonel

*A German trench mortar, still in position on Vimy Ridge, 2013.*

Trimble's orders made clear the purpose of the attack, which were to *"secure identifications (as many prisoners as possible)"*, to kill the enemy and destroy his trench system, and to capture or destroy trench mortars and machine-guns. Unofficially, it was agreed that one trench-mortar in particular, nick-named 'the Goose', would be sought out and dealt with. The 'Goose', it seems, had been unusually troublesome during a previous spell in the trenches opposite.[14]

In support of Colonel Trimble's detailed plans, the battalion was also introduced

---
13 Aubrey Moore A Son of the Rectory (Gloucester) 1982, p.138.
14 J D Hills The Fifth Leicestershire (Loughborough) 1919, p. 207

## "Kudos if it succeeds…"

to a careful reconstruction of the ground to be attacked, which had been laid out at Hesdigneul-lés-Bethune, about ten miles west of the front-lines. The Leicesters were to spend almost every day and some nights too, for over a week attacking across the flagged course. As Captain J. D. Hills recalled, the *"course was set out very elaborately…not only was each trench shown, but small notice boards denoted the position of every supposed machine gun, trench mortar, or deep dug-out…The position of Hulluch village was indicated on the practice ground by a large notice board – HULLUCH – which probably gave any spies there might be in Hesdigneul a vary fair idea of what was intended."*[15]

*Australian troops study a model of Messines Ridge, prior to their attack in 1917. Similar models were constructed across the Western Front and even for training at home.*

---
15 Ibid., pp.208-209.

# Tigers in the Trenches

Aubrey Moore, commanding the 1/5th Battalion's 'C' Company, noted that *"the position of 'Goose' was clearly shown"*, adding sourly, *"and just to make sure everyone should know a large board with the word HULLUCH in about two foot letters was planted. Short of advertising in the German press, we could not have had better publicity. The fact that the Boche could take air photographs as well or better than us did not seem to occur or was forgotten. We practised until we knew the way blindfold..."*[16]

In addition to the 'flagged course', the 5th Leicesters were also put through rigorous physical drill and training in bayonet fighting, bombing, musketry and use of the Lewis Gun – for those not already in machine-gun teams. Time was also found for games and, perhaps most appreciated, baths and disinfection of clothing.

On 14 August the battalion travelled by 'bus to Noyelles, where final preparations for the raid were made. Bombs and flashlights were issued and each man handed in his pay book, badges, identity disks and personal kit; *"no names, numerals, letters, correspondence, or identity discs or any article that might give the enemy an identification"* as Colonel Trimble's *Raid Orders* made clear. In return small round cardboard disks, each bearing an identifying number, were issued, to be handed in on returning from the raid.

The following morning the battalion moved up into the front-line. The journey was not without incident, as an enemy shell, intended for artillery batteries west of Vermelles exploded beside 'B' Company as it passed the Mansion House supply dump. Caught in a column of fours, the company was devastated, with eleven killed and fourteen wounded. One of those killed was No. 240850 Private Frederick Chambers, a thirty-year-old ironstone quarryman, who had been a lodger in Cottesmore, Rutland, until his enlistment in November 1914. According to Captain J. D. Hills 'Freddie' Chambers was the *"self appointed Company humorist, and one of the best known and most cheerful soldiers in*

16 Aubrey Moore Ibid., pp.138-9.

# "Kudos if it succeeds…"

*the Battalion."*[17]

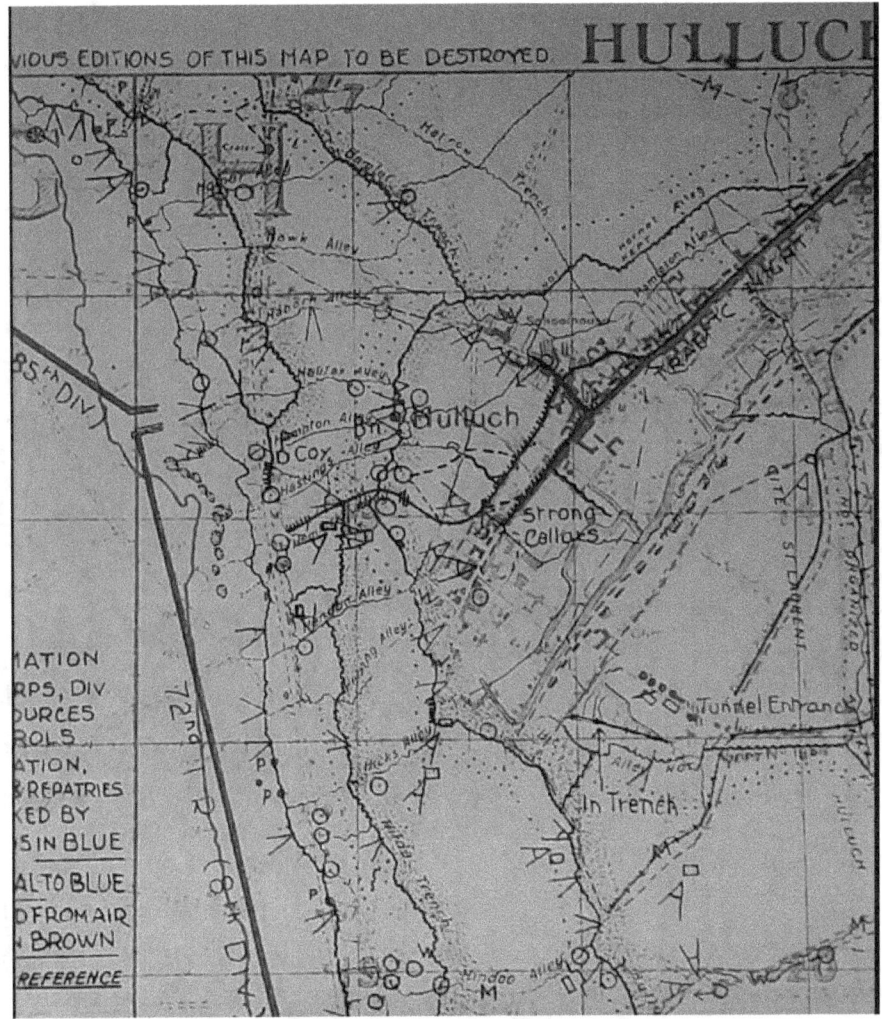

*Trench map of the area raided between Hendon and Hicks Alleys at Hulloch in August 1917. The tunnel is shown, as are machine-gun positions (hairpins or 'A's) and supposed trench mortars (dotted 'O's).*

Bad luck dogged the battalion as it arrived in the front-line. Squeezed into 10th Avenue and Lone Trench, from the raid was to be launched, and presumably

[17] J D Hills Ibid., p. 211.

blackening their faces in preparation (another stipulation of Lieutenant-Colonel Trimble) the Leicesters were then informed that the attack was 'off', postponed for twenty-four hours. Second-Lieutenant Brooke, a skilled and respected patroller of no-man's land, had reported that the German wire was *"not properly cut"*.[18]

*A view of the Hulloch area taken in 2017, a century after the raid.*

Sadly, the delay, whilst it afforded the artillery the necessary time to cut the vital lanes through the German wire, meant that the raid would no longer coincide with a Canadian attack on the nearby Hill 70. Instead, the Leicesters were afforded a grandstand view of the assault and, later, for the battalion machine-gunners to open fire themselves on the resulting German counter-attack.

That night, Lieutenant Brooke was out in no-man's land again, marking the gaps which had been made through the British wire and at 1p.m. on 16 August the artillery again tried, with greater success, to cut lanes in the enemy's.

18 1/5th Battalion War Diary: 15 August 1917.

# "Kudos if it succeeds..."

During the afternoon both the divisional and brigade commanders visited the front-line and to confer with Colonel Trimble; the decision finally being made to go ahead with the raid. Only one modification was made to the planning, as a result of the imperfect wire-cutting, that the attack would be made in small columns rather than waves as had been practised.

At 10.54 p.m., the assault companies, 'A' and 'D', began to thread, or 'dribble' (as their Raid Orders had it) through the gaps in the British wire. At 10.58 p.m., a barrage began from British field guns, and the assault began. The German wire was found to be *"very much damaged (except on the extreme left and extreme right) and little difficulty was found in passing through it"*[19]. They were followed first by 'B' Company in support and then 'C' Company, as 'moppers-up'. Both companies crossed the front-line trench by 'assault footboards' and sped on to the German lines.

The Raid Orders specified what equipment was taken. Officers were dressed as Other Ranks, armed with revolver (a rifle and bayonet was 'optional') and two Mills bombs, but also carrying an electric torch, an aeroplane flare, and responsible for Verey pistols with S.O.S. flares. Behind them came N.C.O.s and riflemen with rifle and bayonet and fifty rounds of ammunition, some N.C.O.s also carrying torches. There were also two Lewis gun teams *per* company (except the 'moppers-up') with fifty rounds small arms ammunition, two grenades and eight drum magazines each.

The Bombing teams were similarly armed and equipped, though the bomb throwers carried only fourteen Mills Bombs and, exotically, a *knobkerry* or club, probably made from an entrenching tool handle topped with iron. Shovels were also provided, while specially designated 'destruction parties' also carried Stokes Mortar shells and explosive charges to blow in enemy dugouts.

The Raid Orders also made clear arrangements for any soldier wounded in the

---
19 Report on the Raid – War Diary (August 1917) Appendices, p. 20

# Tigers in the Trenches

attack. A full page specified the disposition of stretcher bearers, who were divided between the attacking companies and the Regimental Aid Post, which would advance with the battalion to a tunnel off Hay Alley trench. Walking wounded were to be directed there, while a chain of stretcher bearers would operate from the captured German trenches back to the British front-line. Further evacuation was either to Advanced Dressing Stations at Philosophe or Vermelles.

*American artist Cyrus Cuneo's reconstruction of a trench raid: "British soldiers take an enemy trench".*

# "Kudos if it succeeds…"

Within a few minutes, the first of the 'Tigers' were in the German front-line, shouting to signal their arrival. As expected, the German front-line defences were in depth; lightly held at first but the resistance increasing the deeper the attackers went. Some defenders were judged to have withdrawn when *thermite*[20] explosives were projected over the area to be attacked, its golden 'rain' both alarming and warning the Germans.

*"Two enemy were found and killed, but much of the trench was full of wire. The attackers passed on rapidly to the second and third lines, finding the wire thicker in front of each line, but finally reaching their objective and building bombing blocks…mopping up and demolition continued behind the attack. Several Germans were found and killed in the second line, but on the whole very few enemy were seen…"*[21]

There was confusion and possibly some defenders escaped into tunnels. As Captain Hills observed, *"in the dark it was quite impossible to tell what was a tunnel entrance and what merely a dug-out".*[22] No doubt both were blown in by the destruction parties, Corporal Tunks and Private Baker distinguishing themselves in their destructiveness. A party led by 2/Lieutenant John Scott Plummer also set off in search of the 'Goose' trench mortar.

Only a few minutes into 17 August, the decision was made to complete the demolitions and withdraw. As ill luck would have it, the special flares brought for the purpose failed to ignite and, as German resistance strengthened into a counter-attack, runners had to be sent to bring the troops back. Lewis guns held back an assault over open ground to the left, while a strong push up Hicks Alley trench was just contained with much use of hand grenades on both sides of a hastily erected barrier.

---

20 Thermite is an explosive made from iron oxide and a metal powder – usually aluminium. The Raid Orders noted (in Amendment 5) that "the special company R.E. will project Thermite into the northern part of HULLUCH. This thermite appears in the air like golden rain. All ranks should be warned."
21 J D Hills Ibid., pp. 212-13
22 Ibid., p. 213

# Tigers in the Trenches

As the raiders returned, their withdrawal covered by the Support Company and a barrage from four heavy machine guns, the troops made their way towards red lamps, raised above the British trenches on poles. Three posts were set up at the junctions of the front-line and communication trenches to receive the numbered discs from returning raiders. The battalion trench raid on Hulluch was over.

At 9.30 a.m., Major General William Thwaites, commanding the 46th Division, addressed the battalion. They had worked well and fought bravely but, as the battalion War Diary noted, he also *"emphasised the importance of getting identifications."*

In Captain Hills's estimation *"the raid had not been a success... We brought no prisoners and no identifications, though one man had brought back a rifle and some papers from a dug-out. Several of the enemy had undoubtedly been killed, but no one had thought to cut off shoulder straps or search for pay books...We lost Captain Marriott, 2nd Lieut. Plumer, and seven men missing, whom we never heard of again. Three more men were known to be killed, and three others were afterwards reported prisoners, while no less than fifty-one were wounded."*[23]

The fate of 2/Lieutenant Plummer and the seven men who set off after the 'Goose' is not known. Although he appears in Captain Hills's book as 'Plumer', it is clear that the second-lieutenant was John Scott Plummer, a thirty-five year-old Londoner, who had enlisted in the 6th Dragoons before receiving a temporary commission and being attached to the 1/5th Leicesters. Plummer was Secretary to an electrical manufacturer (according to the 1911 Census) unmarried, and living with his widowed mother, Mary Ann, and several brothers and sisters. Mary Ann Plummer later received a pension, from her son's death, of £40 *per annum*.

---

23 Ibid., p. 214

# "Kudos if it succeeds..."

Within a few days the 1/5th Leicesters were back in the line, having spent the afternoon of General Thwaites's inspection, checking kit and bathing and the following three days in vigorous physical training or fatigues. The battalion, described as *"in great fettle"* before the attack, seemed undaunted by the experience – despite its apparent failure.[24]

The last words will go to a participant, Captain Aubrey Moore, whose admiration for his commanding officer's careful planning we have already noted. Moore felt the idea for the raid, to eliminate the 'Goose', had originated with *"somebody high up and well back"* and had not served any useful purpose.

*"We had a lot of casualties. We never knew if 'Goose' was destroyed. If it was it was soon replaced, which should have been obvious from the first. The demolition party was never seen or heard of again…I have written more than I intended about this action, but it is a prime example of the sort of thing going on up and down the whole line in the guise of harassing the Boche or an attempt at one upmanship by the higher up. Kudos if it succeeds, silence if it does not, but a hell of a lot of casualties either way. 'Goose' could have gone on firing at us for the rest of the war and would not have caused a tenth of the casualties the attempt at elimination caused…"*[25]

---

24 War Diary: 16 August 1917.
25 Aubrey Moore Ibid., pp.138-9.

## Chapter Eleven

## *"The Flood-Breakers"*

## The Leicestershire Regiment and the Kaiser's Battle, March 1918

As the Great War entered its fourth year none of the belligerent powers could have considered victory in sight, let alone within grasp. Russia was in a state of Revolution. The French Army having fought itself into a state of mutinous near collapse in 1917, was barely able to contemplate more than limited, minor operations. The British, too, having suffered perhaps as many as 350,000 casualties attacking Passchendaele, were forced to remain on the defensive, while a bitter political battle raged at home between the Prime Minister, Lloyd George, and supporters of General Haig.[1] Both British and French gazed ever hopefully westwards for signs of the American Expeditionary Force.

Germany's allies of the Central Powers were also eager for an end to the war, with Bulgaria overstretched in Macedonia and both Turkey and the Austro-Hungarians exploring avenues for peace. Germany, blockaded by the Royal Navy and increasingly isolated, was starved both of food and the raw materials for war.

The Germans were therefore presented at the beginning of 1918 with both an urgent need and an unprecedented opportunity. The need was to defeat the British and French before the arrival of fresh American troops tilted the balance of war irretrievably against them. The opportunity was peace with Bolshevik Russia, with an armistice in December 1917

---

1. See Denis Winter Haig's Command (Barnsley) 2004, pp.174-177, 180-182. It is clear that neither Haig nor Lloyd George were above mendacious duplicity; Haig exploiting political connections ruthlessly and manipulating casualty figures, while Lloyd George explored implausible alternative theatres of war and possibly deliberately starved the BEF of reinforcements in an effort to curb what he considered excessive casualty figures. In the end Haig survived but under vague French direction, or 'coordination' by General Ferdinand Foch.

# "The Flood-Breakers"

followed by the peace treaty of Brest Litovsk at the beginning of March 1918, which suddenly released fifty fresh divisions for a final attempt to smash through the weakened Allied line before it could be strengthened by the Americans.

The resulting *Kaiserschlacht* or Kaiser's Battle, planned by Erich Ludendorff [left], the First Quartermaster-General of the German Army, was a succession of offensives intended to overwhelm the British Fifth Army (and part of the Third Army) and drive on to cut the B.E.F. off from their French allies and supply bases on the Channel coast.

The point of attack, across the old Somme battlefields, was well chosen; the Fifth Army was under-strength and had only just taken over a sector poorly fortified by the French. Plans were made for a defence in depth but although marked out on the ground, half of the second line of trenches and almost all the third, remained undug. It also seems clear that the Army commander, Hubert Gough, was expected to make a fighting withdrawal if attacked and that his Army was to delay, or absorb, rather than repulse the enemy.

Gough's reputation with rank and file, after Passchendaele, was as a careless, callous 'butcher' and, as Martin Middlebrook observed in his study of the *Kaiserschlacht*, "he had narrowly escaped being returned to England as a failure and he was certainly not in the best of favour with the commander-in-chief who, as a matter of deliberate policy, regarded the Fifth Army's front as expendable and of least priority if the Germans attacked."[2]

---

2 Martin Middlebrook The Kaiser's Battle (London) 1978, p.105

# Tigers in the Trenches

The first German offensive, *Operation Michael,* began at 4.40am on 21 March with a five hour bombardment. High explosive shells sought out British artillery and machine gun positions, while gas mingled with the smoke and mist to hamper counter-battery fire. At 9.40 the shelling ceased and dense waves of storm troops and pioneers, concealed by thick fog, smashed through the devastated British lines. On a fifty mile front the Germans pushed deep into the British defences. Few isolated pockets of resistance remained – elsewhere companies and battalions were either cut off and surrendered or found themselves isolated and forced to withdraw.

The experience of the Leicestershire Regiment's 1st Battalion was typical. Despite half the battalion having spent the night with working parties, including a five mile march there and back, orders were received to advance two companies ('C' and 'D') to a trench line (the Lagnicourt Switch) which skirted the village of Lagnicourt to the south west. German troops had been seen amongst the ruins of Lagnicourt and as the Switch trench was not manned it was feared that the brigade would be outflanked. [See map opposite].

The situation swiftly became more confused and more desperate. Aided by fog and the undulating landscape, bands of Germans had already infiltrated the British defences – which were, in any case, often scarcely more than shallow scrapes. Private George Leedham saw one party of the enemy emerge from the mist: *"About eighty yards away there was a loose bunch of sixty to eighty Germans advancing towards us. I noticed they were big blokes and that they all had new uniforms…they advanced steadily but with the caution of seasoned troops, with the exception of a few eager ones who were brought down first. We managed to get them down on the ground after about thirty yards, well out of 'tater-masher'[hand-grenade] range…I didn't want to die but I thought we were going to…"*[3]

At some time during the morning the Germans broke through between Morchies and the Bois de Vaulx. A platoon of the Leicesters' 'A' Company, occupying a strongpoint at a crossroads in the valley was *"practically*

---
3 No. 17778 Private George Harry Leedham, 1st Leicesters, quoted in Martin Middlebrook Ibid., p.188

# "The Flood-Breakers"

# Tigers in the Trenches

wiped out"; news of the loss not reaching the battalion headquarters until after 8p.m.

By the early afternoon 'B' Company, with the battalion Headquarters, had dug in west of Lagnicourt, to cover the left flank of their comrades in 'C' and 'D' Companies. They drove back a few Germans but found themselves, somewhat alarmingly, under machine-gun fire from the Bois de Vaulx in their rear. Slowly a defensive line along the trackway from Vaulx to Morchies was established with isolated units, from the 2nd South Lancashires, 11th Leicesters and some Royal Engineers all arriving and working feverishly to turn marked-out positions into reality.

"The trench", according to the 1st Leicesters' History, *"was held in greater strength on the left than on the right, but any attempt to equalize matters and distribute the defenders better was fraught with difficulty, owing to the trench here not being continuous, while the many gaps to be crossed were swept by machine-gun fire and marked down by German snipers; also touch could not be obtained with the troops on the right of the Lagnicourt-Maricourt Wood road, since for some distance there was no trench line at all."*[4]

Night brought a lull in the fighting and rations reached the intermingled units of the 71st Infantry Brigade, still clinging to their makeshift defensive line from Vaulx-Vraucourt to Morchies. A roll call of the 1st Leicesters revealed a shocking picture; the battalion having been reduced to 13 officers and 299 men. An attempt to shuffle the units in the firing line, to reunite the Leicesters' 'B' Company with the rest of the battalion also failed when the intervening unit of the South Lancashires declined to move without orders.

Dawn on 22 March brought more fog (the British wire was *"only indistinctly seen"*[5]) and a heavy bombardment from German artillery. Enemy infantry attacked at about 7.30 a.m. but were driven off by the rifles and machine-guns of the Leicesters' 'A' and 'D' Companies. Further attempts were made to cut through the wire and snipers, who settled

---
4 Col H. C. Wylly History of the 1st and 2nd Battalions The Leicestershire Regiment (Aldershot) 1928, p.65
5 War Diary 22nd March, 7.30 a.m.

## "The Flood-Breakers"

at the edge of the wire, caused many casualties and could not be driven back for a lack of stokes mortars and rifle grenades.

At 11.40 a.m., Germans were seen to be massing for another assault in the valley to the east of the Bois de Vaulx; the officer commanding 'C' Company of the 11th Leicesters reporting that he had only thirty-seven men left and that the enemy were in the wood behind his left flank.

*A contemporary periodical's view of the retreat.*

By 3.45p.m., the enemy were *"pouring into the Vaulx-Morchies Line".* [6] The *"breach by this time was effective and the situation was becoming very grave. The withdrawal became somewhat disorderly and the enemy came rapidly through...up to this time only 1 man (wounded, belonging to 'B' Co[mpan]y) of the Battalion, had come back from VAULX- MORCHIES Line."*

The 'disorderly' withdrawal is hardly surprising, given that the Leicesters were, by this time effectively pinned down in their shallow trench. A lack of grenades hampered attempts to block the trench against the advancing enemy and heavy machine-gun fire on all sides made it *"impossible to send any men out of the trench to form any sort of defensive flank..."* and though *"a strong attack developed from the front...as soon as the men lined the parapet they were shot down by M.G. bullets from the rear."*

*Another view of the withdrawal, showing French and British troops mingling in the rapid retreat.*

Late on the afternoon of 22 March a number of tanks (the 1st Leicesters counted sixteen) made an attack up to the Vaulx – Morchies line, driving back the German infantry but bringing down a furious response from enemy artillery and machine-guns. Those tanks not disabled or destroyed eventually withdrew when their ammunition was exhausted, leaving the surviving sections of trench held by a pitifully small remnant of the brigade clustered around its battalion headquarters.[7] A planned counter-attack by the 9th Norfolks and 2nd Sherwood Foresters, also of the 71st Brigade, was abandoned when it was realised how weak in

[7] The 1st Leicesters' war diary records "about 40 all ranks under Lt. Col. F Latham...9th Norfolks about 80 all ranks...2nd Sherwood Foresters about 40 all ranks..."

# "The Flood-Breakers"

numbers those battalions were.[8]

Inevitably, the Leicesters were forced to abandon their trench when it became clear that the German attack had come within a hundred and fifty yards of their sole remaining escape route, into the village of Morchies. The few survivors of the German assault emerged into a hail of machine-gun fire, soon supplemented by 4.2 inch howitzer shells. They took shelter in shell holes, hidden from the enemy at the bottom of a valley between Morchies and Beugny.

The night, mercifully, passed quietly and at 4 a.m. on 23 March 1918, the battalion, such as it was, was relieved. In two days the $1^{st}$ Leicesters had lost six officers and 30 Other Ranks killed, 6 officers and 112 O.R.s wounded, and 8 officers and 316 O.R.s missing. The preponderance of 'missing' rather than killed or wounded clearly indicates the confusion of a fighting withdrawal.

The experience of the $1^{st}$ Leicesters was replicated, with local differences, all along the Forward Zone of the Fifth Army and much of the Third Army's too. As Martin Middlebrook's admirable study of the battle notes: *"The German success in sweeping away the British front-line defences so completely and over such a long stretch of front was a unique achievement by First World War standards...There had been no initial success like this in any other battle on the Western front since the trench lines had been formed..."*[9]

There are, however, always exceptions. One such was the village of Epéhy, half way between Cambrai and Saint Quentin. Epéhy is a small community, incorporating the hamlet of Pezières, which occupies a low ridge, surrounded on all sides by gently sloping valleys. In March 1918 Epéhy was slowly being transformed into a strongpoint by the $110^{th}$ (Leicester) Brigade; two battalions holding Epéhy and Pezières and the other in reserve a couple of miles across the fields at Saulcourt.[10] As

---
8 Col. H. C. Wylly *The Sherwood Foresters in the Great War* (Aldershot) 1926, p. 164.
9 Martin Middlebrook Ibid., p. 203
10 Due to shortages of manpower, brigades in the B.E.F. had been reduced from three to four battalions, the $9^{th}$ Leicesters having been disbanded in February and its men distributed amongst the $6^{th}$, $7^{th}$ and $8^{th}$ Battalions.

# Tigers in the Trenches

Lieutenant E. G. Lane Roberts of the 6th Leicesters recalled, *"the village was of great importance, being on high ground & the capture of it by the enemy would give them observation over several miles of country."*[11]

Epéhy itself had largely been destroyed (particularly by the retreating Germans the year before) but it was defended by three lines of trenches, densely wired, and a series of small, isolated posts or strongpoints, most created from the cellars amongst the ruins. Trouble had been taken to embed telephone cables an almost shell-proof six feet underground and a new line of trenches to the west of the village, the 'Yellow Line', created for all-round defence.[12] The gentle slopes around the village gave an excellent field of fire (at least when not obstructed by fog) and the three Leicestershire battalions knew their business well.

The massive bombardment which opened *Operation Michael* fell just as heavily upon the Epéhy sector. The German shelling, a mixture of high explosive and gas, hit the entire 110th Brigade front, targeting the front line, artillery positions as well as support areas. D. A. Bacon, probably at the brigade headquarters, noted that *"Saulcourt...had been blown up – horse lines demolished – great holes gaped on the roads – and dead replaced the living. The noise denied comments, and the air was darkened and poisoned with Shells, Gas, Powder, Earth and Bricks...All roads and tracks, the junctions especially, had been 'taped'...before 7-0 a.m., the road from Longavesnes to Saulcourt was thickly sprinkled with overturned and demolished wagons, in many cases still attached to the dead drivers and animals."*[13]

The Germans' decision to dilute their fire over so wide an area may have helped the defenders of Epéhy-Pezières. Middlebrook also credits the divisional commander, Major-General Campbell with a wise order to abandon the forward trenches upon which much of the bombardment fell.[14] Nevertheless, the defenders of the hill-top village were bounced from sleep at about 4.30 a.m., to find themselves engulfed in what

---

11 E. G. Lane Roberts *How I was captured* ROLLR: P170/7
12 D. V. Kelly *39 Months with the Tigers* (London) 1930, p.96.
13 D. A. Bacon *History of the 110th The Leicestershire Brigade* ROLLR: 22D63/146
14 Martin Middlebrook *Ibid.,* p. 198

# "The Flood-Breakers"

Captain D. V. Kelly remembered as *"an all-pervading pandemonium"*.[15]

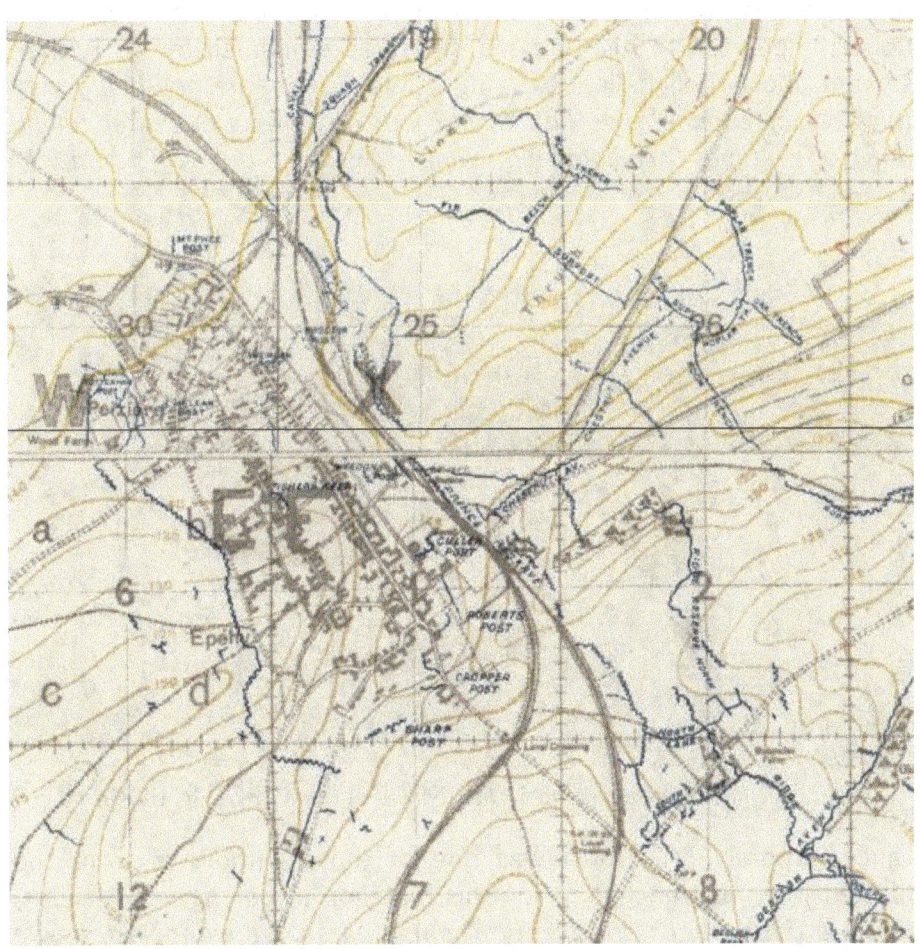

*A composite trench map showing positions held by the 7th and 8th Leicesters.*

The three Leicestershire battalions went immediately to 'Battle Positions', to await the inevitable infantry assault. Thick fog blanketed the ground in front of Epéhy and even after 6 a.m., with daylight, *"it was quite impossible to see the wire in front of the trenches on account of the thickness of the mist"*.[16] The mingling of gas, both phosgene and

---
15 D. V. Kelly *Ibid*.
16 War Diary 8th Leicesters

mustard, amongst the enemy shells also necessitated the wearing of box respirators, which hampered observation even more. Lieutenant Lane Roberts departed to his 'Battle position' accompanied by his runner, servant and two signallers carrying a telephone: *"the gas being very thick & objectionable we had to don our gas-masks but after falling down a few times & colliding with walls etc we took them off again..."*[17]

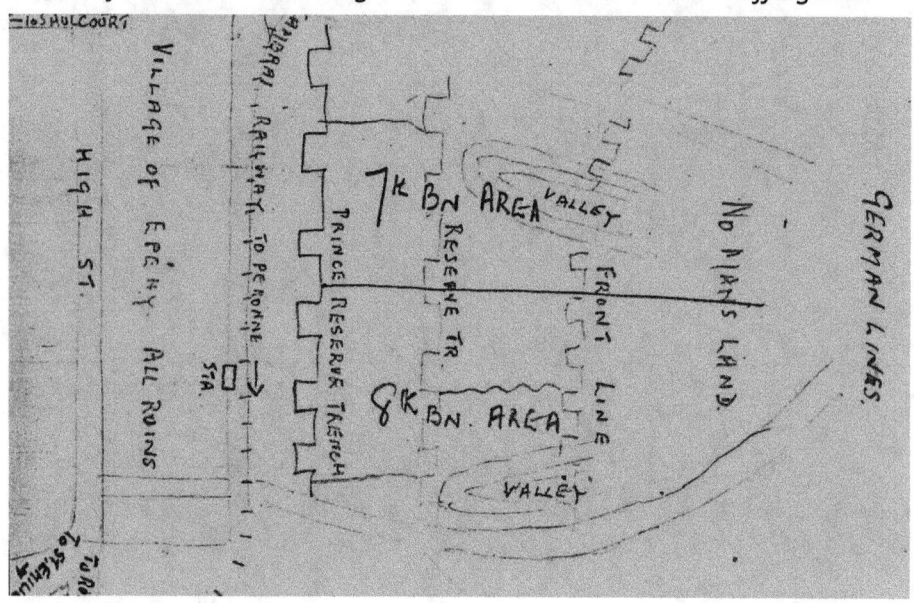

*Lieut Lane Roberts' sketch map of the trenches at Epehy* [ROLLR: P170/7]

Lance-corporal S. T. North was one of those withdrawn from the blasted forward trenches to join his battalion in defence of Pezières: *"With a good trench and plenty of ammunition, we wondered, as we peered into the fog, what lay ahead. We hadn't long to wait. The fog became less dense, the sun broke through and almost at once the fog cleared, revealing an amazing sight. The foremost of the enemy infantry, completely disorganised by the fog, were trying to get sorted out. Not far behind then came several platoons of infantry, moving in sold blocks, four men abreast. Behind them were groups of cavalry...wagons and horse drawn ambulances...The Germans were moving forward as if they expected no opposition. We opened fire. The Lewis guns got busy and*

---
17 E. G. Lane Roberts *Ibid.*, p.26

## "The Flood-Breakers"

*the enemy groups scattered. They had very little cover and no chance of survival.*[18]

Lance-corporal North and his comrades were fortunate that morning. The German attack had been delayed by their own gas and the fog, possibly because of Epéhy's hill-top position, had cleared sooner than in surrounding areas.

From mid-morning Epéhy was subject to unremitting German attacks. Infantry massed on the surrounding slopes and attacked like waves crashing onto a beach. Each attack was driven back, leaving the slopes around Epéhy and Pezières littered with dead, though on both flanks the Leicesters observed the Germans breaking through into open country.

*View from the junction of the 7th and 8th Battalions' positions, looking across the site of the British Princes Reserve, reserve and front-line trenches, from what is now the Rue du Combat. The excellent field of fire over the gently sloping ground is obvious.*

At some time between 10 and 11 a.m. (eyewitness accounts varying) a strong party of Germans worked their way up the railway embankment skirting the northern edge of Pezières and seized Mc Phee Post, an isolated strongpoint there, taking the surviving half dozen defenders prisoner. The 7th Battalion's reserve company, 'C', which had been held back for just such an eventuality, with the support of two tanks, swiftly retook McPhee however, clearing Pezières and rescuing one of the

18 Quoted in Martin Middlebrook *Ibid.,* p. 199. No. 16626 L/cpl Sydney Trueman North, a fitter from Quorn in Leicestershire, had enlisted in January 1915, serving with the 1st Leicesters until 22 March 1917, when he was transferred to the 7th Battalion.

prisoners. 'C' company and the tanks then retired, to sally out again and again as the defensive lines were threatened.

*Lewis gunners of the Royal Scots in June 1918 [IWM Q6776]*

Some time after 3 p.m., the 6$^{th}$ Battalion (which had moved up from Saulcourt) observed the retirement of troops of the neighbouring 16$^{th}$ Division and the hasty retirement of a 6 inch howitzer battery from a position on the road from Epéhy to St Emilie. Three of the guns escaped, the gunners abandoning one. In Pezières, Second-lieutenant Wright and about 20 men held Fir Support Trench all day, against increasingly fierce Germans attacks. The battalion War Diary noted *"flammenwerfers were used but these were stopped on our wire by rifle fire and the cylinders catching alight the enemy were burnt with their own weapons. Good work was done by the whole of this platoon and particularly by Pte HICKIN who on 2 or 3 occasions walked along the parapet firing a Lewis Gun from his hip at the enemy concentrating in the trenches on the*

# "The Flood-Breakers"

flanks. Pte HICKIN was eventually killed in making one of those attacks. This platoon held out until dark when with only 6 men left it was ordered to fall back."

Slowly, the hill-top villages were becoming cut off from their neighbouring divisions. *"Heavy and accurate"* trench mortar fire drove the 8$^{th}$ Leicesters back and between 6 and 8 p.m. there was another bitter struggle for control of Pezières, the two tanks once again rolling through the ruined village in support of four platoons from 'C' company. The enemy were driven back and four dazed Germans from the 123 Grenadier Regiment sent back as prisoners.[19]

As darkness fell, two Royal Engineers Field companies arrived from Brigade Support to join the 6$^{th}$ Leicesters to strengthen and extend the defences south of Epéhy. A company of the 1st East Yorks and three Vickers heavy machine-gun teams who were also sent forward were unable to get through the enemy artillery barrage. While infantry attacks slackened with the growing darkness, eventually ceasing altogether, German artillery remained active, shelling the rear approaches to the village and moving up more guns to batter Epéhy from the south.

The noose was tightening around the hilltop villages. Some time between 4 and 6 a.m. the following morning the German artillery opened fire again and continued for over an hour; deluging Pezières and the northern part of Epéhy with shells. At about 9 a.m., covered by the fire of their guns and a heavy mist, German infantry pushed across the road to St Emilie (south-east of Epéhy) and overwhelmed three posts held by the Leicesters on that edge of the village. Lieut-Colonel W. N. Stewart, commanding the 6$^{th}$ Leicesters, was shot in the head and killed instantly by a sniper.[20]

The fighting was fierce and bitter. Lieutenant Lane Roberts, of the same battalion, was still occupying a ruined house behind the devastated Epéhy

---

19 The 7$^{th}$ Battalion's War Diary states that five prisoners were sent but the surviving message (attached) from Lieutenant H. R. Horne is clear enough: "Herewith 4 prisoners 123 Grenadier Regt. Captured in PROCTOR POST 8 p.m. when our counter attack Coy. Moved up a second time." D. A. Bacon records that members of five different regiments were captured by the Leicesters at Epéhy.
20 6$^{th}$ Battalion War Diary. Major J. C. Burdett assumed command.

cemetery. Having taken a turn around his company's outposts, he was dismayed to be driven to take cover by machine-gun fire from the rear of the position and then to see two Germans entering his headquarters:

*I fired a shot [at] one of them & the other turned and jumped into the trench grasping me as he did so. His rifle fell & we started to struggle in the trench. He was heavily equipped & handicapped by being packed up ready for Paris. 4 times I managed to get my revolver into such a position to shoot him but none of the bullets exploded. Finally at the 5<sup>th</sup> attempt my big burly opponent dropped with a bullet through his heart...Hearing shots my Sergeant Major came along...He was immediately shot down & fell in the trench. A sergeant further along met the same fate. Some few minutes later I saw there were Germans in the cemetery..."*[21]

Lane-Roberts led his men in clearing the cemetery and then worked backwards to deal with yet more Germans infiltrating the position behind him. As the *Official History* noted, quoting the German XXXIX Corps's reports of the day's fighting: there was *"lively resistance especially at Epéhy, which often took the shape of counter-attacks".*[22]

By 11 a.m., the 110<sup>th</sup> brigade was in danger of being cut off, as large numbers of German infantry were fighting their way into the village from the south and others seen massing in dead ground to the west of Epéhy. A brief foray by the two supporting tanks drove the enemy back but they were themselves then "knocked out" on their way back to Saulcourt for more fuel and running repairs.[23]

At the same time orders had been received for the Leicesters to withdraw and to retire firstly on Saulcourt and then Longavesnes. It took nearly an hour for the message to reach every outpost but it was not a moment too soon. While the 8<sup>th</sup> battalion fought on in Epéhy, the 7<sup>th</sup> Leicesters were in danger of being cut off in Pezières, as their War Diary noted:

*"The withdrawal of the Bn. and the extrication of the posts in PEIZIERE was a matter of some difficulty as by the time of the receipt of the order*

---

21 E. G. Lane Roberts *Ibid.*, pp. 29-30.
22 *History of the Great War: Military Operations France and Belgium I, 1918* p.261
23 7<sup>th</sup> Battalion War Diary: 22 March 11a.m.

## "The Flood-Breakers"

*by the Coys. the enemy was in occupation of EPEHY and firing in from the N. The withdrawal was made under heavy M.G. fire from the S.E. and N.E. and a considerable number of casualties were incurred."*

*British infantry on the move, March 1918 [IWM Q8619]*

The fighting withdrawal continued, the brigade still being able to halt and deter close pursuit. More might have been done but German artillery was still dominant and many of the reserve positions were little better than scrapes, barely a foot deep.

By the early afternoon on 22 March, it was clear that the fight for Epéhy and Pezières was over; a few hundred of the defenders had escaped leaving many more dead or in enemy hands. As D. A. Bacon observed; *"so far as formed bodies were concerned, by 1.30 p.m.: Lt. Colonel Utterson D.S.O., commanding 8th Leic. Regt., and practically all the troops* garrisoning Epehy, were, however, missing, having been, so far as could be gathered, completely surrounded."[24] The Leicestershire battalions were, for a time, reduced to composite companies from which a 110th brigade battalion was formed

The massive German breakthrough on 21 March 1918 was a product of careful planning and good luck. Thick fog masked the advancing infantry from even the best placed machine-guns and the careful use of gas, forcing defenders to wear respirators crippled both the British infantry and artillery.

On the entire Front it was only at the twin villages of Epéhy-Peizière, where a system of strongpoints and trenches was held by the 6th, 7th and 8th Battalions of the Leicestershire Regiment, that the onslaught was halted; earning the village (and its defenders) the sobriquet *"the flood breaker"* from the Germans. According to Quartermaster-Sergeant D A Bacon *"it was only when our men were taken in the rear, from the flank and practically surrounded, that the enemy obtained possession of the village."*

For two days, whilst all around them were driven back by an overwhelming force, the three Leicestershire battalions and associated trench mortar battery of the 110th Brigade held firm in Epéhy-Peizière. Fighting for their trenches and then back through the ruins of the village itself, the brigade suffered the loss of 56 officers and 1,304 Other Ranks – two-thirds of its strength. Brigadier-General Hanway Cumming, who had arrived to command the brigade only a day before the attack, could not have been prouder of his men:

*They were a fine upstanding lot of magnificent men, with exceptional* esprit de corps *and proud of their unofficial title...nothing could be finer than their performance and no words of praise are adequate for such men. Their epitaph lies in the text of the German Communiqué, which said: "The Leicester Brigade at Epéhy gave us the most trouble."*

The fact that the British army did not break, that the Flesquières

---

24 D. A. Bacon *Ibid., p. 101*

# "The Flood-Breakers"

salient, in which Epehy stood, did not become a horrific trap for many British divisions, and that Amiens, the vital rail link between Paris and the Channel ports, remained in Allied hands, rendered *Operation Michael*, despite its astounding gains in territory and prisoners, a costly failure. The British Army had been driven back 40 miles across the old Somme battlefield. There the line was held however, while the Germans switched their attention to *Operation Georgette*, an assault on the British line south of Ypres. Some 1200 square miles of territory had been seized but at a cost in men and munitions the Germans could ill afford.

As the much-missed chronicler of the Kaiser's Battle, Martin Middlebrook, observed: *"It had been a very good day for the Leicestershire Regiment. Their 6th, 7th and 8th Battalions had defended Epéhy successfully; the 2/4th Battalion had...stopped the German advance by their stand in the half-dug trench at the rear of the 59th Division's Battle Zone in the neighbouring 6th Division. Few regiments had upheld their reputation so well on this day."*[25]

*Wounded 'tommy' near Merris, 13 April 1918. [IWM Q10293]*

---

[25] Martin Middlebrook Ibid., p. 270 The 2/4th Leicesters, rushed up to plug a gap in the line at Ecoust, between Arras and Bapaume, found themselves defending a line that was little more than the marked-out line of a planned future trench. A succession of mass attacks were driven off by the battalion's rifles and Lewis guns and a German break-through prevented.

# Tigers in the Trenches

## Chapter Twelve

# *"Come along Tigers, show them what you can do!"*

## The Breaking of the Hindenburg Line, September, 1918.

At about 9 p.m. on the evening of 30th September 1918, the headquarters of the 1/5th Battalion, the Leicestershire Regiment took the advice of Bruce Bairnsfather's 'Old Bill' and moved 150 yards to a "better 'ole". Once established in his new home, a German artillery dug-out which he described as *"slightly more comfortable but very full of flies and other insects"*;[1] Captain and Adjutant John David Hills, temporarily commanding the battalion, set about writing its War Diary.

Captain Hills [left] was exhausted but elated. He wrote home to his mother: *"...a very hurried line scribbled at the bottom of a Boche dug-out, unshaved and unwashed for 3 days but feeling uncommonly fit...The battalion has fought two battles in the last few days...and has done magnificently on both occasions. In the first, five platoons of ours – at the most 130 men – went clean through a village held by 3 Boche battalions, brought out some 150 prisoners, and killed most of the rest. I don't believe any troops ever fought better; certainly none could have been in better spirits. They all enjoyed themselves. Even the wounded were yelling with delight and cheering others on. I never want to see better men."*[2]

To the account in the War Diary of his battalion, Hills decided to give an appropriate conclusion. As the flies buzzed about him, Hills's mind must

---
1 1/5th Leicesters War Diary 30 September 1918
2 Copy letters of Capt. J. D. Hills: ROLLR DE9672/13

## "Come along Tigers..."

have drifted back over the past four years. To mobilisation, to the blood bath before the Hohenzollern Redoubt and to the calamitous attack at Gommecourt on 1 July 1916 and Lt. General D'Oyly Snow's scandalous accusations of the North Midland Division's *"lack of offensive spirit".*

Finally, on the St Quentin Canal at Bellenglise, that curse was lifted. It had been a momentous week. Captain Hills's pencil crossed the War diary's page:

*"After 3½ years the 46$^{th}$ Division has at last made a name for itself, and its doings on the 29$^{th}$ are known the world over."*

The failure of their Spring offensives in 1918 doomed Germany to defeat. From then onwards, the Central Powers could only weaken, while the Allies (now including fresh American divisions) grew ever stronger. From July 1918, the German army was in retreat and all about them the forces of their allies crumbled.

By September 1918, as a briefing note issued to the 1/4th Leicesters reports, everywhere the Central Powers were under pressure. Bourlon Wood had fallen (to the Canadians) the French and Americans were advancing in Champagne, the Belgians had retaken Passchendaele, Bulgaria was suing for peace and Turkish forces in Palestine were fragmenting.

On the Western Front, the German answer had been a fighting withdrawal to the *Siegfried Stellung,* or 'Hindenburg Line' as it was known to the British. It was here that the Germans intended to halt the Allies and here that their engineers chose to display everything they had learned of defensive warfare over the past four years. At the unveiling of a post-war memorial to the 46$^{th}$ Division, General Hubert Auguste Garbit later recalled:

*"It was the most formidable of all the German lines, upon which had been lavished all the arts and science of fortification construction.*

*For many months the Germans, in defiance of all the laws of war, had*

# Tigers in the Trenches

*forced their unhappy prisoners and the civilian population to help to construct this formidable position.*

*For kilometres and kilometres barbed wire defences had been erected, trenches, caves and tunnels had been dug, and nests of machine guns guarded the way to the Hindenburg Line. Added to this mine fields, cunningly camouflaged, proved even more formidable obstacles to an advance. ..."[3]*

The strength of the German defences is evident from aerial photographs and trench maps [see opposite]. There, in blue, are three dense lines of barbed wire, front-line and support trenches, linked with snaking communication trenches and studded with concrete dug-outs and pill-boxes. There are signal stations, machine-gun nests and trench-mortar positions – all meticulously identified from aerial reconnaissance. Threading through the line, from north to south is the St Quentin Canal itself, 35 feet wide, part thick mud and in part retaining its water. A perfect anti-tank ditch, *"like the ditch of a fortress, defended by belts of wire in the water and on the banks, and by flanking emplacements."*[4]

Before any assault could be made however, it was decided that a small German salient should be eliminated. A week before the Australian advance had reached the first defensive positions of the Hindenburg Line, while the British division on their right, to the south, had been halted short of the Line by fierce German resistance. On 24 September 1918 the 1/5th Leicesters, in battalion strength, were to straighten out that salient by seizing the ruined village of Pontruet and Forgan's Trench, which was as Captain J D Hills put it *"the Southward continuation of our front line across the valley"*.

The 1/5th Leicesters, in line of companies, would attack Pontruet from the North. One company, 'D', would turn East to capture Forgan's Trench, while 'A' and 'B' Companies would face West to attack Pontruet. 'C' Company would send a platoon to assist in the capture of Forgan's Trench; the rest acting as a reserve to support wherever they were

---
3 Leicester Daily Mercury, 5 October 1922
4 Official History of the Great War 1918, volume 5, p.102.

# "Come along Tigers..."

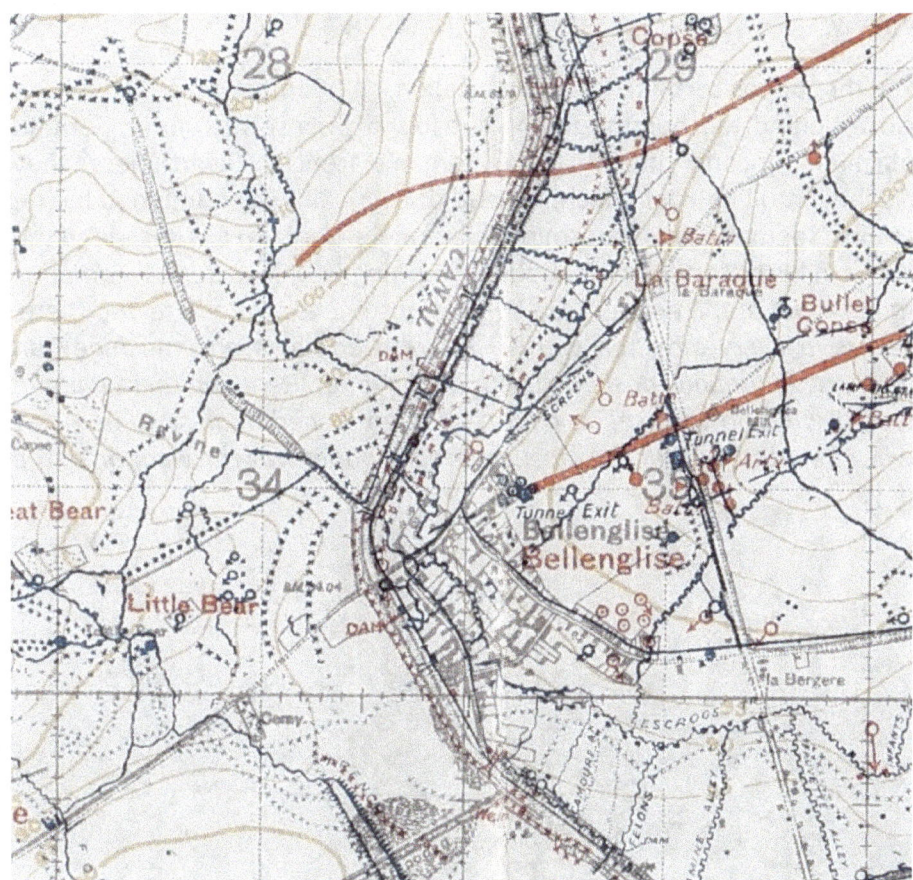

needed. Two officers and forty men of the 1/4th Leicesters also joined the attack. Further South, the 24th Division would also advance – all as a stepping stone to an assault on the canal itself.

At 5 a.m. the supporting creeping artillery barrage opened. Unfortunately, it included a preponderance of smoke which doubtless shielded the attacking infantry but also made the already poor light worse. The Leicesters' 'A' Company, which had the advantage of attacking along the line of a trackway, moved steadily forward while 'B' and elements of 'C' Companies struggled to maintain their alignments. On the left, eastwards, flank, 'D' Company was advancing along Forgan's Trench, having discovered shortly before the attack that it was occupied by the

# Tigers in the Trenches

enemy.

On the opposite flank of the battalion, 'A' Company had advanced close behind the bombardment but found themselves under German machine-gun and rifle fire from Forgan's Trench. Nevertheless, they crashed into Pontruet which, instead of being almost abandoned by the enemy, seemed full of determined defenders. Captain Hills described the scene in his history of the battalion: *"Turning into Pontruet, 'A' Company found it full of the enemy. Odd lengths of trenches were here and there, cellars in every direction were filled with bombers and machine gun teams...'A' Company dashed in with the bayonet. Here and there a bomb was thrown down a cellar, or a Lewis gun turned against some party which resisted, but for the most part the bayonet was the weapon of the day..."*[5]

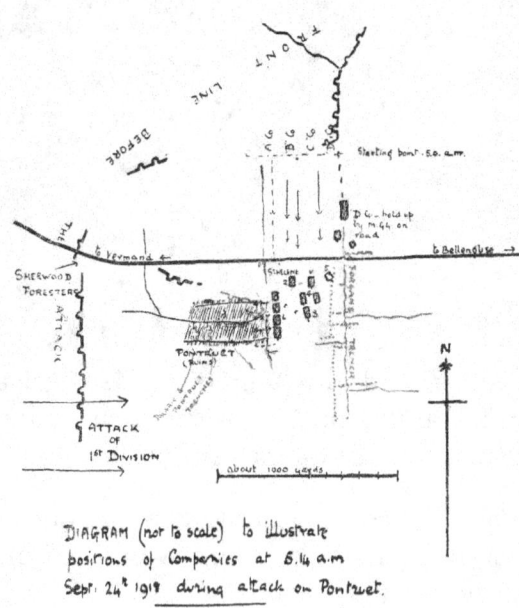

Captain J. D. Hills' sketch map of the attack on Pontruet, from his history of *The Fifth Leicestershire* (1919).

---

5 Captain J. D. Hills *The Fifth Leicestershire* (Loughborough) 1919, p. 285

# "Come along Tigers..."

Enemy resistance grew and the other companies ran into a determined and stiffening resistance. Confusion arose from the discovery of a trench which did not appear on British maps. As the War Diary explains: *"It had in fact been dug during the night. This trench coupled with the smoke and darkness completely baffled the leaders and all who could made for FORGAN'S Trench".* Several disorientated parties entered Forgan's Trench where 'B' Company's commander, Captain Tomson led his men against a succession of machine-guns with a cry of *"Come along Tigers, show them what you can do!"* Tomson captured two guns but was shot and killed by a third, whilst stooping to bandage his wounded Signal Corporal.[6]

*Artist Terence Cuneo at work on his depiction of Lieut. Barrett's attack on Forgan's trench. [ROLLR: GP642]*

---

6 1/5th Battalion War Diary: Report on Operations around Pontruet Sept. 24th 1918, p. 15

# Tigers in the Trenches

Forgan's Trench, far from virtually abandoned, proved to be heavily defended, with machine guns every few yards. Elements of 'B', 'C' and 'D' Companies of the Leicesters became tangled in bitter fighting. It was here that Lieutenant J. C. Barrett earned his Victoria Cross. He had broken into Forgan's Trench with a mixed force from 'B' and 'C' Companies:

" *Without hesitation he collected all available men and charged the nearest group of machine guns, being wounded on the way...he gained the trench and vigorously attacked the garrison, personally disposing of two machine guns and inflicting many casualties. He was again severely wounded, but nevertheless climbed out of the trench in order to fix his position and locate the enemy...despite exhaustion from wounds, [he] gave detailed orders to his men to cut their way back to the battalion. He himself refused help and was again wounded, so seriously that he... had to be carried out. In spite of his wounds he had managed to fight on, and his spirit was magnificent throughout. It was due to his coolness and grasp of the situation that any of his party were able to get out alive.*" [7]

Not all of 'B' Company had turned to attack Forgan's Trench however and two platoons, commanded by Second-lieutenants Lewis and Cosgrove swept into the eastern end of Pontruet in support of 'A' Company. The 1/5th battalion was wild that day and utterly undaunted by losses or enemy resistance. In the furthest south-western corner of the village, two platoon commanders, Quint and Asher, were cut down by machine-gun fire from a blockhouse. Their men persisted in the attack however, a corporal and seven men breaking through almost into open country, only to be killed beside the last few houses.

The War Diary later noted: *"there was no corner of the village which did not contain scenes of the fight: and that the dead of the 5th Leicestershire Regiment were lying with their rifles and bayonets still with them and with all wounds in front."*

By 8 a.m. the attack on Pontruet was virtually over. Almost all ammunition and assuredly every bomb had been expended. The village seemed deserted by the enemy, save for the blockhouse in the south-westerly

---
[7] London Gazette, 14 December 1918.

## "Come along Tigers..."

corner. The appearance of a tank, attracted by the Tigers waving their helmets raised on rifles, offered a brief chance of victory but mechanical failure brought a halt to the attack and shortly afterwards the tank was destroyed by enemy shellfire.

Attempts were made to bring up more ammunition but in daylight, without smoke as cover, any movement brought the attention of snipers, trench mortars and machine-guns. A further machine-gun nest was taken by men of 'D' Company, now under the command of (Acting) Company Sergeant Major Marston as the officers were all wounded. Four prisoners and the machine-gun were taken but the post, under a storm of shot and shell, could not be held; both sides satisfying themselves with depriving the other of it.

The stiff enemy resistance at Pontruet is a reminder that, despite the impending collapse of their allies and week after week of withdrawals and defeats, the Imperial German army was by no means broken and that the Hindenburg Line remained a fearsome obstacle. In storming Pontruet, the 5th Battalion suffered losses of 11 officers and 138 men.

Despite being driven back, the 'Tigers' took pride in their achievements. Congratulations arrived from the brigade's commander, Major-General G. F. Boyd, who declared himself *"quite satisfied. They captured many prisoners and accounted for numbers of the enemy. Owing to unexpected reinforcements they attacked an enemy twice as strong as themselves, and moreover in a strong position."*

Captain Hills, who had been prevented from boarding a leave-train to join the attack felt understandably proud of his men. He observed:

*"We had lost one Company Commander and three subalterns killed, one Company Commander and six subalterns wounded. Of the rank and file, thirty were killed, of whom three were Serjeants, one hundred were wounded, and eight were missing. But we had proved that five platoons could clear a village held by three Battalions (so said one of the prisoners) of the enemy; we had shown that when N.C.O.s become casualties, private soldier were ready to assume command and become*

# Tigers in the Trenches

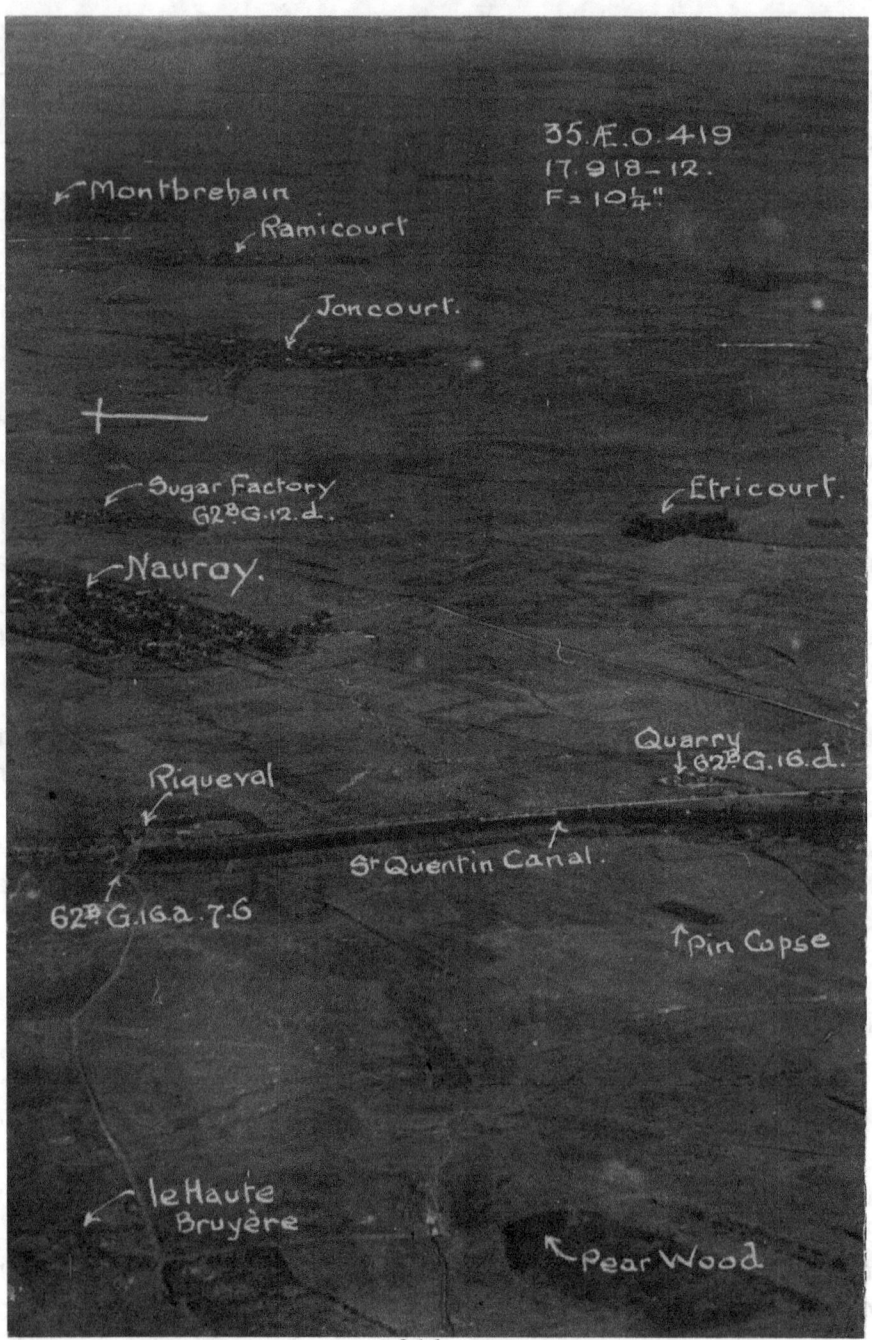

# "Come along Tigers..."

*Aerial photograph taken on 17 September 1918, of the area to be attacked, showing the defences on either side of the St Quentin Canal. [ROLLR: DE1407]*

*leaders, and, most important of all, the battle had proved to each individual soldiers that if he went with his bayonet he was irresistible."*

J.P.Beadle's painting of 'Crossing of the Canal de St Quentin at Bellenglise by the 46th (North Midland) Division, September 1918'

Despite the setback at Pontruet, the stage was set for the next move - a direct assault on the Hindenburg Line. For three days, however, the Leicesters rested, bathed and re-equipped; the $1/5^{th}$ battalion drawing on every spare officer and man to bring it back to battle strength. Both battalions marvelled at the quantity of artillery moving up and few of the soldiers cannot have been aware of the planning conferences and briefings from which senior officers returned frowning and tight-lipped. The Germans remained active, shelling the British front-line and rebuffing any attempts to probe their positions.

On 26 September the $1/4^{th}$ Leicesters received orders to advance into Pike Wood or Copse; another salient slightly in advance of the main German lines, from which any attack on the St Quentin Canal would be bound to receive a devastating enfilade fire. The network of trenches, well-wired in front, was believed to be largely vacated by the enemy but, in fact, proved to be well garrisoned.

An appeal from Lieutenant-Colonel Frederick W. Foster, M.C., commanding the $1/4^{th}$ Battalion, resulted in the support of an Australian

# "Come along Tigers..."

field artillery brigade and so what had been envisaged as the simple occupying of abandoned trenches became a full battalion attack under cover of a creeping, then stationary barrage. Everything was arranged for 7p.m., with only a couple of hours to spare, Colonel Foster racing to intercept his battalion as it prepared to hand over its trenches to a relieving battalion. As Captain John Milne described in *Footprints of the 1/4th Leicestershire Regiment*:

*"The C.O. appeared at 'A' Company H.Q. waving a large map. The C.O. was not given to waving large maps at the time of relief. Obviously something dirty was going to happen..."*[8]

The bridge over the St Quentin Canal at Riqueval, shortly after its miraculous capture - intact - by the North Midland Division.[ROLLR]

It did, although in some ways the attack owed more to the eighteenth century than the grim twentieth. Bathed in the light of the setting sun, and under cover of the Australian barrage, the battalion climbed out the trenches and deployed in no-man's land, some seven hundred yards

8 John Milne *Footprints of the 1/4th Leicestershire Regiment* (Leicester) 1935, p.134

from the two copse-strongholds. As the word to advance had to travel along the front-line trench, the 1/4th's companies moved in series rather than together as one. Worse, the German front-line was not parallel to the British, so 'A' Company waited to conform:

*"Captain Ledward was equal to the occasion and advanced 'B' company from their trenches in time to be on 'A' Company's left at the moment of attack...at the same time part of 'A' Company had to be slowed up while the left platoon...drew level as they had more ground to cross. Captain A. B. Pick commanding 'A' Company did this in the proper parade ground style, blew his whistle, dressed the line and then again signalled the advance. It was well done and showed the steadiness of the men."*[9]

Fortunately the Australian guns did their work and many of the German garrison was still in deep dug-outs when the Tigers began to drop into their trenches. Most surrendered without a fight, though pockets of resistance kept up a fight and fired off what Milne called *"a continual stream of S.O.S. rockets"*. By 7.45 p.m. Pike Wood was secure and 'C' and 'D' companies helping to turn the position into a British rather than German strongpoint.

The recently evicted Germans proved reluctant to give up tenure however and *"a successful evening turned into a dirty night for the 4th Leicesters"*.[10] On the right, 'A' Company fought a vicious battle of bombs, while 'B' company faced a galling fire from the neighbouring Peg Copse. Fresh Germans came in waves up from the canal, only a few hundred yards downhill. Fortunately, the enemy artillery remained largely silent, probably for fear of hitting their own men.

Perhaps overshadowed by the fight for Pontruet and Lieutenant Barrett's V.C., the capture of Pike Wood and nearby Peg Copse deserves to be better known. *"It was a bloody little fight of which any regiment might be proud"* declared John Milne, *"...a battalion, almost a half-battalion show. 'A' company had lost heavily; their C.S.M. was killed and Second-Lieutenant Lacey was wounded. This action demonstrated afresh the

---
9 Ibid.
10 Ibid.

## "Come along Tigers..."

*fighting qualities of the battalion and the dash and initiative with which the junior ranks were imbued. The battalion had advanced 700 yards on a 500 yard front, taken one hundred and fifty prisoners, and with both flanks in the air held the position until relieved."*[11]

Brigadier-General J V Campbell VC addresses men of the 46th Division from the damaged (but still usable) Riqueval Bridge. Many of the troops still wear their borrowed life-jackets, while others wave captured german helmets.

The relief arrived in the form of the 5th and 6th North Staffordshires, festooned to everyone's surprise with ladders and life-preservers borrowed, it appears, from cross channel ferries. Having straightened out the line somewhat, at Pontruet and Pike Copse, the 46th Division was moving on to cross the St Quentin Canal and break through the Hindenburg Line. Lieutenant-General Sir John Monash's Australian Corps, spearheaded by the Americans were to attack at Bellicourt, where the canal passed through a tunnel, but the North Midlanders

11 Ibid., p. 136.

would get their feet wet and storm straight across the St Quentin Canal, partly where it submerged into tunnels south of Riqueval but also north of Bellenglise, where the canal retained much of its water and remained a formidable obstacle in itself.

On 28 September, detailed plans were issued by Major General Boyd, commanding the 46th Division. A copy survives amongst the Regimental archives, written in the hand of Captain and adjutant D. W. Howarth, of the 1/4th Leicesters. Four pages covered everything from the objectives of the attack to synchronisation of watches and the provision of guides and water. Item number one was easier written than done:

*"At hour and date to be notified later 46th Division as part of a larger operation will cross ST QUENTIN CANAL, capture the HINDENBURG LINE, and advance to the GREEN Line."*

Captain Hills, adjutant of the 1/5th Leicesters also received the orders, clarified by maps showing *"the objective of each unit shown in colour. The Staffordshires had the 'Blue,' which was the Hindenburg Line, and the 'Brown' further East to hold till we came up; the 4th Leicestershires had the 'Yellow,'...the 5th Lincolnshires the 'Dotted Blue,' – just beyond Magny village; we had the last of all, the 'Green' line, including a sunken cross-roads, an old mill on some very high ground, and a small copse called Fosse Wood….The day chosen was September 29th – the time, dawn."*[12]

For three days, from the evening of the 26th, the German lines around the St Quentin Canal had been subjected to one of the most punishing bombardments of the war. One thousand and forty-four field and 593 medium and heavy guns had deluged the Hindenburg Line with nearly a million high explosive, shrapnel, mustard gas and even smoke shells; destroying trenches and strongpoints, subduing counter-battery fire and isolating forward units from supply and support.[13]

To Captain Milne the bombardment was one of the war's marvels:

---

12 Captain J. D. Hills Ibid., pp. 300-301
13 Official History of the Great War 1918, volume 5, p.95

# "Come along Tigers…"

Captain J. MILNE.
"G" Company, 4th Leicesters.

*"Dante's Inferno was a mere twitter to this. This was the real thing; there were no two ways about it, this was quite definitely fiery bloody Hell. Hell let loose on earth. Hell with a capital H. Hell with the lid off. Heart-breaking, body-rending, shrieking, blasting HELL."*[14]

At 5.50 a.m. the attack began. Careful plans had been made for the bombardment to lift and move forward with the advancing troops. A pathway was to be swept through the German defences at a rate of 100 yards every 4 minutes. To the North, around Bellicourt, the 27th and 30th US Divisions ran into heavy opposition, fog and inexperience creating a confusion which the German defenders eagerly exploited.

The North Midlanders however had four years' experience and they swept on, hastening through the fog by compass bearing, encumbered with *"three thousand life-belts, small floating piers constructed of petrol tins or corkslabs in wooden framework, light collapsible boats, mudmats, life-lines and scaling ladders".*[15] The first wave of the attack on the Canal was by the South and North Staffords of 137th and Sherwood Foresters of 139th Brigades of the 46th Division. Advancing swiftly behind the bombardment, both helped and hindered by fog thickened by smoke shells, they crashed through the German lines and up to the canal.

Seemingly nothing could stop them. The German defenders were bayoneted or fled, disappearing into the fog. Where the canal was shallow enough, the Sherwood Foresters and Staffords slithered down the banks and across the cold, muddy water. Men of the 6th North Staffords seized the bridge at Riqueval intact, capturing the machine-gun that defended it and driving off an enemy demolition party before

---

14 John Milne Ibid., p.137
15 Official History, p. 102

# Tigers in the Trenches

they could fire their explosive charges. On the far side of the bridge the attackers rounded up one hundred and thirty prisoners including the staff of the battalion dug in there.[16]

The speed of the attack caught everyone, not just Germans, by surprise. The fog and perhaps the fact that the canal and its defences at Bellenglise lay largely hidden from view in a fold of the landscape, meant that the attackers were upon their foe almost before anyone had time to draw breath. The two battalions of Leicesters, in support, hastened on to the canal; bringing forward their start time because of the fog[17] and spurred forward by a succession of scribbled messages:

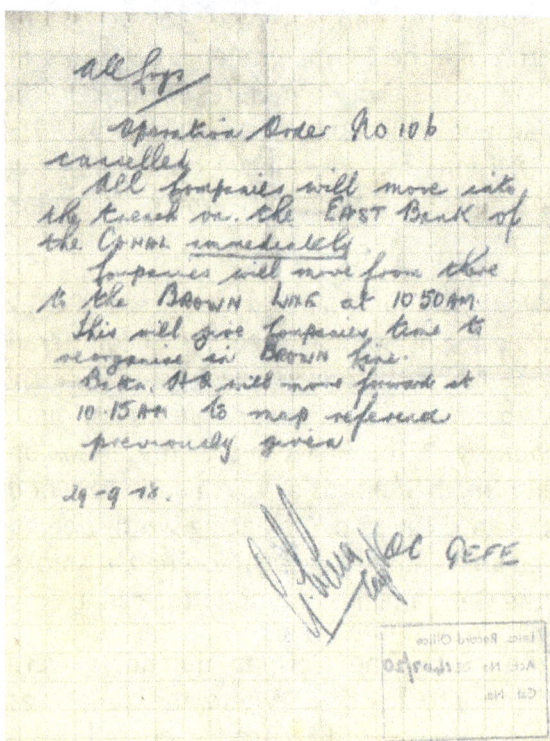

"Operation Order No. 106

The 137th Inf Bde have had little difficulty in reaching the BROWN LINE.

<u>Intention</u> The battalion will moveforward & occupy the BROWN LINE, attacking the YELLOW LINE according to Barrage table..."And then:

"Operation Order No. 106 cancelled.All Companies will move into the trench on the EAST Bank of the CANAL <u>immediately</u>...."[18]

Both Leicestershire battalions suffered from enemy artillery fire and suffered casualties in mopping-up pockets of the enemy. The 1/4th

16 Ibid., p. 103
17 1/5th Battalion War Diary; 29 September 1918
18 ROLLR: DE1407/20

# "Come along Tigers..."

Battalion kept to time despite the loss of both their commanding officer and adjutant. The 1/5th Leicesters were across the canal by 11.20 a.m. and by midday had reached Knobkerry Ridge, overlooking Magny-la-Fosse and the third and final trench and wire of the Hindenburg Line. Ahead of them the 1/4th Leicesters were at the 'Yellow Line', while the 5th Lincolns were pushing on to the 'dotted Blue Line'. American and Australian troops could be seen to the left, while tanks emerged from the swirling mist south of Magny.

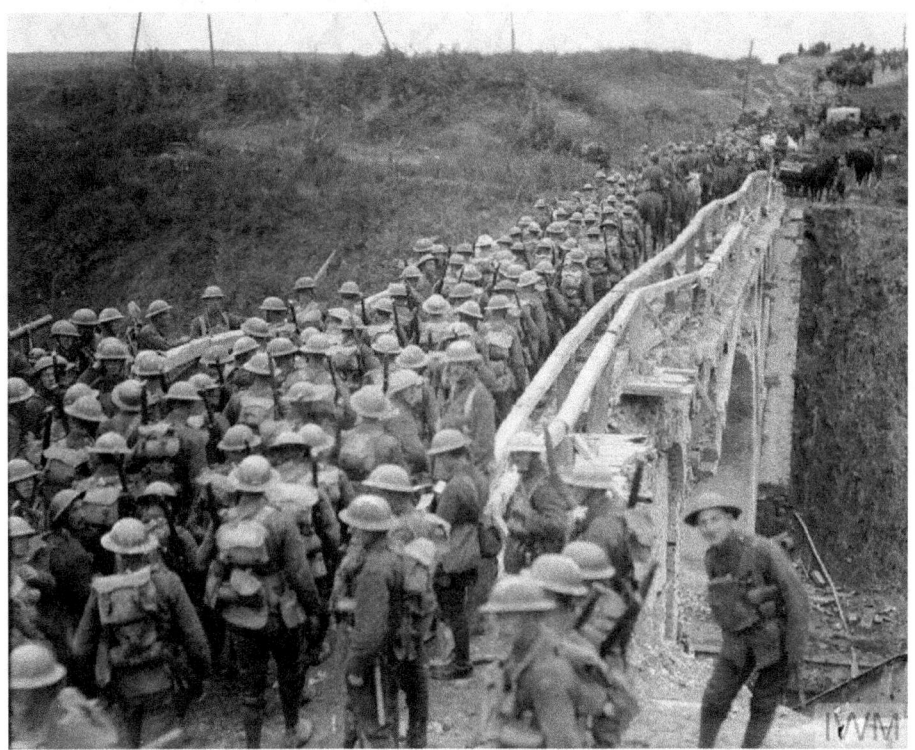

*British troops rush across the newly captured Riqueval Bridge. [IWM Q9511]*

By 1.40 p.m., the objectives everywhere (the Green Line) had been reached and the Leicesters began to dig in. the 1/5th Leicesters had not finished for the day however: *"Opposite MERVILLE old mill a Boche battery could be seen limbering up. Part of C Coy. could not be restrained and went at once through the barrage losing one or two men on the*

# Tigers in the Trenches

way: *horses were killed and gun left but men got away."*[19]

*The view from Riqueval Bridge today.*

Only to the left of the 46th Division's position did the Germans manage to hold some ground, their artillery knocking-out ten tanks on the slopes around the village of Joncourt. A German counter-attack, which alarmed 'D' company of the 1/4th Leicesters, being somewhat out-on-a-limb at the far left of the line, was dispersed by a battery of field guns: *"to see a battery dash hell-for-leather across a bloody battlefield, unlimber, open fire at point-blank range, blow to hell a dangerous counter-attack and restore a doubtful fight - that is a sight for the gods..."*[20]

To some it was a miracle. Not only had the lightning assault broken the Hindenburg Line, it had pushed through into the open country behind. In a few hours some 4,200 prisoners, over 300 machine-guns and 72 artillery pieces were captured. Such victories do not come without a cost however. The division suffered about 800 casualties. While the War

19 1/5th Battalion War Diary; 29 September 1918
20 John Milne Ibid., p.142

# "Come along Tigers..."

Diary of the 1/5th Leicesters records 4 officers killed and 8 wounded, with 31 Other Ranks dead, 114 wounded and 9 missing; that of the 1/4th Leicesters is silent. Their history simply notes that the day was 'bloody'.

Even while the 46th Division continued to advance, fighting a vicious little battle at Ramicourt, celebration of their 29th September attack was growing apace. That very day, the Division's commander, Major General G F Boyd declared: *"I cannot express in words my feelings of intense admiration and pride, in the magnificent effort of the Division today... What appeared well nigh impossible has been carried right through to a great victory. The story of the storming of the St Quentin Canal, the capture of Bellenglise, and the subsequent advance, will make one of the most glorious stories in the History of the War."*

The breaking of the Hindenburg Line at so small a cost swiftly elevated the attack into what the fourth Army commander, Sir Henry Rawlinson [right] called *"one of the finest and most dashing exploits of the war."*[21] Local newspapers had already celebrated the *"North Midlanders feat"*[22] following the Tigers *"through the maze of trenches and redoubts... and out beyond...tunnels and dug-outs were bombed or blocked by mobile charges; prisoners in hundreds taken from these deep retreats...[and]... machine-gun and minenwerfer forts, armoured with steel and concrete were taken and their garrisons killed or captured."*[23]

Hyperbole aside, 29th September 1918 was a day of successful co-operation, of professionalism and experience and of good luck. The

---

21 Sir Henry Rawlinson; address to the division on its leaving the Fourth Army, 23 November 1918.
22 Leicester Daily Post, 5 October 1918.
23 Leicester Daily Post, 11 October 1918.

# Tigers in the Trenches

Germans' most fearsome of defence systems had succumbed, in a single day, to a combination of fog and élan. No wonder J. D. Hills was satisfied, despite his fly-blown quarters: *"... the 46<sup>th</sup> Division has at last made a name for itself, and its doings on the 29<sup>th</sup> are known the world over."*

The memorial unveiled in October 1922 [above] is somewhat neglected now. It lies above Bellenglise on the quiet D1044, which has lost most of its traffic to the fast, new A26 which cuts straight across the Somme battlefields and onwards, from Cambrai to Saint Quentin. Strangely, the bridge at Riqueval remains, almost unchanged, and, gazing across the valley, it is easy to imagine the pell-mell scramble of that attack at the end of September 1918.

On that lonely spot, the words of Général H. A. Garbit, reported by the *Leicester Daily Mercury* of 5 October 1922, resonate still:

*"...the 46th Division dared to attack and won...To the 46th Division was accorded the honour of the hardest task of them all. They crossed the canal where it was most heavily defended and conquered such formidable fortifications as Bellenglise and Vieux Moulin. The gallant 46th overcame all obstruction. Canals, trenches, shot and shell, machine*

## "Come along Tigers..."

guns, grenades - they 'leaped over' them all. Four thousand prisoners and seventy cannon fell into their hands.

*That which was accomplished there was no doubt the finest feat of arms by an army which had already done so much."*

*General Garbit (above) and the 46th Division Memorial as it is today (below)*

## Chapter Thirteen

## *"Worthy of Everlasting Remembrance"*

# The last few shots and the last few casualties: Le Cheval Blanc Crossroads, 8 November 1918.

The sudden silence which followed the Armistice, at 11a.m. on 11 November 1918, found only the two Territorial battalions, the 4th and 5th, of the Leicestershire Regiment in contact with the enemy. The 1st and the Service battalions were at rest or training, having recently come out of the front-line. For the 2nd Battalion, serving with the Egyptian Expeditionary Force in Palestine, the guns had already fallen silent on 7 November.

In all, twelve battalions of the Tigers had seen active service; every one of them for all or part of the war on the Western Front. Of the thousands of men who had served with the Leicestershire Regiment, some 7,300 were killed in action, died of wounds or succumbed to illness or accident.[1] The last five of the Leicesters to lose their lives in the Great War, killed or mortally wounded on 8 November 1918, were five privates of the 5th Battalion, which had been in close pursuit of retreating German forces for several days.

On 7 November, the battalion had caught up with the enemy at the otherwise insignificant cross-roads of Le Cheval Blanc [opposite], roughly half way between Cartignies and the old fortress town of Avesnes-sur-Helpe, not far from the Belgian frontier and perhaps thirty miles from Mons, where Britain's war had begun. Fog had served the battalion well again, as it had at the St Quentin Canal, and the leading platoon, commanded by Second-lieutenant Joseph Bettles,[2] had caught a German artillery battery at rest.

---

1 It is difficult to be precise. The Commonwealth War Graves Commission identifies 7,290 Tigers buried or recorded on memorials between 1914 and 1919 but the deaths of many more were hastened or in some measure attributable to war injuries in subsequent years.
2 Bettles was one of the war's 'temporary gentlemen', a sergeant in the 4th Northamptons granted a war-time commission with the 5th Leicesters.

# "Worthy of Everlasting Remembrance"

The Official History of the war highlights the affair and describes how *"on bursting through a hedge"*, a platoon, *found itself in the midst of a German field battery, the officers and men of which were standing idly about, with the horses tethered close up. The rest of the company came up but the Leicestershires were driven back, managing, nevertheless, to take with them 29 prisoners, 8 horses and a breech block."*[3]

*Le Cheval Blanc crossroads today, a few yards from where Second Lieutenant Coleman's platoon attempted to cross the Brunehaut Road.*

The battalion's war diary and its history, written by Captain and Adjutant J.D. Hills, who had just returned from the leave he forfeited on the eve of the attack on Pontruet, tells a rather more complicated and sadder story. The German artillerymen were, indeed, caught unawares and unhesitatingly Bettles had led his platoon in a desperate bayonet charge to seize the guns.

It was a vicious scrap. A short but bitter fight which saw Bettles killed, with a pistol bullet to the head, but his platoon was eventually supported by 'D' Company of the 5th Battalion, commanded by Lieutenant T. H. Ball,

---
3 Official History of the Great War, 1918, volume 5, p.507

and the position consolidated. An officer and twenty-nine artillerymen, with eight horses, were subdued and sent back as prisoners through the British lines.[4]

Le Cheval Blanc was not a comfortable place. The Germans showed no sign of being a beaten enemy. Their machine-guns to right and left dominated the main road, making any movement across it perilous in the extreme. All attempts to move the captured field guns failed and German reinforcements slowly began to encircle the still isolated 'D' Company. Two attacks were beaten off but with casualties mounting and ammunition becoming scarce, Lieutenant Ball had no alternative but to withdraw. Attempts were made to render the guns unserviceable but, with one exception, they were eventually recovered by the Germans and a few rounds fired from them into Le Cheval Blanc.

*Royal Horse Artillery fording a river, August 1918*

As the late afternoon turned to dusk and then night, two companies of the 4th Leicesters arrived in support, soon after followed by a battery of the Royal Horse Artillery which splashed across the River Semau and

---

4 The War Diary states that 23 prisoners and six horses were taken.

## "Worthy of Everlasting Remembrance"

deployed half a mile or so to the south-west. The Germans remained silent but still in strength and seemingly determined to hold the line of the Avesnes-Étrœungt Road (now the N2) just under two miles to the east. It was a quiet night, save for a few German shells fired at the Le Cheval Blanc crossroads around sunset.

At 6 o'clock the following morning, cavalry patrols from the Scots Greys returned with confirmation that the Germans still held the Avesnes-Étrœungt Road. With artillery support, two companies of the 5th Leicesters attempted to push on, but heavy machine-gun fire once again stopped 'B' Company, commanded by Captain A. D. Pierrepoint [left] from crossing the road. As the battalion war diary records:

*"10.00 After 2 hours leading platoon (H.C. DAVIES) fought their way across and enemy evacuated line of road. A Co (SNAITH) on left were similarly held up until Co on right had crossed the road. 2 Lt COLEMAN and several men were hit in an attempt to push on. 2 Lt BYLES also wounded."*

Second-Lieutenant Davies's platoon had, in fact, crossed the Biwetz road one by one. Finally, in sufficient force, they had fought their way along the opposite side of the road, house by house, until the Germans realised the game was up and withdrew. Second-Lieutenant Coleman's platoon on the other flank, where the land is rather more open, had attempted to rush their machine-gun with bayonets-fixed but Coleman and ten men were wounded and three killed. Two of the wounded died later that day.

The advance continued and by 12.15 p.m. two companies of the 5th Battalion were across the Avesnes-Étrœungt Road. The enemy, according to the war diary, had *"now disappeared again"*. It was the last contact

# Tigers in the Trenches

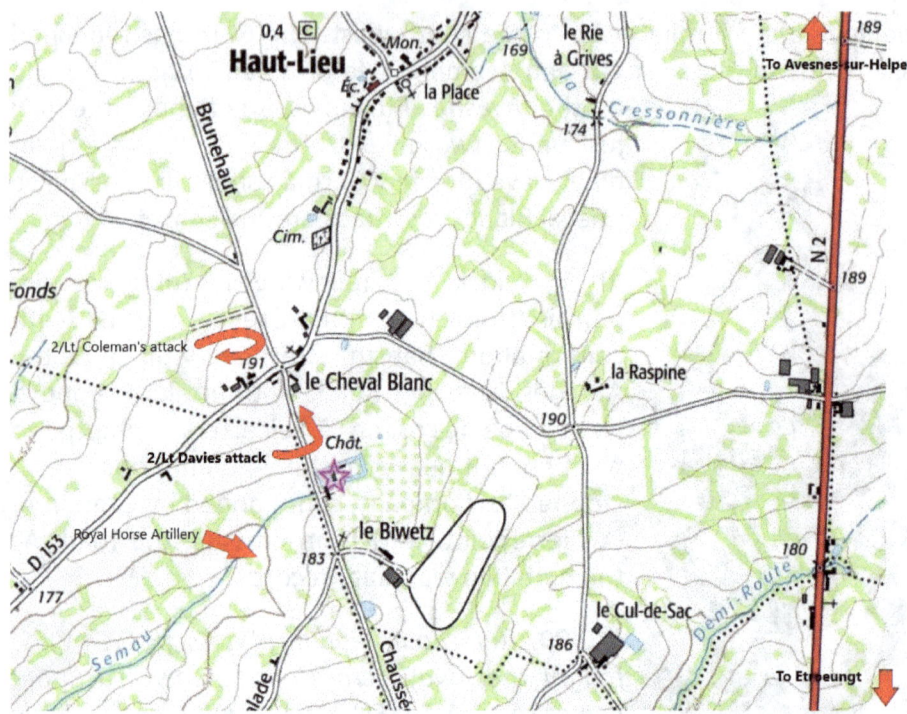

although the order to withdraw was later countermanded, hostilities ceased before they could again catch up with their retreating foe.

Let us return to the casualties from second-lieutenant Coleman's platoon, cut down as they dashed from hedge to hedge and finally through the hedges and across the roadway to Brunehaut. Apart from Second-Lieutenant Coleman the platoon commander, who was probably James Coleman, like Joseph Bettles another sergeant of the Northamptonshire Regiment given a temporary commission, the names of the wounded are unrecorded.

The names of the five dead, the last five 'Tigers' killed, are worth recalling. They were:

No. 48710 Private Herbert Lakin, a twenty-six-year-old coalminer from Whitwick, who left a widow, Elizabeth Jane, behind. They had married in

## "Come along Tigers..."

August 1917 before Lakin had either enlisted or been conscripted.

Next to Lakin, at Cross Roads British Cemetery, Fontaine au Bois lies No. 40771, Private Edward Willars, a Leicester lad of twenty-two. Willars was the son of John and Annie Willars, with whom he was living in 1911; working as a telegraph clerk. It was almost certainly Dorotha, Edward's older sister, who chose the words for his grave: "In Heaven".

*A section of the 1/4th Leicesters skirmishing in open country near Bohain, October 1918 [IWM: Q7103]*

The other three soldiers had originally been buried together at Sains du Nord Communal Cemetery, in what the Commonwealth War Graves Commission records describe as *"an isolated row at the back of the cemetery"*. Sains du Nord is a few miles east of Le Cheval Blanc and it seems likely that the three Tigers had died, presumably from their wounds, whilst in German captivity. They were later exhumed and reburied as part of the Commission's 'concentration' of graves and memorials.

The three were firstly No. 49846 Private Samuel Smith, a twenty-two-year-old coalminer from Ibstock and secondly, No. 260023 Private William Stanley, also twenty-two, the son of William and Lizzie Stanley of Acton Trussell, Staffs., and the husband of Mary Stanley, née Walker of Rickerscote in the same county. It was presumably Mary Stanley who chose "Peace Perfect Peace" for his grave.

Lastly, was No. 49830 Private Thomas Watson, aged twenty-six. Watson had also worked in mining, at the time of the 1911 census as a banksman above ground. His mother, Mrs Louisa Watson, of 8, Waterworks Road, Bardon, provided an epitaph for his gravestone which would stand, no doubt, for all the Leicestershire Regiment's fallen:

*"Dearly loved and worthy of Everlasting Remembrance".*

# Sources & Bibliography

## Sources

### 1. Archival

The richest seam of archival material relating to the Royal Leicestershire Regiment is undoubtedly that held at the Record Office for Leicestershire, Leicester and Rutland, in Wigston Magna. This collection consists not only of the archive of the Regiment and its associated bodies, such as the Territorial Association, but also of material collected over many years from individuals whose papers, diaries, correspondence and photographs supplement and often cast a valuably different light upon the official record.

More 'official' records, including copies of the *War Diaries* held in Wigston, may be found at the National Archives. The Imperial War Museum also has important personal archives, deposited by old 'Tigers' or their relatives.

References to all this material will be found throughout this book.

### 2. Periodicals, etc.

Local newspapers and periodicals, at least until 1916, often printed reports and correspondence from the Front. Once again, specific references are to be found as footnotes wherever they are used. Almost all local newspapers are to be found at the local record office, nationally through the British Library and, increasingly, *on-line* through national newspaper collections. Study of the Christmas Truce in 1914 demonstrates perfectly how far afield the keen researcher should be prepared to go in search of material; and that Leicestershire Regiment soldiers wrote home to families throughout the Kingdom.

## 3. Printed Sources

Many books were consulted in the preparation of this volume. For clarity, this bibliography contains only the most useful and they are divided into memoirs of soldiers serving with the Leicesters, histories of the Regiment's various battalions, and general studies of campaigns or aspects of the war. Others may be found amongst the footnotes.

# Bibliography

## General Sources

| | | | |
|---|---|---|---|
| Arthur, Max | *Forgotten Voices of the Great War* | (London) | 2002 |
| Ashworth, Tony | *Trench Warfare 1914-1918* | (London) | 2000 |
| Babington, Anthony | *For the Sake of Example* | London) | 1983 |
| Barton, Peter | *Passchendaele* | (London) | 2007 |
| Barton, Peter | *The Somme* | (London) | 2006 |
| Barton, Peter | *Arras* | (London) | 2010 |
| Beckett, Ian F & Simpson, Keith | *A Nation in Arms* | (Barnsley) | 2014 |
| Brown, Malcolm | *The Western Front* | (London) | 1993 |
| Brown, Malcolm & Seaton, Shirley | *Christmas Truce* | (London) | 1984 |
| Carrington, Charles | *Soldier from the Wars Returning* | (Barnsley) | 2015 |
| Cherry, Niall | *Most Unfavourable Ground: Loos 1915* | (Solihull) | 2008 |
| Corns, Cathryn & Hughes-Wilson, John | *Blindfold and Alone* | (London) | 2001 |
| Corrigan, Gordon | *Mud, Blood, and Poppycock* | (London) | 2004 |
| Corrigan, Gordon | *Sepoys in the Trenches* | (Stroud) | 2008 |
| Downing, Taylor | *Breakdown: The Crisis of Shell Shock* | (London) | 2016 |

# Sources & Bibliography

| | | | | |
|---|---|---|---|---|
| Duffy, Christopher | *Through German Eyes* (London) 2006 | | | |
| Edmunds, Sir James (et al) 1935 | *History of the Great War: Military Operations* | | HMSO | 1922- |
| Farrar-Hockley, A. H. | *The Somme* (London) 1971 | | | |
| Farrar-Hockley, A. H. | *Ypres 1914: Death of an Army* (London) 1970 | | | |
| Hancock, Edward | *Bazentin Ridge* (Barnsley) 2001 | | | |
| Hart, Peter | *1918: A very British Victory* (London) 2008 | | | |
| Howard, Michael (ed.) | *A Part of History* (London) 2008 | | | |
| Hudson, John | *Christmas 1914* (Stroud) 2014 | | | |
| Levine, Joshua (ed) | *Forgotten Voices of the Somme* (London) 2009 | | | |
| Lloyd, Nick | *Passchendaele* (London) 2017 | | | |
| MacDonald, Lyn | *Somme* (London) 1993 | | | |
| MacDonald, Lyn | *1915: The death of Innocence* (London) 1997 | | | |
| MacDonald, Lyn | *They called it Passchendaele* (London) 1993 | | | |
| Mead, Gary | *The Good Soldier* (London) 2008 | | | |
| Messenger, Charles | *Call to Arms: the British Army 1914-18* (London) 2005 | | | |
| Middlebrook, Martin | *The Kaiser's Battle* (London) 1978 | | | |
| Mitchinson, K W | *Epehy - Hindenburg Line* (Barnsley) 2012 | | | |
| Morton-Jack, George | *The Indian Empire at War* (London) 2018 | | | |
| Murland, Jerry | *Battle on the Aisne 1914* (Barnsley) 2012 | | | |
| Neillands, Robin | *The Death of Glory* (London) 2006 | | | |
| Nicholls, Jonathan | *Cheerful Sacrifice: The Battle of Arras 1917* (Barnsley) 2015 | | | |
| Saunders, Anthony | *Raiding on the Western Front* (Barnsley) 2012 | | | |
| Sellers, Leonard | *Death for Desertion* (Barnsley) 2003 | | | |
| Sheffield, Gary | *The Somme* (London) 2004 | | | |
| Sheldon, Jack | *Fighting the Somme* (Barnsley) 2017 | | | |
| Sheldon, Jack | *The German Army on the Somme* (Barnsley) 2012 | | | |
| Sheldon, Jack | *The German Army at Passchendaele* (Barnsley) 2007 | | | |

# Tigers in the Trenches

Steel, Nigel & Hart, Peter    *Passchendaele*    (London) 2003

Terraine, John    *General Jack's Diary*    (London) 2001

Weintraub, Stanley    *Silent Night*    (London) 2008

Westlake, Ray    *The British Army of 1914*    (Staplehurst)    2005

Winter, Denis    *Haig's Command*    (Barnsley) 2004

Winter, Denis    *Death's Men*    (London) 1979


*King's Regulations*    HMSO    1914

*Manual of Military Law*    HMSO    1914


## Leicestershire Regiment histories

Atter, Nigel    *With Valour and Distinction: 2nd Leics. Regt 1914-1918* (Warwick) 2019

Middlebrook, Martin    *Captain Staniland's Journey: The North Midland Territorials go to War* (Barnsley) 2003

Peaple, Simon    *Mud, Blood and Determination: the 46th (North Midland) Division* (Solihull) 2015

Richardson, Matthew    *The Tigers* (Barnsley) 2000

Richardson, Matthew    *Fighting Tigers*    (Barnsley) 2002

Wylly, Col. H C    *History of the 1st & 2nd Battalions the Leicestershire Regiment* (Aldershot) 1928


## Personal memoirs (or histories with a personal element)

Eyre, Giles E M    *Somme harvest*    (Eastbourne)    1991

Hills, J D    *The Fifth Leicestershire*    (Loughborough)    1919

Jamie, Lt-Col. J P W    *The 177th Brigade 1914-1918*    (Leicester) 1931

Junger, Ernst    *The Storm of Steel*    (London)    1929

Kelly, D V    *39 Months with the Tigers, 1915-1918*    (London)    1930

Milne, John    *Footprints of the 1/4th Leicestershire Regiment*    (Leicester) 1935

Moore, Aubrey    *A Son of the Rectory*    (Gloucester)    1982

Read, I L 'Dick'    *Of Those We Loved*    (Barnsley) 2013

# Index

| | |
|---|---|
| 2nd North Midland Field Ambulance (TF) | 21 |
| 5th Northern General Hospital | 21 |
| 46th Division, BEF, memorial near Bellenglise (inc. photographs) | 258-259 |
| Aircraft (enemy) | 176, 191 |
| Aldworth, Captain & Adjutant (later Lieut-Col) Albert Arthur | 144, 158 |
| Alexander, 2/Lieut. John, 8th Bn. | 155 |
| Alexander, Private Claude, 1/4th Bn. | 127 |
| Allenby, General Sir Edmund, commander 3rd | 99 |
| Allum, Corporal (later sergeant) Thomas, 2nd Bn., court-martial witness | 89 |
| Alrewas, staffs., National Memorial Aboretum at | 109 |
| Anderson, Lieut-General C. A., commanding Meerut Divisio | 94 |
| Anderson, Major Harry Edward Courtland, 8th Bn. | 177 |
| Armitage, Capt. C., 1st King's Shropshire Light Infantry | 101 |
| Army Act (1881) | 80 |
| Artillery: shellfire and bombardments | 72, 118, 120, 133, 145, 173, 178, 252 |
| Ashby de la Zouch, Leics. | 9 |
| At Risk War Memorials Project (Leicester City, County & Rutland) | 56 |
| Australian & New Zealand Army Corps (ANZACs) | 171, 251 |
| Bacchus, Captain Julian, 1st Bn. | 13, 44 |
| Bacon, QM & Colour Sergeant D.A., 9th Bn. | 144, 147, 156, 158, 172-173, 228, 235 |
| Bailiss, Private Herbert, 1st Bn. | 43 |
| Bailleul, French Flanders | 195 |
| Baker, Private, 1/5th Bn. | 217 |
| Balfourier, General Maurice, assessment of Bazentin Wood plan and portrait | 141 |
| Ball, Lieut. T. H., 1/5th Bn. | 261-262 |

| | |
|---|---|
| Bantry, Co. Cork, Ireland; 1st Bn. Detachment at | 13 |
| Bareilly, Uttar Pradesh, India | 15 |
| Barrett, Lieut. (later Colonel) John Cridlan, VC | 244 |
| Barrowden, Rutland | 9 (footnote) |
| Basher, Captain George Hedley, Governor at Blargies Military Prison | 99 |
| Bayonets, use of | 65-66 |
| Bazentin Wood, attack on | 144-162 |
| Bazentin Wood, map of shifting artillery bombardment, 14 July 1916 | 146 |
| Beardsley, Captain Herbert Luis, MC | 159 |
| Beaumarais, Calais, No. 4 Medical Base Depot at | 100 |
| Beaumont Hamel, burial of Newfoundlanders at, by 1st Bn. | 139 |
| Beaumont, Private Arthur, 2nd Bn. | 65-66 |
| Beaumont, Private Ernest Alfred, 2nd Bn., shot at dawn, trial and execution | 87-96 |
| Beck, L/cpl. Arthur, 1st Bn., court-martial witness | 100 |
| Belgians, soldiers' opinions and experience of | 197 |
| Bennett, Private, 7th Battalion, sentenced to 15 years imprisonment | 85 |
| Bent, Lieut-Colonel Philip E. , VC, commander 9th Bn. | 174-175, 176 |
| Bent, Lieut-Colonel Philip E. , VC, commander 9th Bn. Portrait | 175 |
| Bent, Lieut-Colonel Philip E. , VC, commander 9th Bn. Telegram reporting his deat | 176 |
| Berehaven, Co. Cork, Ireland; 1st Bn detachment | 13 |
| Bettles, 2/Lieut Joseph, 1/5th Bn. | 260-261 |
| Bisbrooke, Rutland | 9 (footnote) |
| Blackader, Lieut-Col.(later General) Charles Guinand | 17, 62, 77, 92, 94, 200-203 |
| Blakeney, Rev Canon | 24 |

# Index

| | |
|---|---|
| Blargies, military prison at | 99 |
| Bois de Biez, Neuve Chapelle | 72 |
| Bombs, see *hand grenades* | |
| Borelli, Leutnant, German 106th Machine Gun Company 148-149 | |
| Bottesford, Leics. | 9 |
| Boyd, Major-General Sir Gerald Farrell, commander 46th Division | 245, 252, 257 |
| Bradford, Private William Robert, 1st Bn. | 44 (footnote) |
| Braemar Castle, troopship | 15 |
| Bray, L/cpl. T. W., 1st Bn. (footnote) | 44 |
| Brewin, Private Hargreave, 6th Bn. | 82 (footnote) |
| Bridlington, E. Yorks. | 21 |
| Brooke, 2/Lieut. (later Captain) Jack Russell, MC, 1/5th Bn. | 214 |
| Brown, Lieut. Hugh Barrington, 1st Bn. | 44 |
| Buchanan-Dunlop, Major Archibald, 1st Bn. | 54-55 |
| Buckingham, Private William VC, 2nd Bn. | 71 |
| Buckle-Pickett, Lieut. George, 9th Bn (and 110 Trench Mortar Batter | 186, 190 |
| Burchmore, Private F. N., 8th Bn. | 150 |
| Burdett, Major James Charles MC assumes command of 6th Bn. | 233 (footnote) |
| Burton, Private Harry, 1st Bn. | 49 |
| Byers, Private joseph, 1st Royal Scots, shot at daw | 88 |
| Byles, 2/Lieut Harold Bower, 1/5th Bn. | 263 |
| Byng, Admiral John, executed 'pour encourager les autres' | 108 |
| Campbell, Major-general John Vaughan, VC | 228, 251 |

## Tigers in the Trenches

| | |
|---|---|
| Carr, Capt. A. R. Appleton, RAMC, att. 1st Bn., certifies death of Private Nesbit | 106 |
| Carter, Private W. R., signaller, 8th Bn. | 154, 161 |
| Casualties, effect of, on Leicester | 128 |
| Casualties, total number in Leicestershire Regimen | 260 |
| Cavalry, brief appearance of, on Bazentin Ridge | 161 |
| Chambers, Private Frederick, 1/5th Bn., killed near Hulluch, 1917 | 212 |
| Christmas funds (Leicester Mercury and Princess Mary's) | 50-51 |
| Christmas Truce | 50-58 |
| Cigarettes, impact on morale | 34, 183 |
| Coalville, Leics. | 9 |
| Cobh, Co. Cork, Ireland, 1st Bn embarks from | 14 |
| Codrington, General Sir Alf | 38 (footnote) |
| Coldham Common, Cambs., 1st Bn camp at | 15 |
| Coleman, 2/Lieut. James, 1/5th Bn. | 263-26 |
| Communications, problems of | 63 |
| Cooper, Private F., 1st Bn. | 57 (footnote) |
| Cottesmore, Rutland | 9 |
| Courts-martial, heirarchy of | 80-82 |
| Cross, Private Harry, 7th Bn., killed on raid June 1916 | 209 |
| Cumming, Brigadier-General Hanway, commanding 110th Brigade | 236 |
| Cummins, Captain W. A., Chief Medical Officer to 19th Corps | 101 |
| Cuneo, Terence, artist | 243 |
| Cunningham, Sergeant Frank, 1st Bn. | 182 |
| Dalgleish, Lieut-Col. R | 19 |
| Davies, 2/Lieut. Hubert Cecil Davies, 1/5th Bn. | 263 |

# Index

| | |
|---|---|
| Davis, Capt.& Adjutant Richard Nevill, MC, 1st Bn., prosecutes court martial | 101 |
| De Lisle, Lieut. Alexander C. N. | 142, 151-152 |
| Deane, Capt. E. C., RAMC, certifies death of Private Beaumon | 95 |
| Dehra Dun Brigade, Indian Army | 73 |
| Delhi, India | 15 |
| Dent, Major B.C., 1st Bn. | 44 (footnote) |
| Derry, Private A., 2nd Bn. | 195 |
| Deserters, gangs of | 83 |
| *Devanha*, HM Transport | 17 |
| Diggins, CSM Frederick, 1st Bn. | 45 |
| Discipline, inc. punishments and military justice generally | 78-109 |
| Dods, Lieut. William Henry Gordon, 1st Bn. | 46 |
| Dowell, 2/Lieut. Walter Thomas | 177 (footnote) |
| Drysdale, Lieut-Colonel William, 7th Battalion | 144, 158 |
| Durand Group (Great War archaeologists) | 110 |
| Durham Light Infantry | 98 |
| Dyett, Sub-Lieut., Royal Naval Division, court-martial of | 86 |
| East Yorkshire Regiment, 1st Bn., joins in defence of Epehy, March 1918 | 233 |
| Ecoust-Saint-Mein, defence of by 2/4th Bn, March 1918 | 237 |
| *Elephanta*, HM Transport | 17 |
| Elliott, Capt. C.A.B. | 40 (footnote), 41-42, 156, 159-160, 188, 196 |
| Epehy, German assessments of defence of, March 1918 | 234, 236 |
| Epehy, Somme, France; held by 110th Brigade 191 | 227-237 |
| Everard, John Breedon, chairman of Leicester Petty Sessi | 128 |

# Tigers in the Trenches

| | |
|---|---:|
| Eyre, Rifleman Giles, King's Royal Rifle corps, att. Leics. Brigade. | 147, 149 |
| Fagan, Private G., 2nd Bn. | 84 |
| Farrell, Private James, 1st Bn. | 57 |
| Fermoy, Co. Cork, Ireland, 1st battalion barracks | 9, 13 |
| Field Punishment No. 1 | 78-81, 99 |
| Fleckney, Leics. | 9 (footnote), 13 |
| Fontaine-les-Croisilles, attack on by 110th Brigad | 167-169 |
| Food, provision and availability of | 34-35, 194-195 |
| Ford, Captain Frederick Ingram, 1st Bn. | 55 |
| Forgan's Trench, attacked by Lieut. J.C. Barrett VC | 243-244 |
| Fort Widley, Portsmouth | 18 |
| Foster, Lieut-Colonel Frederick W., 1/4th Bn. | 248-249 |
| French, Field Marshal Sir John, Commander-in-Chief | 92, 95 |
| French, Field Marshal Sir John, Commander-in-Chief, portrait | 112 |
| French, soldiers' opinions and experience of | 197 |
| Garbit, General Hubert Auguste, unveils 46th Division memorial | 239, 258 |
| Garwhal Rifles | 63,67 |
| Garwhwal Brigade, Indian Army | 15, 66, 72, 76 |
| Gas, poison | 119-120, 150, 185 |
| Gaton, Drummer, 1/4th Bn. | 124 |
| Geary, CSM Amos Arthur, 7th Bn. | 152 |
| Geddes, Lieut. Samuel McKee, 1st Bn. | 101 |
| George V, HM King | 38, 50, 59 |
| Germans, opinions of (see also Christmas Truce) | 47, 183 |

# Index

| | |
|---|---|
| Glen Parva, Leics.; Regimental Depot | 1, 11, 199 |
| Glen Parva, Leics.; Regimental Depot Mobilization Staff | 11 |
| Goadby, L/cpl. A, /4th Bn., wounded at Spanbroekmolen | 206 |
| Goadby, Private, J., 1st Bn. | 44 (footnote) |
| Gommecourt, 46th Division attack on | 135-139 |
| Gommecourt, diversionary attack on | 135-138 |
| Gommecourt, map of German defences, July 1916 | 136 |
| *Goose, The*; German trench mortar | 210 |
| Gordon, Lieut-Colonel (later Brigadier-general) Herbert, 2nd Bn. | 64, 70-71, 92-93 |
| Gough, General Sir Hubert de la Poer, commander 5th Army BEF | 167, 221 |
| Graham, Private James Stephen, 1st Bn. | 44 (footnote) |
| Granger, Capt. Edward H., RAMC, att. 1st Bn., court-martial witness | 100 |
| Grantchester, Cambs. | 15 |
| Gurkha Rifles | 63, 200-201 |
| Hackett, Private J, sentenced to death | 81 |
| Hagon, 2/Lieut. C. Stanley | 180 |
| Haig, General Sir Douglas | 60, 94, 106, 111 |
| Hamilton, General Sir Ian | 38 |
| Hand grenades | 65,70, 115, 124, 127, 142, 149, 155, 212, 215 |
| Harbutt, Mrs (of Evington) recipient of soldier's letter | 194 |
| Harby, Leics. | 9 |
| Harrison, Lieut-Col. William Augustus, commanding. 4th Bn | 23, 25-26,28 |
| Hawes, Captain Robert F., 1st Bn. | 44 |
| Haylock, Captain Henry E., 1/4th Bn., mortally wounded | 206 |
| Henderson Scott, Capt. A. M., DAAG, Indian Corps | 95 |

# Tigers in the Trenches

| | |
|---|---|
| *Heroic*, Belfast Steamship Co. ferry | 14 |
| Hesdigneul-les-Bethune, trench raid 'model' at | 211 |
| Hessey, Brigadier-General William Francis, commanding 110th Infantry Brigade | 156, 160 |
| Hetton-le-Hole, Co. Durham | 97 |
| Hickin, Private Thomas, 7th Bn. | 232-233 |
| Hills, Capt. J. D., 5th Bn. historian | 23, 26, 33, 36, 38, 80, 87, 115, 127, 129, 135, 195, 211, 217, 238, 242, 261 |
| Hills, Major R. C., DAAG to XIX Corps | 105 |
| Hinckley, Leics. | 9 (footnote) |
| Hindenburg Line | 164-166, 239-241, 246-258 |
| Hindenburg Line, map of defences at Bellenglise | 241 |
| Hoddinott, Sergeant Bert, 1st Bn., court-martial witness | 100 |
| Hohenzollern Redoubt, aerial photograph of | 113 |
| Hohenzollern Redoubt, attack on (1915) | 111-132 |
| Hohenzollern Redoubt, description of | 114, 130 |
| *Hohenzollernwerk*, see Hohenzollern Redoubt | |
| Holden, Private M. S., 1/4th Bn. | 195 |
| Holt, Private W., 5th Bn | 35 |
| Horner, Private John W., 6th and 8th Bns. | 84-85, 147 |
| Hovell, Lieut-Col. Hugh de Berdt, commanding. 8th Bn. | 41 |
| Howard, L/cpl. J., 1st Bn. | 50 |
| Howarth, Captain & Adjutant D. W., 1/4th Bn. | 252 |
| Howitt, Major Thomas Cecil, DSO, commanding 7th Bn. | 176 |
| Hubbard, Private Wilfred Henry, 2nd Bn., sentenced to death | 82-83 |
| Hulluch Raid, August 1917 | 210-219 |

# Index

| | |
|---|---|
| Hulluch Raid, August 1917, Captain A. Moore's dim view of | 219 |
| Hulluch trench map (excerpt) | 213 |
| Hutchinson, Private W., 1/4th Bn. | 118, 122 |
| Identity disks | 212 |
| Iliffe, Private Arthur, 1/4th Bn., death whilst prisoner of the Germans | 207 |
| Illston, Sergeant Arthur, 1st Bn. | 53, 54 |
| Imperial Service Obligation | 25 |
| Ingouville-Williams, Brigadier-general Charles, commanding. 16th Brigade | 13 |
| Ingram, Captain Thomas, R.A.M.C. | 57 |
| Ireland, Private C., 1st Bn. | 48 |
| Jack, James Lochhead, Lieut-Colonel, later Brigadier General | 130-131 |
| Jacques, Sergeant James, 1/4th Bn., killed at Spanbroekmolen | 206 |
| Joffre, General Joseph Jacques Césaire, French commander-in-chief | 111 |
| Jones, Lieut-Colonel Herbert, 1/5th Bn., halts attack on Gommecourt | 138 |
| Jones, Lieut-Colonel Herbert, 1/5th Bn., portrait | 138 |
| Junger, Ernst, portrait | 164 |
| Keitley, Corporal R., 2nd Bn. | 71 |
| Kelly, Capt. David V., Leics. Brigade staff | 143, 164, 169, 173, 228-229 |
| Kemball, Major A. G., 31st Punjabis (att. 2/8 Gurkha Rifles) presides over court-martial | 88 |
| Ketton, Rutland | 9 (footnote) |
| Kibworth, Leics. | 9 (footnote) |
| *Kilkenny*, Dublin Steam Packet Co. ferry | 14 |
| Kitchener, Herbert, 1st Earl, Secretary of State for War | 29 |
| Klann, Officer-Deputy, German Reserve Infantry Regiment No. 226 | 168 |

## Tigers in the Trenches

| | |
|---|---|
| Knight, Private, 7th Battalion, sentenced to 15 years imprisonment | 85 |
| Kumme, Oberstleutnant, (German) Lehr Infantry Regiment, captured at Bazentin le Petit | 153 |
| Kunhardt, 74th Punjabis (att. Garwhal Rifles) member of court-martial | 88 |
| Labbett, L/cpl Cecil Henry, 9th Bn., battalion runner | 168 |
| Lacy, 2/Lieut. H.N. | 250 |
| Ladysmith, Natal, South Africa | 76 |
| Lagnicourt (-Marcel), Pas-de-calais, France, 1st Bn. Engagement at (1918) inc. map | 222-224 |
| Lakin, Private Herbert Lakin, 1/5th Bn | 264 |
| Lane Roberts, Lieut. E.G., 6th Bn. | 228, 233-234 |
| Lane Roberts, Lieut. E.G., 6th Bn., sketch map of Epehy, 1918 | 230 |
| Latham, Captain & Adjutant (later Lieut-Col) Francis, 2nd Bn., later 1st Bn. | 91, 103, 226 |
| Ledward, Captain Jocelyn Charles, 1/4th Bn. | 250 |
| Leedham, Private George, 1st Bn. | 222 |
| Leicester | 22-23 |
| Leicester Tramways, war memorial | 56 |
| Leicester, Bridge Road School, old pupils' letters home | 64, 75, 113, 150, 185-186 |
| Leicester, Great Central Station | 21-22 |
| Leicester, Simpkin & James (provision merchants) | 194 |
| Leics. Royal Horse Artillery | 21 |
| Lilley, Lieut. A. A., 1st Bn. The Buffs | 101 |
| Lomas, Sergeant George, Orderly Room Sergeant, Rouen, court-martial witness | 88 |
| *Londonderry*, Midland Railway ferry | 14 |
| Loos offensive | 111-112 |
| Loughborough, 5th Battalion depot | 9, 23-24, 27 |

# Index

| | |
|---|---|
| Ludendorff, Erich, German Quarter-Master General | 221 |
| Luton Hoo House, Beds. | 38 |
| Luton, Beds. | 32 |
| Luxmore, Rev. H. Cyril | 24 |
| Machine-guns (German) | 121, 199, 202 |
| MacIntyre, 2/Lieut. A.S., 2nd Bn. | 76 |
| Maidstone Prison, Kent | 99 |
| Mametz Wood | 140, 143 |
| Marden, Major-General Thomas Owen, commander 6th Division | 105 |
| Market Harborough, Leics. | 9 (footnote) |
| Marriott, Captain Norman Clarke, 1/5th Bn. | 218 |
| Marston, Sergeant (Acting CSM) Thomas, MM | 245 |
| Martin, Lieut-Col. Robert E., 5th Bn. | 35, 121 |
| Mason, Lieut. Alan E. G., 7th Bn., mortally wounded on raid June 1916 | 209 |
| Mason, Private John Thomas, 7th Bn., sentenced to death | 82 |
| MCEwan, Major H., commanding 8th Bn | 41 |
| McIntyre, Captain R.J., 2nd Bn. | 75 |
| *Mecklenberg-Schweriner Weg* (German trench) | 169 |
| Meerut Division, Indian Army | 60, 63 |
| Midland Pioneers (11th Bn.) | 171 |
| Mignon, Lieut-Colonel Jepson George, commanding 8th Bn. | 155 |
| Milne, Captain John, 1/4th Bn. | 124, 129, 181, 186, 206, 207fn, 249fn, 250, 252, 256 |
| Milward, Lieut-Colonel, commanding 71st Infantry Brigade | 100-101, 104 |
| Minor Enterprise Company created by 7th Bn. for raids, etc | 208 |

## Tigers in the Trenches

| | |
|---|---|
| Mobilisation, planning for | 9 |
| Mogridge, 2/Lieut. Basil F. W. , 1/4th Bn. | 131 |
| Moore, Captain Aubrey, 5th Bn. | 32, 137, 210-212, 219 |
| Moran, Charles Wilson, 1st Baron, opinion on courage as finite resource | 107 |
| Morchies, German breakthrough at (1918) | 222-227 |
| Morgan, Captain Noel, 2nd Bn. | 63 |
| Morris, Private George, Portsmouth mutineer | 85-86 |
| Mosse, Lieut. J. W. E., 1st Bn. | 14 |
| Moulin du Pietre, German strongpoint attacked by 1st Bn. | 112 |
| Mountsorrel, Leics. | 9 (footnote) |
| Mud, problems of | 172-173, 178, 190-191 |
| Murray, Cpl. C., 1/4th Bn. | 185 |
| Music (inc. bands) | 195-196 |
| Musketry, skill and effectiveness of Leicestershire Regiment | 48, 75 |
| Mutiny, of 3rd Bn. reservists at Portsmouth, 1914 | 85 |
| National Memorial Aboretum, Alrewas | 109 |
| National Reserve & Reservists | 18-20 |
| Neuve Chapelle, battle of, | 59-77 |
| Newby, Private Albert, 1st Bn. | 51 |
| Newfoundland Regiment, casualties on Somme | 140 |
| Nine Elms Cemetery, Poperingue | 106 |
| Nisbet, Private Joseph, 1st Bn., shot at dawn, trial and execution | 81, 97-108 |
| Nivelle, General Robert Georges, portrait | 163 |
| North Midland Division (46th) | 37, 114, 139, 239, 258-259 |

# Index

| | |
|---|---|
| North Midland Mounted Brigade (TF) | 21 |
| North Staffordshire Regiment | 135, 253 |
| North, L/cpl. S. T., 7th Bn. | 230-231 |
| Nourish, Thomas A. (Coldstream Guards) | 13 |
| Oakes, Private C., 2nd Bn. | 71 |
| Oakham, Rutland | 9 |
| Oxley, Captain & Adjutant Harold Gordon, 14th Bn. | 198 |
| Passchendaele campaign (3rd Ypres) | 170-179 |
| Passingham, L/cpl., court-martial witness | 100 |
| Pegg, Drummer Bernard, 1st Bn. | 44 (footnote) |
| Pets | 35 |
| Pexton, L/cpl. Harry, 1/4th Bn. | 118, 120 |
| Pierrepoint, Capt. A. D., 1/5th Bn. | 263 |
| Pill boxes | 177 |
| Plumer, 2/Lieut, 1/5th Bn., *see* Plummer, 2/Lieut. John Scott, 1/5th Bn. | |
| Plumer, General Sir Herbert, commander 2nd Army, BEF | 170 |
| Plummer, 2/Lieut. John Scott, 1/5th Bn. | 217 |
| Pochin, Private Eric, 1/4th Bn. | 126 |
| Polygon Wood, capture and defence of | 171-179 |
| Polygon Wood, trench map | 172 |
| Pontruet, Aisne, France, attacked by 1/5th Bn. | 240-245 |
| Poole, Corporal T., 2nd Bn., court-martial witness | 90 |
| Portsmouth, Hants. | 18 |
| Preston, Private F. W., 1/4th Bn. | 203 |

| | |
|---|---:|
| Prin, Lieut. Theodore, 1st Bn. | 46 |
| Prisoners, varying treatment of | 150-151 |
| Queenstown, Co. Cork, *see* Cobh | |
| Raiding – *see* Minor Enterprise Company | |
| Ranikhet (India); 2nd Battalion depot | 9, 15 |
| Ratcliffe, Private Frederick Rowland, 1/4th Bn. | 82 (footnote) |
| Rawlinson, General Sir Henry, commander 4th Army, BEF | 133, 257 |
| Read, Private later Lieutenant I. L. 'Dick' | 79, 83, 152-153, 159, 165, 185, 188, 190, 194 |
| Reading, Corporal William Cyril, 1/4th Bn., wounded at Spanbroekmole | 206 |
| Richebourg l'Avoue, Pas de Calais, France, trench raid at | 200 |
| Richebourg St Vaast, Pas de Calais, France | 61, 95 |
| Richmond, Private James, 1/4th Bn. | 203 |
| Riqueval, Bridge over the St Quentin Canal at (inc. photographs) | 251, 253-256 |
| Robbins, Private A.J., 2nd Bn. | 76 |
| Rolph, Captain Charles Colwyn, 1st Bn. | 49 |
| Romilly, Captain Francis, 2nd Bn. | 70-71 |
| Royal Field Artillery | 35 |
| Royal Flying Corps | 34 |
| Royal Garrison Artillery | 49 |
| Royal Welch Fusiliers | 166 |
| Ruckledge, Sergeant H.E., 2nd Bn. | 71 |
| Rue du Bois, Pas de Calais, France | 45-46, 61 |
| Rutland, Duchess of | 28 |
| Sanitation (inc. absence of) | 45, 187-188, 195, 206, 212 |

# Index

| | |
|---|---|
| Sarson, Colonel J. E. | 19 |
| Saxons, inc. fancied preferability to Prussians | 54-56, 74 |
| Scalford, parish church | 132 |
| Scottish Rifles (Cameronians) | 198 |
| Serot, Capitaine, French staff officer | 161 |
| Sheffield, Corporal John Davenport, 2nd Bn. | 76 |
| Shepherd, Col. C. H., commanding. 8th Bn. | 42 |
| Shepshed, Leics. | 9 (footnote) |
| Sherwood Foresters (Notts, & Derbys Regiment) | 135, 253 |
| Shirts, remarkable diversity in colour | 37 |
| Shortus, Private, later l/cpl William, 2nd Bn., sentenced to death | 82 |
| Shot at Dawn pardons, 2006 | 109 |
| *Siegfried Stellung*, see Hindenburg line | |
| Signalling, problems of | 63 |
| Simms, Private A., 6th Bn. | 196 |
| Sint Hubertushoek, Flanders, Belgium | 100 |
| Sirhind Brigade, Indian Army | 76 |
| Skinner, Private Arthur Horace, 1st Bn. (footnote) | 44 |
| Slater, Private - later Sergeant - Arthur, 1st Bn. | 58 |
| Slater, Private Horace Charles, 2nd Bn. | 183 |
| Smeathman, Lieut. Cecil, 1st Bn. | 46 |
| Smith, Private Albert, 4th Bn., death sentence commuted | 82 (footnote) |
| Smith, Private Samuel, 1/5th Bn. | 265 |
| Smoke, tactical use of | 208 |

| | |
|---|---|
| Snaith, Lieut. Eric George, MC, 1/5th Bn. | 263 |
| Snow, Lieut-Gen. Sir Thomas D'Oyly, contradictory assessments of 46th Division | 139, 239 |
| South Staffordshire Regiment | 135, 253 |
| South Wigston, Leics. | 11 |
| Southampton, Netley Hospital | 23 |
| Spanbroekmolen, plan of trenches at | 205 |
| St Asaph, Denbighshire | 21 |
| St Nazaire, Loire-Atlantique, France | 15 |
| St. Mary's Advanced Dressing Station Cemetery, Haisnes, Pas de Calais, France | 110 |
| Stanley, Private William, 1/5th Bn. | 265-266 |
| Startin, Private Harold, 1st Bn. | 53, 139 |
| Steeples, Private J., 2nd Bn. | 71 |
| Stewart, Lieut-Colonel William Norman, DSO; killed by sniper at Epehy, March 1918 | 233 |
| Stewart, Sergeant D., King's Own Scottish Borderers, court-martial witness | 100 |
| Stoney Smith, Major (later Colonel) Herbert, 1st Bn | 50 |
| Sutcliffe, 1/3 Royal Fusiliers | 88 |
| Sutton, Private George Henry, 1st Bn. | 56-57 |
| Tennant, Lieut. C., 1/4th Seaforth Highlanders | 66 |
| Territorial Force Association (Leics. & Rutland) | 19 |
| Teynham, Major Henry john Sidney Roper-Curzon, 18th Baron, 1st Bn. The Buffs | 101 |
| Thermite, description of, and instructions for use | 217 (footnote) |
| Thwaites, Major General William, commanding 46th Division | 218 |
| Tidswell, ER.S.W., 1st Bn. | 44 (footnote) |
| Tomson, Captain James Wyndham, 1/5th Bn. | 243 |

# Index

| | |
|---|---|
| Trench mortars, effective German use of. See also *'Goose, The'* | 157, 210 |
| Trench raid equipment | 215 |
| Trench raiding, origins of | 200 |
| Trenches, experience of life in (hardships, etc.) | 43, 45, 49, 180-198 |
| Trenches, practice | 33, 35 |
| Trimble, Lieut-Colonel John Brereton Owst, MC, commanding 1/5th Bn. | 209 |
| Trophies, war | 199 |
| Tunks, Private, 1/5th Bn. | 217 |
| Tunnel Trench, see Hindenburg Line | |
| Tyler, Lieut. Herbert William Henry, MC, 7th Bn, Bombing Officer | 161-162, 208 |
| Uppingham, Rutland | 9, 138 |
| Utterson, Lieut-Colonel Archibald Tito Le Marchant, commanding 8th Bn. | 177, 235 |
| Vauban, Sébastien Le Prestre, Marquis of | 170 |
| Vaulx, Bois de, held by 11th Bn. in 1918 | 225 |
| Vermin (rats, lice, etc) | 185-186 |
| Vermorel (chemical spray) | 188 |
| Wakefield, Private, 1st Bn. | 47 |
| Waring, Private H., 7th Bn. | 84 |
| Water, importance of, shortages for cleaning, etc. | 45, 183, 187 |
| Watson, Private Thomas, 1/5th Bn. | 266 |
| Watts, Lieut-General Herbert, commander XIXth Corps | 105 |
| Weather, inclemency of | 49 |
| Weir, Captain Donald | 75, 188 (footnote) |
| Whissendine, Leics. | 9 |

# Tigers in the Trenches

Wigston, Two Steeples Co., recruits from — 29

Willars, Private Edward, 1/5th Bn. — 265

Willcocks, Lieut-General Sir James — 76-77, 94

Williamson, Private Fred, 1/5th Bn. — 124

Wissbangs Concert Party — 196

Wokingham, practice trench digging — 33

Wolff, Hauptmann Ludwig, (German) Infantry Regiment No. 104 — 120, 123 (footnote)

Wollaston, Lieutenant (later Lieut-Col.) Charles Henry Fox, MC, 1/5th Bn. — 125

Wood, Field Marshal Sir Evelyn — 38

Woodhouse Eaves, Leics. — 9 (footnote)

Wright, 2/Lieut. George, 7th Bn. — 232

Wymondham, Leics. — 9

Yalland, Major (later Lieut-Col.) commanding 6th and 9th Bns. — 177

# Available Now from Lookout Press (Leicester)

**NURSING IN SERBIA WITH LADY PAGET IN 1915**
The Adventures of Flora Scott of Leicester
Jess Jenkins

**The Base Hospital**
The 5th Northern General Hospital R.A.M.C. (T) and its satellites during the Great War, 1914-1918.
Robin P. Jenkins

From all good on-line booksellers or from
www.heritageco.co.uk

LOOK-OUT PRESS (LEICESTER)

www.ingramcontent.com/pod-product-compliance
Lightning Source LLC
Chambersburg PA
CBHW052133070526
44585CB00017B/1809